Coming On Center
English
Education in Evolution

James Moffett

Boynton/Cook Publishers, Inc.

The quotation from William Butler Yeats' "Oxford, Autumn 1920" on page
154 is reprinted by permission of Macmillan, Inc.

For information address Boynton/Cook Publishers, Inc.
206 Claremont Avenue, Montclair, NJ 07042

ISBN: 0-86709-005-7

Printed in the United States of America

81 82 83 84 85 10 9 8 7 6 5 4 3 2 1

Preface

I wish I could say that these talks and articles produced between 1970 and 1980 were dated. That would mean that the political dangers to education that I and others warned about had been averted and that curricular proposals we made had been realized. Instead, however, these dangers have been realized and the sorely needed new curriculum averted. But these essays addressed increasingly, as the decade went on, the futuristic possibilities we should be thinking about in the very midst of the darkening '70s. I felt, and still feel, that cultural trends of a positive sort will mature in the '80s and, abetted by fiscal desperation, force the issue of educational change to the point of either drastically improving public schooling or pretty well abolishing it. So in one way or another the items forming this collection have spoken already to where English education is now and where it may go. I hope they will bridge usefully between past and future.

Roughly in chronological order, these utterances sketch an interaction between educator and society in the crucial area of language learning. I had published at the end of the '60s two companion volumes of theory and practice about teaching English that, as methods textbooks, soon enjoyed much use and influence—*Teaching the Universe of Discourse* and (retitled slightly in its revised version) *Student-Centered Language Arts and Reading, K–13.* The first, like this present volume, was a collection of talks and articles that, though not intended to eventuate as a book, naturally cohered because of a certain unity and continuity in the author's preoccupations. But I was also responding to responses: the interaction consisted of my addressing issues I was asked to talk or write on by various professional organizations or institutions who knew of my work. During the '70s I acted in some measure as a weather vane, a freelancer invited to hold forth on integration of the language arts or behavioral objectives or reading or humanities or writing or consciousness-expansion, according to current trends and funding. I tried to honor what some part or other of the society held important, all the while holding firmly to the development of my own ideas and ideals of growth. Shifts in both naturally formed a record that is part of what I have to say.

The bulk of this writing, however, comprises ideas about curriculum and methods intended to have some enduring utility—practical teacher talk or analysis of learning principles that aim to help educators think more effectively about what they are doing. I hope very much, for example, that some suggestions here may facilitate the teaching of reading and writing and that other suggestions will enlarge far beyond these activities our notion of language learning and curriculum development. In addition to weaving throughout a thread of personal chronicle for secondary interest and enhancement, background notes should make some thematic connections to tie together the variety of learning matters dealt with at one time or another.

Robert Boynton and I have deleted some material that seemed to repeat key ideas an intolerable amount but at the same time permitted some redundance to remain as themes recurred within different frameworks. Totally eliminating all redundance seemed unwise to us on the grounds, as Editor Boynton expressed the matter in a note, "that each piece was, and is, of a piece and not simply a politician's theme mouthed on cue after the chicken and peas." I'm grateful indeed to him for being willing to help me prepare these items for publication and to let final decisions rest with me.

In selecting only those items that would balance and complement each other, I have also kept an eye out for variety of register employed, given that all are expository. Some were carefully composed then delivered live or simply printed; some were extemporized from a very bare outline then transcribed and edited to tighten; one is an interview. Since readers interested in language teaching are usually interested also in such distinctions, background notes try to bring these out by relating certain circumstances of production.

Contents

1

Coming on Center

Background

Delivered on the very eve of the '70s, at the convention of the National Council of Teachers of English in November 1969, this talk interweaves rapidly many of the themes developed by later essays in this book. So it may serve well as overture.

Convention programmers had assigned me the topic "A Student-Centered Curriculum" in reference to my methods textbook of that title published the year before. Although I appreciated this reference and this opportunity to expound my curriculum, I couldn't resist reacting to the implications of the program title under which my talk had been placed—"Alternative Centers for English Curricula"—which seemed to reflect euphemistically the traditional prejudice that a curriculum daring to center on the student was second-class. At any rate, fussing with their classification helped me organize my thoughts around notions of centering.

Behind this effort to whirl together many matters not usually dealt with as a whole lay an equal diversity of personal experience both remote and distant. I had just moved with family from east coast to west coast, Cambridge to Berkeley, after recuperating from finishing two books at once by spending a year relatively idle on a Caribbean island. From there I watched with some detachment the cresting and repression, in '68–'69, of reformative forces in my native land. Then suddenly we were in Berserkeley, as columnist Herb Caen calls this subtropically gorgeous hometown of radicalism (more deeply rooted in maverick middle-aged people than in students).

Three years before the convention, I had served as one of fifty participants in the Anglo-American Seminar on the Teaching and Learning of English, held for a month at Dartmouth in the summer of '66. This meeting had fallen in the middle of two years afforded me by a Carnegie Corporation grant to work full time at the Harvard Graduate School of Education on the development of a new English curriculum, which I was writing up as the two books of theory and practice. From many of the British at Dartmouth I received a gratifying corroboration of my approach, which included much drama and other peer interaction and which resembled the open classroom, though I had known nothing of what the British were doing. Many of the American participants were involved either in government-sponsored curriculum centers that were more often than not perpetuating wrongheaded tradition or in efforts to found a new English on recent linguistic triumphs.

For ten years before that I had taught English (and for a while, French) at Phillips Exeter Academy, an old boys' boarding school in New Hampshire, where I had done everything from personal counseling in the dormitory to coaching lacrosse to directing drama and debating. During my later years there, Exeter flirted with coeducation in their summer school, which was open to public high school students. There and in the local town high school I transferred experiments in writing and in selection of literature to average students. The teacher's freedom at Exeter to experiment tempted me so deeply into curricular innovation that I left to carry my ideas out where they were needed more—in the public schools, first around Boston and then points west.

Having cleared my head underwater around the reefs of Barbados, I plunged back into the maelstrom of changing America as it emerged from the '60s and, barely uncrated in a new end of the country, tried to pack all I could into a carefully worded half-hour talk. It was published in the *English Journal,* April 1970.

━━━━◄●►━━━━

Why are you here today? What do you hope to get from me? From *any* speaker on English teaching? Bright ideas? New techniques? But is it bright ideas or new techniques you need most?

A new focus? Student-centered? What other kind of focus *can* there be, what*ever* your philosophy? Isn't the learner the active ingredient? And isn't the subject, his native language, already within the student, one functioning in fact of the student as human being? So why take an organic part of a person, thingify it, process it, package it, and lodge it back in him as a foreign object? Shall I *tell* you why? Would that be what you came to hear? Tell you why a student-centered curriculum is an "alternate" curriculum? Eccentric?

But what's the hurry? Let's take the case of the blue-eyed black, once a student of mine, hanging fire between his ghetto origin and his gentleman role in a famous prep school. When he talked, I understood him. When he wrote, I was lost in a bastard language no one ever heard before, a tortured syntax of false starts, obscure fusions, and never-ending self-collisions that perfectly uttered this Caucasian Negro of Mother Harlem and Father Exeter. E for English. So O.K., give our blue-eyed black a language-centered curriculum and show him what real sentences are like. You know, the kind his standard-dialect father would probably speak to him, had he stayed. Learn about our language heritage and how our language changes under the impact of social change. Or a literature-centered curriculum. Show him the masterpieces his "forefathers" created and how they can be reduced to a few mythic types for easy handling as he wends his way toward the white college of his mother's choice. Let him find himself in whichever literary selections the textbook adoption committees and their scared constituencies will permit publishers to put into literature series for him. It's a seller's market for black writers, but no vulgar language please, or sex, or politics, or controversy, or negative emotions— or even positive emotions if they get *too* high. I can center the curriculum wherever I like, but that student will center it where he must—somewhere between what people have been to him in the past and what I am to him in the present.

A freak case, this blue-eyed black. Yeah, sure. But every case is. Take a sophisticated WASP from New York City, *entitled* to blue eyes, of wealthy family, smarter than I, driven into schizophrenia. He communicates through double-binding messages as his parents taught him, sets traps for me in class, misreads literature despite his intelligence because every text is a pretext for his fantasies of abjection and domination. He stays furious at the rest of the class. They disagree with his readings and can't follow his themes . . . or smile at each other. Do I care enough for him, he wants to know after class, to immolate my other students for him? I ask him if that's the going price for love where he comes from, and he weeps and curses and is grateful. But the next day he sets another trap for me in class. And this goes on for a year.

He and I both came through, but if today—when he is himself teaching in Harlem—if today he can read perceptively, write clearly, and converse without trying to subjugate, it is not because I taught him those things. What I did was supply him with some real response to what he was expressing and support him when the response was too painful. He did the rest. His education was a lot more important to him than it was to me. Student-centered.

But the case is too freaky still. Forget minorites and neurotics and pick a normal kid (say from New Goshen, Indiana[1]). O.K. How about a nice, industrious, conscientious, Midwestern Scandinavian paper boy, eager to succeed, eager to please, thoroughly housebroken? He would bless me if I were to put into his hands a factual language book or a composition text with do's and dont's. If I were to give him five questions to answer about the short story for tomorrow. But I don't. I'm cruel. I ask him instead to write about his experience, and I don't grade his paper. I ask him to talk to the students across from him about anything in the short story, and I look toward them whenever he looks at me. To read their writing and tell them what he thinks and feels about it.

Problems come up fast. He tenses in discussion: who knows what'll get said next, and will I be equal to it? His fellows respond politely to his writing, and he understands that they are bored. Following the rules

---

[1]The home town of a young soldier who said he killed thirty to forty civilians at My Lai in Vietnam.

isn't enough. He's shaken. But he doesn't ask them, "What does he *want* anyway?" He asks me, "What do they *want* anyway?" I say I agree they're a hard lot but all they want is what any audience wants—you. He stares at me, and I can see the awful truth sinking in. He had me figured for the indefinite, permissive type who's a real pain because he won't come right out and say anything so you know where you stand. But it's much worse than that even. I really am tough. The course requires *full* attendance. He wants to send a stand-in, to *dance* attendance. And he wants me to give him something he has already, but I'm selfish—I want to give him something he doesn't have. Maybe by now he's forgiven me for being student-centered when he was authority-centered.

Not typical enough yet? An immigrant's grandson from the heartland? You're a hard lot too. So, next case. A tall pretty girl catches me before class and says her theme isn't ready yet because her period is on. She stands there forthright and looks level at me. She knows I'm no stickler for deadlines, and I know she's no whiner. There's just this fact of her womanhood that she wants established between us. Female first, student second. Fair enough. Besides, her steadfast look is rapidly convincing me. So I say all right, not to the late theme but to her womanhood. After all, teaching communication is my job.

The girl turns out to be a leader. She writes real and interesting stuff and reads it off in class without blinking. When she debates with boys, she doesn't act dumb and passive for fear of not attracting them. She doesn't need to cut down the other girls when they talk or write. She can like literature without embarrassment or apology. This kind of behavior bears looking into. The others do look into it. They see it's possible to be liked by both sexes even though involved in an adult-sponsored activity. She hasn't copped out, she's just exploiting me and my class for her own benefit. She can do that because I'm not trying to cover any material— nothing except what students bring up as they respond to each other and to books.

One of the people impressed by our young woman is a girl who dyes her hair one night with four cronies in a fit of fun but is mortified to sally forth the next morning. Who always grimaces in the prescribed ways, manipulates boys according to time-honored rules, and isn't about to risk losing status by showing interest in learning. But she gets taken off guard more and more, becomes rapt watching and listening, forgets her face until it mirrors each passing feeling. Kids are talking seriously to each other, *in a classroom,* about reality as she knows it. They've forgotten the teacher, and yet they do not speak as they speak in the gang. Or a girl is acting a role with a passion she shows nowhere else. It's awesome. Or that boy there reading his theme aloud, she never heard such intensity and sensitivity from him before. Where has *that* voice been? Then in her lovely, self-forgetting face you see it dawn: they haven't *begun* to show themselves to her, these boys, on dates, in gangs. Suddenly they're more than just objects to reflect her desired image back to her. She's caught up. Freed from the code—they can't help it if I force them to do all these weird things—they catch each other up until their group contagion works to open instead of to close them. Students center on each other.

But take the case of ourselves. You remember, I promised to tell you why a student-centered curriculum is an alternate—a fourth or fifth alternate, in fact. Well, hang on, this may be a dizzy trip. You've heard of the military-industrial complex, perpetrated by those other professionals, the wicked ones over there in the defense industry. Defense, it is true, is the nation's largest industry, but do you know which is second? Yours, my poetry-loving friends. Education. A booming business that people get rich off, nearly as dirty as the defense industry, hardly more moral when you consider that those who make war to make money are graduates of our *own* industry. We're dreadfully implicated in the very dehumanizing forces that are strangling our own profession. We *taught* those crazy people. Besides shopping the bazaars for bright ideas to take home and put into action, I suggest we take a long look at the system we're a part of, to grasp why it is we have not already had these bright ideas and done something about them.

So without further ado: the educational-industrial complex. An unsavory comparison, to be sure, but after you've finished recoiling, consider this. Both schooling and soldiering are compulsory. How differently would you teach if your students did not *have* to come to class? That question should haunt teachers. Thinking about it will give you more bright ideas than a century of NCTE conventions. Second, both are tax-supported, which means that, besides a captive clientele, we enjoy a monopoly business. Why innovate when the customers have to come and there's no competition? This would be a pretty good deal except that we are accountable to the public, which has an ignorant notion of education because it was educated by us. Now, education means of course that something in somebody gets changed, but taxpayers want their children to stay the way they made them. They didn't work on them all those years for *nothing*. So to educate really means to infantalize, to retard. Defense, too, is not what it says it is. We haven't been attacked for a long time, and the last occasion or so may have been rigged. Like education, defense is a *1984* term for its opposite. To defend means to menace the rest of the world with apocalyptic weapons. Actually, despite different window dressing, both industries have the same secret function—to solve certain economic, social, biological, and psychological problems of society that no one has had a creative enough education so far to solve any other way. Like overpopulation, employment, the need for outlets independent

of the market, civil disorder, personality disintegration in our kaleido-
scopic culture. Things like that. Cool the young and the poor in schoolroom and barracks. Keep the kids out of politics, jobs, and girls. Issue a
uniform . . . thought and speech.

So much for vague resemblances. As a salute to systems-analysis, I'd
like to break these resemblances down into five components. First, the
compulsory element, the draftees or students, who do the work and in
whose name a vast quantity of equipment is purchased which they use
but do not choose. Proxy consumership (which, come to think of it, just
about describes the status of the Vietnamese at this moment). Second is
the officer class, the professionals, the teachers. For them the complex
provides employment (working on those very young people who might
otherwise compete with them in the labor market). These jobs are fairly
secure, since schooling and soldiering are too well built into the social
process to fluctuate on the market like other commodities. (Admittedly,
the military has a rougher time in this regard, foreign outlets being harder
to control than home consumption.)

A governing elite makes up the third component—the equivalent of
Pentagon and Congress—such as school superintendents, schoolboards,
education officials in state and federal government. These people usually
transcend the profession, which is to say they are administrators and have
all the power. The center of the complex—where lies the possibility of
colossal mischief—is in the overlap between this group and the next,
which is made up of the leaders of industry—builders and suppliers of
school plants, manufacturers of learning materials, educational testers and
researchers, and teacher trainers. What happens is that government officials and leaders of industry swap hats or swap favors and thus create demands which they also supply, as that radical Eisenhower was the first
to point out in his own profession. This is what a complex is all about—
the same people controlling the whole cycle of policy, procurement, production, and profits. There is no conflict of interest; left and right hands
are beautifully coordinated. In your industry too. These two power
groups, however, are dependent on the enlistees and the draftees, who
make up together the effective consumership and who keep the complex
running by playing along with it, one because he wants a job, the other
because he has to.

The whole complex is supported by, or rather bathed in, the fifth element, which I can only call a national mystique. This is a kind of body
steam given off by the mass of the taxpaying public, an aura that becomes
epitomized in certain master symbols or slogans, that is to say, certain
blank checks. The mystique that mandates the defense industry is "con-
taining Communism." For education it's something like "speaking good
English," or as they said when I was a kid, "not talking common." Actually both are sub-mystiques of the grand mystique called "upholding

the American heritage," sometimes amended as "common" heritage or even, in Great Books fashion, "upholding the values of Western civilization." As if someone in our culture could *avoid* being an Aristotelian or Newtonian or Freudian.

The same fear behind both mystiques. Losing status, losing identity, being a nothing. "Contain Communism" means *don't let them blend with us.* "Speak good English" means *don't sound like those others.* Keep differences because differences will define us. Color. How you talk. Foreign ideology. It is indeed very American to be unsure who you are, because look where we came from. Trauma of the frontier, trauma of the melting pot.

But I digress, or as we English teachers write in the margin, "poor organization." I'm sure you're all panting to know how this systems-analysis relates to a student-centered curriculum. Well, I'll try to pull this all together in a climactic burst of incoherence. It happens like this. Let's say you want to let students talk and write and read and act in small groups. All the time, until the fantastic power of those groups is unlocked and carries those kids way beyond the paltry standards we now stretch for. To start with, you don't know anything about small-group process or dramatic improvisation and hardly anything about writing, because you never did these things. You never did them because whoever taught you to be a teacher never did them. Teacher trainers usually don't know about such things. People who do aren't in teacher-training institutions. What your teacher trainer is going to do instead is train you to center on textbooks and to be unable to teach without something in your hands, if only by default through not teaching you any alternatives. Deliberately or not, he programs you to need the kind of materials he's just been authoring. Furthermore, he's the same person who gets government funds to run experiments and set up workshops that omit, naturally enough, what he doesn't know about and that play up, naturally enough, the kinds of things his materials feature. He reads proposals and passes on them. Writes national exams. Consults for school systems, may even have worked for one once, or for a publisher. He's not an evil person probably, but by controlling both ends of the industrial cycle he plays a part in sending the whole system out of control, from the *educational* point of view.

But you're one of the happy few. You know how to set up improvisations and dramatizations, use small-group dynamics, build pre-writing into writing, and get all these processes feeding into each other. Fine! But when are you going to have the class time to do this? You'll have to throw out the spellers, grammar-language books, composition books, basal readers, skill builders—the whole mean, miserable lot of time-filling, tranquillizing commodities designed to market your own mind back to you. But we can no more throw that junk out than we can disarm. Everyone's investments are too great, including yours and even your students'. MIRVs and ABMs, composition texts, and practice readers—all discredited by practical experience but still around because once an industry winds up, it isn't fair to leave the poor fellow out on a limb. We can't afford peace, and we can't afford real education. They're too cheap.

But other rubbish has got to go. All those tests, you know. Second haunting question: How differently would you teach if you never had to test? But you don't have a choice, do you? There're not only those standardized achievement tests that test you, the school, and the curriculum while the kids are being tested, but teacher's turn to test comes around too. Besides your *candid* quizzes, you have your tests disguised as teaching—your book reports and research papers and essay questions. Oh, don't kid me now! We all know they're a check on the reading. Did he read it and if he did, did he comprehend it? Oh, if we could only look in their heads with a fluoroscope machine! Some way to monitor their minds.—Be reasonable. To evaluate you must see the results.—You might ask the student.—Too unscientific. The taxpayers, the colleges—they want body counts. Besides, the essay question kills two birds with one stone.—I agree with you there.

You yourself can't stop testing because you're impressed into the service of accountability, and standardized testing is no more easily dropped than cigarette manufacturing, however injurious to your health. It is packaged into materials and nested down in the souls of administrators. It evaluates curriculums and therefore dictates curriculums. Teachers teach toward the tests, and it's amazing how fast their good intentions dissolve about teaching anything else. All this has taken place haphazardly so far in English, but now that the behaviorists have teamed up with the Pentagon cost accountants imported from Ford and G.M., we're about to take the guesswork out of accountability, with the same efficiency that the Defense Department took the guesswork out of killing. We're writing behavioral goals in English which will become tests which will shrink the curriculum to observable behavior, only a lot of learning in English can't be seen unless you make the student do something to show it, so we can't teach for testing. But one thing we can say: the educational budget is well accounted for even if the education is of no account. Overt behavior. . . . Eight years out of high school a man understands in the master bedroom what his wife is saying to him, despite what she says. Are you and I going to be there to evaluate this effect of our teaching at the moment it becomes overt? Since few will get funds henceforth in English unless their project is behaviorally framed, it seems fair to say that the trend will be *self-reinforcing.* But this is necessary because we must be efficient and not waste money, in education. We must save our money to kill off those red yellow people.

Other examples I leave to your imagination. If, say, you wanted to make your homogeneous class heterogeneous, what obstacles would you encounter? It's time for teachers to quit playing dumb and passive, even if that *was* part of their teacher training. Again and again I have found that English teachers don't believe much in what they're doing, agree with a student-centered approach, and are really quite eager to make a change. But they feel powerless and don't trust their perceptions. These are effects of the educational-industrial complex we're embedded in.

I remember a dedication in a book I have forgotten. It read: "To So-and so, who taught me what I know." No, no, it didn't read that; my cliché-ridden mind read that. I looked again: "who taught me *that* I know." Who taught me that I know. What I know that's of use to you is that you know. Sweeping aside the intervening clutter, recall yourself as a young learner, then review those learners in front of you. You know. But you must assume the power to do what you know.

2

Misbehavioral Subjectives

Background

The following essay originated as part of a drama that says as much as the essay itself. By 1969, enough federal funding had been channeled into schools to raise issues of strict evaluation, supposedly to guarantee cost-effectiveness. Faculty representatives from Purdue, Illinois, and Indiana Universities had received a two-year grant from the U.S. Office of Education to produce "A Catalog of Representative Behavioral Objectives in English, Grades 9-12" with built-in suggestions for evaluative procedures. This was called the Tri-University Project in Behavioral Objectives. During its first year, a couple dozen "consultants," including me, were to convene twice for a total of five days to write objectives for this catalog. Consultants comprised some leaders in English education and administrators representing schools where the objectives were to be field-tested during the second year in a "controlled" comparison between schools not using the objectives and those blessed with them. The latter, the ones represented at the meetings, were called "ES 70 Schools"—"Experimental Schools for the '70s." With this federal notion of "experimental" it's no wonder the '70s got off to a bad start.

The Tri-University directors were to revise and edit our objectives and, after field-testing and garnering reactions from outside readers, publish the Catalog for the profession. One of the directors was also the in-house behavioral psychologist and was charged with visiting all school sites. Directors worked closely with "major consultants" David Krathwohl, co-author of a continuation into the "affective domain" of Benjamin Bloom's *Taxonomy of Educational Objectives, Cognitive Domain,* and Robert Mager, author of the project bible, *Preparing Objectives for Programmed Instruction.* The very telling title of the latter had a more innocent air then than it could possibly get by with today. The same for some statements in the abstract of the Project's USOE proposal distributed to participants for study before we met:

> Behavioral scientists may provide some assistance [in defining the subject of English]. They focus upon the learner—the learner as a doer, as a reactor, as a person whose behavior can be influenced in measurable and desirable ways by the classroom and by his reading, viewing, listening, speaking, reading, and reasoning.

To equate *doer* and *reactor* is symptomatic of this approach, whose advocates had not yet learned to mask the technocratic manipulation of students so well as later, after they came under fire. Admitting that English is not typing, the Proposal rationale continued:

> Nevertheless, despite the impossibility of eliciting for English many statements as exact as "type fifty words a minute," the search for behaviorally phrased statements has value because of the constant focus upon the child and upon the outcomes of instruction as reflected in what the child does.

Posing as child-centered while actually generating a very destructive "constant focus upon the child" struck me as exactly parallel to the fraudulent doublespeak claims of programmed instruction to be "individualized." No one has ever tried to measure the incalculable negative effects of keeping children perpetually under this kind of spotlight and of regarding them as score-sources while they are trying to grow up. This is not education but child molestation.

Similar efforts to manipulate the consultants themselves bothered me more and more after we arrived for three days, in October 1969, at the Speedway Motel in Indianapolis (no cheap symbolism, please). I might have been flattered to find that the handout called "Categories for Behavioral Objectives," which was used to group us into working parties, employed concepts and even specific terms from my two books published the year before, but when I tried to open some discussion during plenary sessions on the ideas and principles underlying the project, the "major consultants" became hostile and the directors (mostly English education professors) embarrassed. Clearly, we were to get out into those motel rooms in our small groups and write our objectives as directed, not question assumptions and intentions and ramifications. Some of the other consultants privately expressed misgivings or disgust, or satirized the project, but the mood seemed to be, "What can you do in the face of the feds? Better we're in on it."

For two days I was a good boy and went along; then at a cocktail party the evening before the third day I told the directors I couldn't stomach it any longer. They understood, they said, and we agreed that I would spend the last day writing a paper on my position. We did not discuss what I might do when we all reconvened for the final two days in St. Louis the following March. So in about four hours the next morning—having so much to get out in one sustained deadline session was rather like doing once again a long college bluebook exam—I wrote longhand the following statement, dictated it to the Project secretary, took one last look at the historic racing cars reposing in the Final Parking Lot of the lobby, and boarded a plane for the return to San Francisco.

I spent the flight trying to assimilate an experience I had never had before. At breakfast, one of the directors had offered me the presidency of the National Council of Teachers of English for the next available term, knowing full well that as soon as I finished my scrambled eggs I was going off to my room to write a dissenting view that, according to agreement, would be distributed to participants and included in the Project papers. Why hadn't he made this offer during the three nights and two days we had already spent together? And why was the offer never repeated for another year, as agreed when I declined? I know that the directors wanted badly to pull off the Project so that English could get federal support and to this end tried hard to accommodate consultants like me who were idealistic enough to be potential troublemakers. They no doubt felt justified because they were trying to protect our profession from our government. My purpose in relating this is not to embarrass these well-intentioned people but to point out what we very much need to face in the future— that it's better to do without funding than to become enslaved to its source. Schooling in the United States is supposed to be a function of municipal or county government, not of state or federal government, but we have sold it out to those centralized bureaucracies. More tax money should be retained locally so that the community can control its own schooling.

Under the title "Misbehaviorist English: A Position Paper," Anthony Tovatt and John Maxwell included this essay in their collection *On Writing Behavioral Objectives for English,* which the Commission on the English Curriculum of the National Council of Teachers of English published in 1970, prefaced by a resolution cautioning that "real danger to English instruction may result from definitions of English in the behavioral mode." This book includes articles by directors of the Tri-University Project, one of which replies directly to my article. While their collection was being compiled, the NCTE Director of Publications telephoned me to ask if I would be willing to delete the final sentence, to which some people involved in the book objected. Later, after he had left the Council, he told me that he had been hoping I would refuse, as I did.

Of course, the real drama at the Speedway Motel was an invasion of Tony Tovatt's room by a squad of field mice that forced him to bunk with me for a couple of nights. How could this be the same motel where, in the movie *Winning,* Paul Newman found his wife in bed with a faster racer?

————————◀●▶————————

As an exercise in clear thinking, it might be a helpful thing for English teachers to write behavioral objectives—and then throw them away. We probably tend to be more fuzzy-headed about what we are doing than math or science teachers. At any rate, we often operate intuitively. As a result, a lot of research in English education has probably wasted

government money. To concede all of this, however, is not to yield pen-
itentially to cost accountants' preference for evaluation models. English
is difficult and different, because a native language is enmeshed in the
vast and intricate fabric of interpersonal and intrapersonal life. For this
reason, to waste money on research in English may be necessary for a
while before results are satisfactory. (More money is being wasted on
more dubious enterprises.)

What I see as negative in the formulation of behavioral objectives for
English concerns three areas: the inadequacy of such formulation to do
justice to the goals of English, the unintended mischief that will almost
surely result from publishing behavioral goals, and the bad precedent set
for future relations between government and education.

Some goals in English imply overt behaviors and some do not. In insisting that desirable behaviors be *observable,* the behavioral approach rules
out a great deal of learning—too much to merely mention in a cautionary
note prefacing the goals. Consider, for example, what may be happening
in a more taciturn member of a discussion group. The effects of certain
reading, acting, and writing on a student's social, emotional, and cognitive
growth tend of course to be long-range and inextricable. Although it
helps to acknowledge that many of these effects will occur years later and
often out of school, in practice these effects will either not be observed
by evaluators or be falsely attributed to more recent school treatment—
or, most likely, be ignored because they cannot be causally traced. The
greater the time-space span, the less likely it is that effects can be ascribed
to their proper causes. A behavioral approach will tend to favor short-
span, well-segmented teaching fragments, because observed "responses"
can then be more easily related to the applied "stimuli."

Even at short range, observed behavior can be badly misinterpreted
by a psychology that in the name of objectivity refuses to infer what is
going on in the black box of our head but does not refuse to infer the
meaning of observed behaviors because the latter are supposedly self-
evident and entail no inferences. But any observation entails inference.
The claim to be an objective observer is really unscientific. The mere fact
of being overt does not make a behavior objective. Einstein said that the
observer is the essence of the situation. (In this regard, incidentally, the
claim that the behavioral approach is centered on the learner is not very
honest. A premium is placed on the favored viewpoint of the observer.)

In order to reduce the observer's inference to an "objective" level, it
is necessary to control the stimulus-response situation to an extreme degree. In education this means to simulate laboratory conditions within a
classroom—to systematically vary one factor at a time. For this reason,
the protest that trivia need not result rings hollow; it is built into the
"objective-observer" emphasis, which requires oversystematized frag-
menting of learning. Without a respect for inner processes, such as ge-

netic development, an observer can misinterpret certain confusions in the thought and speech of students as task failures when actually these confusions indicate arrival at a more complex stage of growth where more errors *can* be made. A student who describes dialectical differences very well after a session of hearing recordings of different dialects may be drawing on previous personal experience unknown to the observer.

So mainly, what is unscientific is limiting observation to the external view and repudiating all introspective statements. Since truth surely cannot inhere in one point of view alone, it must follow that an inside-outside view is more truthful. Overreacting to the mystical elements in earlier vitalist and mentalist psychologies, S–R psychology adopted another extreme in denying truth to the individual's own description of his inner life and consequently in denying his self-assessment of his learning. The only hope for truth through observation is to synthesize the totality of observations—from different times and vantage points—into a full picture. This certainly must include the student's statements about what he has or has not learned, how and when. The interior and external views correct and corroborate each other. Discrepancies stimulate new insights.

Also, because objectives determine evaluation, it is absolutely essential that the learner have a hand in formulating objectives. Otherwise, some kinds of learning behavior of value to him will never be written into the curriculum because they are not destined to be assessed. It is of course just this exclusion of students from decision-making that has helped to fire campus rebellions. One need not be sentimental about students or blind to their excesses to recognize nonetheless how wise and practical it is to include their view—in fact, to do more than that, to permit their groping for self-determination and power to become itself a driving force in their education. But S–R psychology is not inclined to champion this "vitalist" view that action originates in the individual as well as in the environment.

The kind of curriculum that I have been trying to evolve in collaboration with others could not be successfully evaluated by measures derived from behavioral goals. Not only could it not be assessed, it would never get off the ground because the amount and kind of activities that would have to be run off in the classroom in order to evaluate behavioristically would drive out and distort hopelessly the learning activities themselves. What I have proposed is to settle on a handful of general verbal processes that, if only from a purely logical standpoint, can't fail to develop the growth of thought and language because they are basic sending-and-receiving activities that can be varied in infinite ways, and to back these activities to the hilt without asking either teachers or students to engage in other activities merely or principally for the sake of evaluation. Assessment would occur in two main ways, one informal and the other formal: teachers would constantly match their observations against the statements of students about what they are learning and what they need to learn. Outside raters, experts in discursive learning, would assess samples of student discourse—tapes of discussion, finished compositions along with early drafts, tapes of rehearsed poetry readings, videotapes of acting and improvising—all taken in slice-of-life fashion from the normal learning activities. Rater evaluation acknowledges the subjectivity of any observer, but the subjectivity can be somewhat offset by quantifying and correlating rater judgments. This sort of observer can combine cues and get a total "reading" about which aspects of reading or composition or conversing a certain group is weak or strong on. This assesses the curriculum, but it does not necessarily tell which student has mastered which sentence structure or been sensitized to which dialectical differences. But to make sure that every student has mastered every specific should not be a goal anyway. Such uniformity at such a level of particularity is not desirable in itself, and, more important, can be bought only at a ruinous price that I, for one, would never be willing to pay.

To appreciate fully the price entailed in behavioral specification of English teaching, we have to envision realistically what will probably be done with such a list of objectives when promulgated by a prestigious leadership corps to the rest of the profession. First of all, I have noticed again and again that when second-level objectives are further specified as third-level objectives,[1] they not only become transformed into activities, which is necessary since this third level is the one that is actually behavioral or observable, but that at least half of these activities are ones I would consider undesirable, such as filling in cloze passages or listing the items of evidence in a speech or essay. The latter might very likely occur, and occur many times, in discussion, but I would be willing to trust that years of small-group discussion would, if teachers knew how to run the process well, naturally cause students to itemize evidence either individually or collectively. I would never be willing, however, to program a curriculum so minutely as to ensure that every student gave observable proof at every developmental stage that he could list someone else's evidence, because to ensure that, along with the myriad other mini-objectives, would pervert the curriculum into one vast testing system that would not leave enough room for something like small-group discussion even to become effective. In fact, most major drawbacks in the present curriculum stem from just this self-defeating effort at systematization. Instead of reading, talking, acting, and writing for real, students are taking comprehension tests, doing book reports, writing "critical" papers about literature, parsing sentences, filling in blanks, etc., to make their learning visible to the teacher. Thus the main impact of behavioral formulation in English will be to perfect the error of our present ways.

---

[1]According to guidelines issued at the conference, it is at the third of five levels of increasing specificity that objectives first become "behaviorally phrased."

It is reasonable to assume that a representative list of behavioral goals would be rather eagerly seized upon by (a) administrators at funding sources who are accountable to taxpayers (officials in state and federal education departments and school superintendents), (b) curriculum directors in school systems and all English teachers looking for guidance about how to teach the subject, (c) the testing industry, and (d) teachers of teachers, who wish to bring teacher education in line with the current notions of curriculum and methods. Despite all protestations to the contrary, the scenario will probably play like this. The third- and fourth-level objectives will almost automatically become measures of evaluation because they are, by virtue of being behavioral, almost in testing form already. Since tests are used to measure the performance of curriculum, teachers, and students, everyone concerned has an investment in doing only what can be tested. The testing industry certainly has little motive to pass on to schools the reservations and qualifications about behavioral objectives that the writers of them might feel. Cautionary notes and prefaces are virtually certain to be stripped away. In the familiar circular fashion of all state and national exams so far, these tests will act backward to determine the curriculum, and teachers will teach to them. This shrinking of the curriculum to fit the measuring standards is precisely what the Dartmouth Seminar denounced. Furthermore, only those projects whose objectives are stated in behavioral terms will stand much chance of receiving local, state, and federal money. Since this budgeting bias will bias research and experimentation, the S–R trend will be self-reinforcing, as indeed it has been for some time. After all, the essential motive behind the writing of behavioral objectives is to take the guesswork out of accountability.

Clearly, all areas of education have been advised to conform or lose out. To permit this kind of relationship between government and education is to encourage an already pernicious national trend. A marriage of convenience has taken place between the cost-accounting procedures developed in the Defense Department and the operant-conditioning principles of some behavioral scientists. What they have in common is a manipulative one-sided approach to human affairs and a rejection of two-way transactional models of action. Both gain. Cost-accounting administrators have mated with the psychology that suits their needs and problems best. It is the same psychology that the advertising industry has picked, and for the same reasons—manipulation of others toward one's own ends. The education industry has invested heavily in it by marketing teaching machines and other small-step programmed materials. To the extent that teachers and parents misunderstand what education is about, they too sometimes "buy" the operant-conditioning model of education—to remove choice from the "subjects" and make them do what teachers and parents want them to. On the other side, what the S–R school of behavioral science itself gains is a support that it has increasingly failed to get among the great leaders within its own discipline. This is an unholy wedding indeed.

English educators should have been asked to write goals according to their best lights but also in the light of an honest presentation of the government's accounting problems. We should never have been asked to fit English to a model chosen for these reasons and with this history. Losing this battle means losing a lot more in the future.

In short, we are being MacNamara-ed, and we should fight it. But, I am told, if we don't write these behavioral objectives, "they" will. If this is true, then let's recognize this for just what it is—extortion. Lend your name and support to this project or else you-know-who will write these objectives instead of you. I simply cannot accept these conditions. I respect the directors of BOE, appreciate their good intentions, and sympathize with their own conflicts about possibly contradictory commitments, but with the submission of this position paper I must withdraw from the project.

3

Making Schools Pay Off

or

A Student-Centered Language Arts Curriculum

Background

At the same time that I was being dragged by the heels into the educational politics and economics of the '70s, so thoroughly enshrined today that few struggle much anymore, I was signing on—with eyes wide open, I thought—to direct a large and intricate kindergarten-to-college language arts and reading program called *Interaction,* destined to be published in 1973. I had decided that school curriculum really issued from commercial corporations, and so that was where I was going to place myself. I became a capitalist lackey. For once, I resolved, a publisher was going to do a program the way it ought to be. Like my many brave co-authors, I knew such innovative materials would be a financial risk. (If you want to make money in textbooks, it's obvious how to do it, and if you can't see, the publisher will tell you.) For me personally, this meant becoming one of those dangerous people I had described as making the educational-industrial complex what it is. But I was going to save true language learning in this country by incarnating it in school materials that would make a revolutionary approach respectable to those outside the classroom and feasible for those in it. The real risk was that I wouldn't know until after the three or four years it would take to produce the program whether I had sold my soul or not. (Old Faust had to deal only with the Devil, whose contract stipulated very clearly in advance what you would have to pay, whereas corporation deals are more ambiguous or, if you like, more sporting.)

While I was senior-editing some 275 paperback anthologies replete with recordings and senior-authoring some 800 activity cards, two film series, and dozens of games, I was fighting alongside other English educators in California the now rapidly rolling movement toward state-leg-

From *Interaction: A Student-Centered Arts and Reading Program.* Teacher's Guides, pp. v-vii. Copyright © 1973 by Houghton Mifflin Company. Reprinted by permission of the publisher.

From *The Florida English Journal,* Spring, 1973, Vol. II, No. 1.

islated (but federally "inspired") fiscal accountability based on locking behavioral-objectivized standardized tests directly into educational decision-making and hence into curriculum determination. We debated in special forums against proponents of PPBS (Planning, Programming, Budgeting Systems), gave talks and wrote articles on the folly of applying Detroit/Pentagon cost-benefit systems approaches to human learning, and even presented our cause before the State Board of Education, which didn't know much about how the state legislature's commission on school evaluation was, in effect, taking curriculum sovereignty away from districts through "accountability" bills. I was rewarded for addressing the Board on this by having my hand shaken afterwards by the rascally Max Rafferty, who was still California's Commissioner of Education and who opposed accountability for reasons very different, I suspect, from ours. Soon I found myself on mailing lists for right-wing groups in Southern California who believed not only in curbing centralized government, as I did, but also in militarism, abolition of sex education, phonics, and "literal" interpretation of the Bible.

We won the battles but lost the war. PPBS as such was never adopted in California and hence nowhere else in the nation, and before the end of the '70s we ceased hearing much about behavioral objectives. But only the names changed. PPBS took other forms. Behavioral objectives became performance objectives, and the whole movement goes today by the labels of "minimal criteria," "competencies," or "proficiency standards." The more educators combated the virus, the more virulent a strain of it evolved. It was hellbent, and nothing ever stopped it, because too many forces in government and industry wanted it and could exploit for their own motives the public's cry to make schools pay off better.

The following article says nothing directly about any of this struggle. Rather, it's about the kind of learning I was trying to protect, make a way for, keep a door open on. Essentially a nonpolitical person, I had lobbied and jousted only because I knew the curriculum that I had developed and that *Interaction* embodied was headed on a collision course with the technocratic management of youth being railroaded through schools over the heads and behind the backs of teachers. I wrote this piece as the lead statement of the curriculum in the *Interaction* teacher's guides at all four levels of the program. I entitled it "Making Schools Pay Off" to connect the philosophy of the program as directly as possible with the chief educational issue of that day, 1973, as it still is today. While writing it, I was invited to address in Miami a joint conference of the Florida Association of Teachers of English and the Florida affiliate of the International Reading Association. Many educators there knew that *Interaction* was about to appear, in time to be a candidate for upcoming state adoptions in language arts and reading, so in assigning me the topic "A Student-Centered Language Arts Curriculum" they were asking me to present the philosophy underlying the program. Under this title the *Florida English Journal* published the piece in the issue of Spring, 1973. To retain the original connection I affix both titles here.

———————— ◄●► ————————

Children do their most difficult and important learning before they come to school. Researchers constantly tell us this, but we can also see it for ourselves. Learning language, for example, is not new to the child entering kindergarten or first grade. In learning to speak, he or she has already accomplished a feat far surpassing learning to read or write, or any other task attempted in schools.

Speech occurs during the first year of life, with no specialized teacher, no curriculum and methods, no planning, and without even a fully developed nervous system—and also with no failures, no dropouts, and no underachievers. This marvel happens simply because the child is human and is therefore especially gifted for making sense of the kaleidoscope of life. From the crib on, this organism is busily processing data—classifying, relating, inferring generalizations. If it did not, it would never speak; for in order to speak, the child must: perceive and classify in the chaos around him those things to which words refer; discriminate human speech from other sound and one vocal sound from another; match these classified vocal sounds with the things they stand for; infer from dialogue all the basic grammatical rules that enable him to interpret and make up sentences he has never heard before. Motivation is the best ever—to join the human race and survive.

Preschool children have already done superbly some of the very things that we in schools arrogantly list as our goals for them. We are going to teach them all about auditory and visual discrimination, comprehension, composition, how to classify, how to draw conclusions, how to think. The fact is that we cannot teach any of these faculties, because they are part of being human and account for evolutionary survival. It helps not at all to play God. We would do very well just to avoid playing the Devil. What schools *can* do is open up all the ways and means by which a child can *continue* to exercise these faculties.

This view of children is not romantic or sentimental or permissive. Both homely observation and the best scientific findings fairly shout at us to abandon, once and for all, the notion that children come to school as empty vessels to be poured into, blank clay to be imprinted, or passive products outputted by a programmed assembly line. The real truth, as everybody knows, is that students are entirely too full of themselves for schools to bear. Instead of trying to make kids do something different from what they have been doing, we should be helping them to carry to maturity the very successful, if limited, knowledge structures they have already evolved. Instead of making them shut up in school, we should show them more ways to talk and more things to talk about. Children have been comprehending and composing all their lives. Quite literally, to comprehend and to compose mean to "take together" and to "put together." They are two sides of humanity's chief talent, which is to make sense of things by selecting and ordering experience into useful symbols.

If schools have too much ignored what the students are and what they know in favor of other, nearly disastrous approaches, the reason may lie less in some lack of insight than in some classic problems of institutions that hamstring and blindfold their staffs. As an institution, a school has an honest problem of numbers. As a *public* institution, it also has some not-so-honest problems of tampering by selfish or unthinking interests in government, industry, and community. If you multiply one set of problems by the other, you get a curriculum determined by mere standardization and politics, not by the practical realities of learning. So it fails, the public cries that it is not getting its money's worth, tighter accountability systems are installed, the original problems of standardization and politics are thereby worsened; and so the cycle goes. You do not solve a problem of numbers by playing numbers games. You solve it by *offsetting* quantification with qualification, mechanization with humanization. The great irony of performance-contracting was that school systems paid outsiders to do what they did not permit their own personnel to do—get out from under their own institutionalism.

Long analysis with many other educators has thoroughly convinced me that the famous problems of learning to read and write so plaguing public schools are not *learning* problems at all, but *institutional* problems. Learning to read and write is far easier than learning to speak, being merely a media shift from ear to eye, but *appears* much more difficult when attempted in school. Kids for whom, in fact, literacy is no problem learn it mostly at home. Those students unsuccessful at it are mainly those dependent on school for literacy. In other words, the most effective language learning requires precisely the spontaneous, responsive, personal, small-group circumstances of the home that seem impossible in any institution.

But such favorable circumstances are not impossible. Furthermore, numbers are not all bad. School has one great advantage over the home—more people and other resources. After basic speech has been acquired, a youngster can develop language power better outside the home, by communicating with a variety of people. Also, where numbers congregate, there also can be assembled more media and materials than at home. So an institution is not a hopeless place to learn in: the trick is to make numbers work for us instead of against us. This is, after all, the original purpose of any institution.

So far, public schools have been losing this struggle. In a nutshell, we have drastically overcontrolled the learning resources, in an effort to simplify management. We should *use* numbers to generate the vast quantities of practice that kids require in order to continue to develop language. The result of tidy uniformity is only chaos, of course, because everybody is prevented from doing what the institution exists to do. When reading has to be chosen, administered, and monitored by the teacher, students cannot read nearly enough, and furthermore they dislike reading. When the teacher has to process all the writing, students cannot write nearly enough, and furthermore hate to write. When speaking is outlawed as bad behavior or restricted to "class discussion" led by the teacher, students can't exercise the chief means of developing both oral and written expression. The more these target activities thus stagnate or regress, the more we feel we have to look for new methods, or ride herd on accountability. But the real problem is that making the teacher the center makes the teacher a stumbling block.

Programmed materials do not solve the problem, because, for one thing, they shunt the teachers aside instead of allotting them a more creative role. Programmed learning utilizes new technology and managerial ideas to cinch up old failures. It flies banners of "individualization," but it is merely *isolated* learning. Like other traditional approaches, it tries to wish away numbers instead of capitalizing on them. That is, it resorts to standardization. Students all do virtually the same things, and in the same order, but at somewhat different speeds. To vary pace alone is to trivialize the idea of individualization, which, to mean anything, must mean that students pursue different and unpredictable courses. What is efficient is to accommodate *all* individual differences in background and in makeup, not just speed. Furthermore, language is so thoroughly social in origin and function that it cannot be learned without interaction. We can capitalize on numbers only by making full use of people resources—the teacher, other students, and other adults—and by making the classroom a cornucopia of ways and means to learn.

Trends toward the open classroom in elementary school and elective courses in secondary school show that many people are trying to make school adjustable to individual differences in motivation and modes of learning. These individual differences derive largely from out-of-school learning of some sort; so any efforts to individualize schooling will strengthen continuity between life in and outside the classroom. The same rich variety of materials, methods, modes, and media needed to ensure each learner's finding his right way will also permit him to keep his life whole.

As variety must offset an institution's natural drift toward uniformity, wholeness must offset the tendency to fragmentation. Again, to simplify management, many schools have broken down learning into unreal units that nobody can learn. Each long-vowel spelling is made a teaching target for beginning reading, even though we know that learning to read often happens with no phonics instruction at all. Or, even with phonics instruction, it happens by *pulling together* different phonetic understandings. Later reading is broken down into scores of "skills," such as "singling out details," that are psychologically meaningless. Composition is decomposed into artificial particles like "transitions" or "topic sentences" or "paragraph structures" that can no more be factored out of the total composing act and separately taught and tested than the pound of flesh can be cut out of the body without killing both. After all, we are not dealing with carburetors or mufflers that can be taken out, fixed up, and replaced without damage to anything. Learning is organic in the true sense of being a live organization, a system of interrelationships. Further learning is *reorganization.* It may be handy to *speak* of parts of an organism, but to try to isolate them out *in actual practice* is a mad scientist's kind of fatal play.

The fragmentation of reading and writing cuts in several deadly ways. It cuts at the roots of language learning by separating reading from "language arts" and both from "oral skills," "creative writing," and "drama." "English" becomes just literature and therefore rules out huge areas of reading and writing treated nowhere else in the school curriculum. Because isolated words and sentences are easy to check out, vocabulary is thought to be learned by memorizing words out of context, and sentence structure is thought to be learned by analyzing separate sentences, whereas in truth vocabulary and sentence structure are expanded far better by pulling out all the stops on talking, reading, and writing. To atomize reading into "skill-building" passages, or composition into "practice paragraphs" simply severs action from motivation, because purpose and meaning have only wholes as goals. If these unreal units must, in addition, be sequenced, the unreality is multiplied. Although done in the name of scientific objectivity, this way of proceeding is thoroughly unscientific. All that results is a self-defeating overcontrol.

Again, we really know better, but the institutional need to monitor and account for itself pushes schools to such excesses. It seems easier to check out and report on what's going on if the action is chopped up fine. But this is the tail wagging the dog, in the worst way. Ironically, the public, in whose name these vivisections are committeed, does not assess schools in this mincing fashion but rather in a gross-gauge, rule-of-thumb way. "Can my child read?" "What does he read?" "Can he express himself well?" "Does he talk the right way for getting a job?" "Does he like to write?" etc. When parents talk accountability, they do not mean what management-by-objectives, cost-effectiveness specialists mean by it. Parents, in fact, clamor about their money's worth, but their goals are wholes—broad and humanistic—like students', and like most perceptive and experienced teachers'. Schools would do well to assess on the basis of goals as whole, motivated acts.

The program I have been working on attempts to restore wholeness—whether it is the totality of the writing act, the interrelation of reading with speaking and writing, the continuity of personal life with school life, the unity of will and action, or the integrity of individual growth. What can make this possible is a classroom array of materials and activities that are themselves wholes—that is, complete acts for common language motives. Second, each learner sequences these activities and materials differently according to the interplay of forces acting in and on him as he or she goes about evolving his or her own knowledge structures. So what this program does is set up such a powerful field that virtually anything that happens in it produces language-learning.

Personal choice is at the center, not only so that the learner *cares* about what he is doing, but so that good judgment will develop—whether the option is which book to turn to next, which activity card to select, which medium to say something in, whom to ask for help, which phrasing to express an idea in, or which way to interpret a line of poetry. But personal choice does not operate in a vacuum; in this program it operates as elsewhere, influenced by peers, elders, alluring variety in the environmental array, and intrinsic connections among things and actions. Thus, the student-centered curriculum is never "permissive" or "unstructured." It is not based on some empty and faddish notion of "doing your own thing." An individual is always a force in a field of other forces and very hard-put indeed to tell inside from outside.

Nothing can be "unstructured"; when we say that, we mean that we don't *recognize* the structure of what we're looking at. The word only expresses our ignorance. A bystander, observing a truly individualized classroom in action, may be tempted to call it "chaotic," because it is impossible for him to know what each student is doing, what he has been doing, and what knowledge structure he is building within. But any learner using this program will be learning to exercise language choices wisely, which has surely been the main goal of any traditional curriculum. The wisest decision for educators to make is to stock a classroom with as many things as possible to *choose among*. The traditional classroom has not had *enough* structures. This is one way in which it has been over-controlled. One lesson plan for all each day, one sequence for all for the year—that is not to structure *more;* it is simply to let a single structure monopolize the learning field. This monopoly rules out any real possibility of learning to develop judgment, which requires that the learner be structur*ing* in school, not structur*ed* by the school. Structuring is choosing. Comprehending, composing, making sense of the world—these are structuring. School should be harder and more fun. It should be a place where youngsters can structure for themselves, not have it done for them before they arrive. For one thing, we can't *stop* a child from structuring. For another, we have already tried that way.

The classroom should be a microcosm of what is most positive about America—its diversity and flexibility. The hybrid strength that comes from continued synthesis seems to be humanity's chief adaptation for survival in a very rapidly changing world. And the youth of the nation that serves as the growing edge of this world cannot afford to be hung up by false problems at our present rudimentary level of language teaching. There are simply too many other things schools must start teaching that we don't now have time for because language learning gets stalled in institutional problems. The future will require that children not only learn language well and fast but that they *transcend* language, liberate themselves from it, that is, go all the way through and out the other side to subtler, more powerful ways of proving and communicating that lie beyond and beneath language.

4

Interview
by David Sohn

Background
English teachers at Exeter admired a book called *Stop, Look, and Write* co-authored by Hart Leavitt, a teacher at our rival prep school, Phillips Andover, and by David Sohn. These two deserve credit for first putting across the idea of writing about photographs. By the time I met Dave years later, he was coordinator of language arts for Evanston, Illinois, schools and a contributing editor to *Media & Methods.* He heard me talk to the Illinois Council of Teachers of English and asked me to meet him at the New Orleans NCTE convention in 1974 to do an interview. The result follows here.

By the mid-70s my hands were good and dirty as capitalist lackey and political activist in education. But it was time for a shift. *Interaction* and a much-revised version of *Student-Centered Language Arts and Reading* (with new co-author Betty Jane Wagner) were launched and now at the mercy of corporate and cultural forces that were too big for me. I needed to develop myself more and resume earlier searches outside of education for influences to bring inside. In the late '50s and early '60s I had experienced some small-group dynamics and interdisciplinary, mind–body integration and tried to incorporate these into curriculum development. Such movements later evolved as "encounter groups" and the "holistic" and "consciousness" activities. So much of my career seems to have been trying things out personally and then making use of them later professionally. In 1971 my wife and I began practicing meditation. Then, already in the habit of doing some yoga postures, we took in 1973 a class in prana yoga given by Swami Sivalingam, a hatha yogi and an extraordinarily developed South Indian who specializes in breath-control exercises, which we had been wanting to learn about. Thus began a very important association from which I was to learn far more of the realities of inner disciplines than I had gained from my reading in zen, yoga, shamanism, and Western mystics. I was also following at the layman level some research in brain functioning, consciousness, and neurophysiology.

This interview, which was taped in my New Orleans hotel room and published in the February 1975 issue of *Media & Methods,* captured in its dialogical movements some of the interplay between activities in English teaching and ideas from outside the field. Coincidentally, James Squire had at that same NCTE convention brought together six English education people, including me, to do a group interview with him on "The Future Direction of English Teaching," which later became Chapter Ten in *The Teaching of English,* the 76th yearbook of the National Society for the Study of Education, edited by Squire and published in 1977 by NSSE and the University of Chicago Press. It touched at times on some of the matters David and I dealt with and reflected a new tendency of the profession to enlarge its view of English and to probe the future. Again as weather vane, I felt the winds blowing in topics coming my way such as "Consciousness Expansion and the Future of English," a significant linking that arose not only at the next NCTE convention but at other meetings in variant ways.

SOHN: Individualized instruction is pretty hot now in a lot of circles. "Self-concept" is also quite big. Should we be placing so much emphasis on these approaches, or are they just another flash in the educational pan?

MOFFETT: Well, I think for education to improve it's going to have to go very, very far in the direction of individualization, but an individualization quite different from the way the word is generally used. I think it got preempted very early in the game by narrowly programmed materials, so that right now it often means learning small things in small steps. My impression is that these materials—usually with a behavioristic approach—take all students through the same program, except for some difference in pacing. Basically they are doing the same things in the same order, and I think that that's a fraud and a terrible misleading of the profession and the public. It gives the impression that we have done something that we haven't. And what we need to do remains still to be done.

SOHN: What's that?

MOFFETT: We need an honest, deep, thoroughgoing individualization in the sense that learning really accommodates individual differences in people as they vary both by background and by personal makeup. That includes a tremendous amount. It covers the differences in ethnic and familial upbringing, the incredibly varied uses of language and dialects in different families and ethnic backgrounds. Then you get into differences in personality: what people understand by different words, what experiences they've had, which things they have or don't have concepts for, even the different sensory modalities which individual students learn best from—the auditory, the visual, the motor-oriented, the kinesthetic.

If we give these differences the critical attention they deserve, then we must have a much broader spectrum of materials, methods, media, et cetera, that kids can learn from. If we don't, we're simply not individualizing.

SOHN: Well, I wonder about the term "individualization." A lot of people use it, but I don't think they are really doing it.

MOFFETT: Actually, I prefer the term *student-centered* because it gets away from the connotations of narrowly programmed materials and kids working alone in carrels. Part of the problem with that sort of individualization is that it's isolated learning. Language learning in particular has to be social, has to be interactive. So if you put kids off alone with a machine or a carrel too much of the time, you cut them off from the social resources, you bypass the human interaction needed to learn language.

Now until this interaction occurs, we won't have really open classrooms in this country, no matter what we call them. The idea of the open classroom was to accommodate differences in kids, not just differences in timing. To do this requires a totally different classroom management, one that is very seldom seen in this country—and may not even be all that common in England, where the idea originated. It means having different working groups doing different things at the same time. And that's very hard to manage. At least it's a very different management. It looks chaotic to people who don't understand it.

SOHN: Doesn't it take a lot more work to individualize than it does to use a more traditional mode of teaching?

MOFFETT: It does. But it's also terribly hard to teach the conventional way. Many teachers are trying to emcee their classes. So you have twenty-five to forty different kids straying off in all sorts of directions. You wind up fighting them constantly, trying to keep them on one thing at the same time. This produces horrendous disciplinary problems because it's impossible for that many kids to be interested in doing the same thing at the same time. And it takes a tremendous toll on teachers; they're demoralized by the constant strain and the poor results of their efforts.

Take lesson plans, for example. Lesson planning, or "What Do I Do on Monday Morning?" is, you know, a chronic question. But I think it's the *wrong* question because it arises only when you're emceeing the show. I think you should always *know* what to do on Monday morning. It's a basic process of individualized management, small-group work that goes on all the time.

SOHN: Well, when is a group experience valid? Or is it? Are there occasions when the whole class should experience a common event?

MOFFETT: I think so. Certainly you don't want to close any doors by saying that a whole class mustn't ever meet. There are times when you want numbers. The whole idea is to explore human resources, to have one-to-one relations, small-group relations, and large-group relations. Each uses numbers in a very different way.

I think, for example, that choral reading and large-group improvisations are very useful. Also, you want to get together as a whole class so that different working groups can present their products to each other, perform for each other. If the students are all doing something together, there's no audience within the class, and therefore there is a tremendous loss of motivation. I think the real motivation in communication comes from doing something and getting a response. Writing something, for example, and having the rest of the class read it, or performing something and having the rest of the class respond. So for that, you need the whole class. Some teachers plan certain sharing times; others play it by ear when certain groups are ready to make presentations.

SOHN: How about viewing a film as a group experience?

MOFFETT: Well, there's a little of the same problem as in reading the same book together. Are they all ready to be interested in that? And the problem also of choice: Who does the deciding for whom? If the whole class is "given" a film, they may react the same way as when "given" any other assignment—that is, when they don't have any choice in the matter. That's the only problem I see and it has nothing to do with films. It has to do again with the whole basic process in the classroom.

Certainly there is a value in sharing a film together, as there is in a book. Then the students can compare responses. That's tremendously important—to compare their responses to either reading or viewing. But I think you can do that more effectively in a small group. I'd rather see six or eight kids view a film together and then talk about it in a practical way. It's kind of hard with a whole class, I think, particularly if the teacher is leading.

SOHN: Especially if the teacher is imposing his or her own viewpoint. One of the toughest aspects of working with film is letting the ideas and responses come from the kids. It's an easy trap when teachers think they know what the film means.

MOFFETT: Right. One reason the teacher wants the kids to see the film is that he or she has a strong feeling about it, and wants the kids to have that same feeling. Not just film, though. It also happens with poetry. A classic disappointment of English teachers is trying a poem they love dearly with a class and having the kids go "uuuuuhhhhh." And then they hate the class for not sharing their feeling.

SOHN: Some teachers, in an effort to not prejudice the responses of the students, go to the other extreme and refuse to voice their own feelings. Is that the answer? Or should teachers contribute their reactions in a discussion?

MOFFETT: I would play it very much by ear according to the kind of students I had. If they're experienced in talking with each other, expressing ideas, listening to other people, and are confident about their own thinking, then I'd feel much freer to play my own thoughts into the discussion. Kids like that can accept or reject the teacher's ideas and will benefit from knowing what you think and what perspective you bring to the discussion. They note what you say, they listen to it, but you know they're not awed by it, they don't feel they have to push their own ideas out of their minds. But if the students don't have that kind of confidence, your ideas could easily short-circuit their thinking, and that's bad teaching. The main problem is to make sure you give them plenty of time to think, that you don't foreclose the issue. It has nothing to do with an authoritarian-permissive dichotomy. It's simply not a practical way to teach—to assert too much too soon if it closes the issue. It takes a lot of independence for a young person to continue to think in the face of strong, maybe good, ideas from you, the teacher.

SOHN: What about John Holt's idea that we're training students to be answer-oriented? Shouldn't teaching be inductive?

MOFFETT: The thing about what Holt called "answer-pulling" on the part of the teacher is that it implies you know something ahead of time—you have in mind some piece of information, some statement, some conclusion. It's just a question of how you're going to get the kids there. Will you use the old-fashioned approach of just plain-out telling them, or will you trick them a bit, lead them up to it? In class discussions of literature, I used to do something that I guess would be considered inductive. I'd have a carefully planned series of questions that I thought led brilliantly up to the main point of the story. But I found it was guiding too much. Also, I often got frustrated because their minds went off in different directions. They didn't follow my lead. I had to come to value the fact that the directions they went off in—even if they were bad in the sense that I felt the kids were misunderstanding the work—made me go that way in order to find the cause of the incomprehension. You have to get the incomprehension out before you can get to the problems. Why did they misread something, you know? Or did they all? Was it just one student?

The trick is to let them compare what they feel, how they respond to the film or the literary work. And they discover that they don't agree. That, I think, is really enlightening. They expect a disparity between what you think and what they think. It doesn't impress them too much, because there's always a gap, you know, a generation gap—adults are different people anyway. But when their own flesh-and-blood peers respond very differently to a short story or a film, interpret it quite differently, then they have to stop and think. It breaks their egocentricity by forcing them to compare their own ideas with those of their peers. And that's an important aspect of learning, to break egocentricity.

SOHN: Don't we learn most things by comparison and contrast?

MOFFETT: I think that's very much the secret of it. I've been reading recently and thinking about research on the two hemispheres of the brain. Apparently the human brain specializes, that's why we have two hemispheres. The left hemisphere, which governs the right side of the body, is digital, linear, it moves in time and works like a computer would. It's analytical-intellectual. The right hemisphere, on the other hand, is spatial and visual. It functions holistically, and deals in the metaphoric mode. While the left is verbal, the right is nonverbal.

This has been demonstrated in experiments that present a visual problem to one hemisphere or the other. The right hemisphere can process the spatial problems, but the left sometimes just creates static. For example, if you're asked to define "spiral," most people start with words and then say, "To hell with it," and make a spiral in the air with their hand. It's a much quicker way to define a visual or spatial concept. The whole reason for the specialization, apparently, is to keep one hemisphere from interfering with the other. Some things are better processed one way, some another. Of course, they also collaborate. How well they collaborate is a vital factor in education and learning.

I think it's really critical to set up learning circumstances that permit kids to coordinate the two hemispheres. Many people who know this brain research—which is very solid at this point—feel that our culture has been overemphasizing the left hemisphere, the analytical-linear, for some time. They see this overdevelopment as one of the reasons why we can't solve so many of the culture's problems—pollution, ecology, world coordination. We're thinking too much with the left half, while the other half, the holistic and metaphorical, is precisely what would help most to solve such problems.

The reason is that today's problems—whether you're talking about the individual's own life, or whether you're talking about international coordination—center on *intricacy*. And intricate things are not linear; they involve several simultaneous happenings. It's the difference between playing a melody—a series of individual, separate notes in time—and striking a *chord*. The right hemisphere is always striking chords. It is made to process intricacy, to handle information about several things happening at the same time from several different sources. And this is, I think, the whole function of metaphor, figurative language, most literature, and, I suspect, of many films that are more metaphor than literal realism.

This imbalance in favor of the linear-analytic is dismaying and a real culture-wide problem. McLuhan hit on it from another angle. Though I don't believe his thinking was related to the brain hemispheres—the research hadn't come out with much yet—he talked about print being linear and analytic, and said we were overbalanced that way. From what I know of him, however, I don't think he allows for the fact that reading tends to combine the two hemispheres—at least it can if the material is metaphorical. On the other hand, something like television is also linear; you have a succession of images. Films and television both have that linear aspect. When he talks about the graphic media being different from linear-analytic books, it seems to me that that's only part of the story. A movie is also a succession of images. In that sense, it's like a novel.

SOHN: If it's a traditional movie. You've seen multiple-image movies.

MOFFETT: Well, it's a succession, even if it's not a time-order. It may be completely jumbled.

SOHN: It has to be a succession if you have time involved at all.

MOFFETT: That's what I mean. And I think literature—figurative, metaphorical writing—although it's based on the linear processing of the left hemisphere, can be intuitive because it includes *equivocal* symbols. Like the musical chord, it conveys several meanings at one time. That's what Melville was doing, I think, in *Moby Dick* with the image of the white whale. In other words, the intuitive, right hemisphere, the metaphorical mode, has a way of sneaking itself into the left hemisphere, so that both sides collaborate. And this new perception about the specialized hemispheres of the brain undergirds literature in the metaphorical mode, the visual metaphor. It supports metaphor in a rational, practical way that we haven't had before in schools.

Let me explain a bit further. Both literature and movies tend to be regarded as entertaining rather than utilitarian. Now if you talk to administrators and the public about where to put their money priorities, you know damned well which one they are going to pick. It's going to be the utilitarian over the pretty or the pleasurable. But now we're saying that the problem is with the dichotomy. It forces us to use just half our brain. But the metaphorical mode is not only practical, it's essential—without it we're dying. The culture is strangling on its own problems because it scorns that part of the human organism which is really made to process the intricacies of simultaneous phenomena. The right hemisphere—the intuitive and metaphorical—is atrophying in our culture. . . .

SOHN: This would suggest, then, that a lot more emphasis should probably be placed on—I hate to use another label—what is called the "affective" type of education. Art, music, poetry, film—things which lean toward the aesthetic.

MOFFETT: Yes, well, you know I've always regretted that cognitive/affective dichotomy. I don't think it's been helpful, and you know, I've heard people speak so technocratically about the affective domain that I kind of shiver when I hear it said too much. I can tell by the way it's being said that it's going to come out the same old way. I think it would be more useful to use the dichotomy that is based on our biology, that's based on these two hemispheres. Analysis and synthesis—that's what it amounts to—and they are both cognitive. But as long as we talk about cognitive and affective, there's going to be this bias.

SOHN: I've always suspected that somebody invented the affective domain to make an excuse for what can't be measured.

MOFFETT: It was an afterthought. I think that's historically true. Wasn't it Bloom and those people, with the taxonomy. I think they did the cognitive first, and people said, "Hey, look! There's more to life than that." And they said okay, and they went back as an afterthought. It's like that old utilitarian-pleasurable dichotomy—given the choice, we know where the money and the energy and so on is going to go. It's going to go to the cognitive. I'd like to think that people would begin to consider the metaphorical mode for what it really is—cognitive. We simply think in two different ways. Referring to it as affective makes it emotional. It's like saying "It's there, it's part of us, but we don't think with it." And that's not true. We think metaphorically.

Scientists have been saying that for a long time. Bruner talked about it in his *Essays for the Left Hand.* The problem was that, in his own educational research, he tended to emphasize the cognitive—the post-Sputnik reaction—and, as I think he realizes now, he spun us off too much in the direction that the culture was going already.

SOHN: Is the trouble with a lot of education that teachers tend to want to "unwrap the chord"? To take each separate note and look at it and investigate it?

MOFFETT: I think that's very true. It's one reason why I turned against the "lit-crit" approach—in both English and French. We played the old "lit-crit" game, where you take literature, the metaphorical mode, and translate it from the deliberately equivocal back to the univocal, the literal. It's paraphrasing a poem. And you're absolutely right. What it does is demythologize something. Literature was put in the metaphorical mode for a damned good reason to begin with. Because it's addressing itself to our right hemisphere. As soon as you force kids to paraphrase poetry or to tell the meaning of *The Red Badge of Courage* or *Moby Dick*—to give a univocal readout on the book—you're forcing them back into the other mode. Now that's the mode they're most often in anyway, the left-analytic. The whole point of studying literature is to exercise the metaphorical mode, so you're undoing the whole thing. I think this is why kids hate it. And it's interesting that kids and writers are united in their opposition to this kind of paraphrasing of literature. I think they sense that this is destroying the whole point of the thing. We do it to get a grade. It's evaluation, basically. Because kids view a film or read a book, and we want to know if they understand it. And the only way to find out, we think, is to get them to paraphrase it.

SOHN: Frost used to say, "Read the poems. They're there. Why should I say it in another way."

MOFFETT: He used to satirize questions about "What did it mean?"

SOHN: That's probably why a lot of artists can't talk about their art. And why should they?

MOFFETT: Talking just hits one level, and they don't want to take just one level.

SOHN: I wonder if this is why the Russians get so agitated about art. You remember when they ran over an art exhibit with a tank? And they get very upset about writers like Solzhenitsyn who writes interesting, truthful novels, presumably.

MOFFETT: As you were asking the question, I thought of the Underground movement in France during the Occupation. A lot of the poetry, plays, and novels that came out of France at that time were tremendously metaphorical and allegorical. That was the only way you could write about the Occupation under the Nazis and get away with it. I think totalitarian governments suspect anything in the metaphorical mode. Part of the ambiguity gets to them, and they're not sure, you know.

SOHN: It makes them uneasy.

MOFFETT: It's a way of escaping censorship. A lot of rock lyrics referring to drugs resorted to this too. To get drugs and sex across the airwaves on most radio stations, you have to speak figuratively. That explains part of the style of rock lyrics. The same was true of the euphemistic style of Victorian writers like Dickens.

SOHN: Many of the films coming out of satellite countries are so allegorical. I suppose an artist jumps on the allegory wagon to avoid censorship.

MOFFETT: Also, you reach more people. Children, for example, really have to do their thinking about the inner psychic life in story form. They don't have concepts and names for all that's going on in there. The same is true with primitive people. *Beowulf* was the sociological treatise of its time. That's the way you did sociology in those days, in the metaphorical mode. Kids today tend to do all their thinking that way. It's a kind of dream compression—a condensation in dreams, which have many levels. I think that's a prime example of the right hemisphere operating. The function of dreams, and it's apparently a definite biological function, is to help solve problems. A person whose dreams are continually interrupted gets into a near-psychotic state, because it's functionally very practical to dream—to try to solve problems in the metaphorical mode. If that's true, then it follows that in our waking life metaphor has the same practical function.

SOHN: What would this suggest about the student who is a dreamer?

MOFFETT: It could mean that he or she has a lot of problems. In yoga, for example, the yogis who have reached a very advanced stage of development stop dreaming. They hardly sleep at all. Still they have tremendous energy; they may work till 2:00 A.M. and then sleep for a few hours. When they do sleep, it's very deep and they purr like a cat—a constant snore. I think this means that they have resolved most of the problems of the inner life that we're still dealing with. They have simplified and unified their behavior, their thinking, their feeling. So you can say that the person who dreams a lot has a lot of problems. We dream because we haven't resolved our psychic life.

SOHN: Have you ever noticed that in education, a pedagogical idea will emerge, and you almost have to make a medium out of it to put the idea across? "Programmed instruction" and "visual literacy" are examples. Carpenter talks about each medium having its singular grammar—the elements that cause it to communicate.

MOFFETT: The rules of relating.

SOHN: To me, this is a critical insight, because I feel it is important to relate back and forth among the media, understanding all the time that the elements that make film communicate, for example, are different from the way that words communicate in a book.

MOFFETT: You were saying earlier that the idea of comparison was probably central to learning. Going along with that, I think that the comparing of media themselves is a tremendous part of what students should learn in school. It's putting language and all the other media in kind of an array, as alternative ways in which to inform oneself and to communicate with others. We should offer students opportunities to go to all these media and find out what each can and can't do, when one is more expressive than another. Also, I don't think we really understand language until we turn it off and work with something else. This is very hard for people who teach language, who have a professional investment in teaching English. They feel it's self-defeating to talk about turning off language and going to something else for a while. But I think you really don't understand language until you do that. I think the most sophisticated verbalizers, from Shakespeare on, have been people who see through language. They have a perspective bigger than language itself, a sort of metacommunication that can go beyond the communicating process. This, I think, is one of the most powerful arguments for working in other media—for visual literacy, or media sophistication, or however you want to put it. Each medium can give us perspective on the other.

SOHN: McLuhan suggests that the environment becomes invisible to us.

MOFFETT: Including the language environment.... We have to get more sophisticated about how language gets produced. I mean, you look at the language level because that's visible and you can see it, but, underneath that, there's a tremendous amount going on psychologically. Like the states of consciousness in which people do things or don't do things. There's a correlation, for example, between absorption in reading and hypnotic susceptibility. This just reinforces what a lot of us suspect, you know. The people who love to read, avid readers, go into an altered state of consciousness. My parents used to laugh at me. When I was reading, they had a hard time attracting my attention. I think the same thing is true of film viewing; you go into a different state. And writing—to get back to what you were saying a moment ago—also requires a certain state. Talk about the language constraints—you know: Write a paragraph that goes from big to little or little to big, or is based on comparison, or something like that. That's not the way writing happens, I think. We all know that. I don't know what this hypocrisy is about.

SOHN: A lot of teachers don't know that, or they won't admit it. They don't recognize it. . . .

MOFFETT: I think that people who value language value poetry most of all because it can make language do things that it ought not to be able to do. Poetry has the capacity to push language to its breaking point, to depict accurately in words a nonverbal reality. That's very hard to do because language isn't really a help in representing reality very well, you know. It's too selective a medium. What it does is to stereotype reality, and that limits originality, which is the breaking of stereotypes.

SOHN: That's interesting. I never thought of it, but language has to be fairly superficial.

MOFFETT: It's interesting that we speak of the best and the worst moments as "unspeakable." The word "unspeakable" is ambiguous. It can mean some ultimate horror, or it can mean ineffable bliss. Things that are off either end of the scale are beyond language. They're too big for words. And when you use words, you have to realize that this is second best, and all it can do is represent reality with the limits inherent in the medium.

But we tend to think that somehow language escapes the laws of other media, that it can represent reality more truly, that everything can be *said.* This is not so. I don't think that everything can be *said.*

SOHN: And yet we revere the printed word. In fact we revere it so much that we ignore the other potentially powerful resources that we have in education, like film and television.

MOFFETT: Well, if you speak about the limits of language, this upsets a lot of teachers because they feel that their kids don't use language very much anyway. The kids, they say, are basically nonverbal; why encourage them to grow more nonverbal? They're practically inarticulate and mute as it is. They need more language, not less.

That's a hard argument to face because there's a lot of truth to it. I guess my response is that they need more of both. There are many kids who are pretty undeveloped in *any* medium. Sure, they need to talk a lot more. They need to develop speech, and really get interested in it. But they need to work a lot in the other media, too, so they can get perspective on them. Then when they choose speech, it will be because they understand the capabilities and limitations of this medium.

SOHN: Some teachers will not even admit that there are other media. They don't understand them. They don't understand that they are so much a part of our lives, and they need to be used and understood. We can't even measure the profound effects that television, for example, is having on our society.

MOFFETT: Well, the interweaving of the media is a very useful thing for teaching, because it provides ways for kids to use language and to get away from language at the same time. What we tried to do in *Interaction* was interweave talking, reading, and writing with drawing, photography, making slide shows, slide-tapes, working with tape recorders, so that it would be very natural for kids to become fluent with all of these at once. We don't make a big deal out of the fact that we're shifting media. We just allow the kids to do it. They improvise with the tape recorder on, they transcribe their improvisation, and then they've got a script. Well, there's talking, there's transcribing, they have to spell and punctuate their own speech—the basic skills come in there—and they are interested in their own speech. They're really motivated to do that. Then they give this script to other kids who read it and act it out. You set up these wonderful chains of activities that go on and on endlessly.

The main thing is to keep them going long enough. Some ancient doctor was supposed to have said, "All medical diagnoses come down to just one—congestion. And there's only one remedy—circulation." I think it's very wise, because the more you apply it, the more you see it holds up, medically and educationally. Both. You can say that part of the whole problem with the schools today is just tremendous congestion. There's really not enough going on. There's not enough volume and variety of exercise and practice. The constraints of controlling and managing in a mass institution are so great that not enough of anything occurs to know whether it's worthwhile or not. This is part of the problem with educational research. The constraints are so great that you can't tell from the trial of this or that whether it's any good or not. Activities that have great possibilities simply need to be done with greater frequency. . . .

5

Teaching Literacy

Background

Although pre-service teacher training relies too much on unwise conventional wisdom and commercial materials, and seldom affords experience in such things as small-group process, writing, or drama, an encouraging trend among both districts and colleges partly compensates for this through in-service institutes, workshops, and conferences that go beyond the limitations of regular training. These are usually regional, and some fine ones I was invited to participate in exemplified a very valuable collaboration between colleges and school districts. The address coming up here was elicited from me by a very high-caliber reading institute called *The Reading Experience: Social Dimensions of Language and Reading Development,* given in the summer of 1976 by the School of Education at Fordham University's Lincoln Center campus in New York City. Although I have expounded to many groups my approach to reading, I felt this effort was especially clear, coherent, and complete, partly, I believe, because the institute had created a good situation for me by emphasizing the *contexts* of reading, the social and psychological dimensions that make it an intricate process and are too often stripped off in the hurly-burly of school life.

To say that I never had any formal preparation in the teaching of reading is simply to say that I've never taken training in *any* area of teaching. Such innocence amounts to a real advantage in the field of reading, I realized, because it's a battlefield, and the smoke of war obscures it so badly that you have to step outside to perceive anything. I never had to strive to be broadminded and overcome the partisanship of being professionally brought up a certain way. I came upon the phonics approach, look-say, and "reading for meaning" as an astonished outsider who couldn't believe that the nurses were all fighting among themselves while the baby was crying untended. I never had to learn to integrate reading with the other language arts, because for me it has never been a separate subject. At first, I did take too seriously the research in comparing reading methods that Jeanne Chall reported in *Learning to Read: The Great Debate,* before I realized such research omitted or slighted some means to literacy and reflected what schools do and publishers put out, not what schools might do or ought to do. But I always assumed that literacy learning, as I prefer to call it to include beginning writing as well, occurs as an organic part of total language experience.

If I have been able to contribute to reading—or any other language art, for that matter—it has been more from working with teachers than with children. There's a good reason for this. Most problems children have learning literacy in school are artificial and unnecessary, but it's very difficult for teachers, caught in a frenetic world they never made, to see how much these problems are school- or teacher-induced. My approach is to try to restore learning conditions in school to something like what they might be naturally, i.e., when no professional is trying to teach at a special learning site. I'm not worried about children learning to read and write when only that is involved. If I can clear up the teachers' problems, I know the children will have trouble only if they're clearly damaged in some way. Most of my ideas about literacy come from listening to teachers talk about their problems with it and from matching what I know of children's general learning processes against the materials and methods schools offer. I've also learned a lot from reading with my own children when they were small and from working on literacy materials for the *Interaction* program, which contained no textbooks, only reading selections. When you have to commit yourself to definite school materials but repudiate basal readers and programmed "skill-builders," you start really thinking about the basic nature of literacy acquisition. Mainly, I felt I had to shun convention and reconceive the two R's, to create a perspective on reading within which problems looked different and would become soluble. I've met countless reading specialists and teachers in reading labs who, despite working for years with kids, were so blinded by conventions not founded on actual learning processes that they really could not see the issues well enough to troubleshoot for themselves. Sometimes I feel embarrassed telling grown-ups things that seem obvious or commonsensical to me, but I think that schooling has operated for so long on undetected irrelevance that teachers can be at least partly excused for not being able to have the needed insights. So for me, an institute like the one

LITERACY GOALS

I. To sound out with normal intonation any text one could understand if heard.

II. To write down with correct spelling and punctuation anything one could say.

at Fordham offers a fine chance to help teachers raise the quality of their thinking, so that even if they reject some of my practical suggestions, they'll be better able to see the way to go.

The text here is an edited transcription, in which I tried to retain as much of the flavor of the original as possible, consistent with reading ease. Illustrations recapitulate the transparencies referred to during the talk. I used these visuals also as cues to supplement some sparse notes.

In the Appendix I have included an open proposal to the profession, "People Reading," to which I invite responses toward the goal of eliminating illiteracy as a serious issue in U.S. education. Dr. Gabriel Della-Piana, Director of the University of Utah's Bureau of Educational Research, has already begun, for 1981, a USOE-funded project based on it, "Parent Participation." Such an idea could and should be replicated on a national scale, I believe, in much the same manner that the National Writing Project has grown out of the Bay Area Writing Project.

I find it's very important to have a certain theoretical underpinning for teaching practices in literacy because I think there's tremendous confusion in the field and has been for some time due partly to an ambiguity in the term "reading." It really means two things at once in speaking of school learning. The same thing is true of writing. I could put it this way. A friend of mine in the Boston area, Joel Weinberg, a reading specialist at Simmons College, said, "I can read Hebrew aloud faultlessly, but I don't understand a word of it. Friends of mine who do can understand perfectly well without looking at the text what I am saying." There are two very different meanings of reading right there. This duality is commonly recognized in the field of reading by referring to decoding versus comprehension.

The decoding is the part that Joel was doing, that is, translating the words right off the page into vocal sounds. That's often referred to also as word attack. The other is the comprehension aspect; his friends would be listening and not looking at the text but would understand it. Now, the same thing occurs with people reading to the blind, for example, or reading aloud to a sick person, where you split these dual functions of reading off from each other. These examples dramatize what is always true of any reader. In solo silent reading, the same thing is true. The two totally different processes are going on at the same time. Now, as teachers, we have the problem of confusing these. Though fused in the mind of the reader, they should not be confused in the minds—as I think they traditionally are—of people in the teaching profession. So, I'd like to disengage a bit these two different activities. It's true that, functionally, when one reads, one does everything at once and that's the way it should be, but I think as teachers we have to separate these functions in order to understand them more clearly.

Decoding is a term borrowed from communication engineers, who speak generally of coding, which subdivides into decoding as the receptive, and encoding as the writing, end of literacy. You don't hear much about encoding in school because we're more interested in passive, receptive activity, but literacy should be symmetrical. At any rate, I start with the engineer's term "coding" and recognize three levels of coding—putting raw experience into thought, then thought into speech, and then speech into print (see Fig. 1). I think it's important to distinguish these three levels that, in a certain sense, lead in an order; that is, each presupposes the prerequisite of the one before. Before speech can be encoded into print or decoded from print, there must be the prior level of the thought-speech relationship, thought into speech, and, before that, the prerequisite of experience into thought. I'm going to translate those three levels into somewhat different terms here to develop the idea.

The experience-into-thought level is the nonverbal level of *conceptualization,* where experience is first coded into concepts. We speak of concept formation. The second level is the level of *verbalization.* To verbalize is to put thought into speech. That's the oral level. The last—and we note— the most dependent, the most derived level is speech-into-print, the written level of *literacy* (see Fig. 2). Now, we are speaking of two-way coding, encoding and decoding. Nonverbal, oral, written—literacy being the two R's, reading and writing.

LEVELS OF
CODING

- *Experience into thought*

- *Thought into speech*

- *Speech into print*   Figure 1

LEVELS OF CODING

- *Experience into thought*

-NON-VERBAL-
Conceptualization

- *Thought into speech*

—ORAL—
Verbalization

- *Speech into print*

-WRITTEN-
Literacy

Figure 2

Let me translate these a little further. On the left of Fig. 3 are the three levels I just mentioned. I want to translate them over to the right into skills. So, reading down the left is the conceptualization level, which, when translated into school skills, let's say, comes out as the thinking skills—again, concept formation. The level of verbalization comes out as the speaking skills or oral language skills, as schools will call them, and then I have a very heavy bar down here to distinguish those two levels from the third, the literacy level or the two R's. That translates in school terms into the skills of word attack—that is to say, decoding and spelling, depending on whether one is talking about the reading direction or the writing direction.

Now, those traditionally are called the basic skills, but what justifies calling the most derived, the most dependent level, *basic* skills? Two other levels have to exist before that level can exist. We hear talk constantly about the two R's, word attack and spelling, as the basic skills. Well, from my point of view, there is kind of a misnomer involved. Those two skills are basic to literacy only. They are basic to that level, but, in the broader perspective of the total development of the learner, they are derived rather than basic. The real basic skills are thinking and speaking, right? Those are the really basic ones. So, I use "basic skills" always in quotation marks. You're not going to have basic skills in the sense of two R's until the true basic skills of thinking and speaking are thoroughly developed.

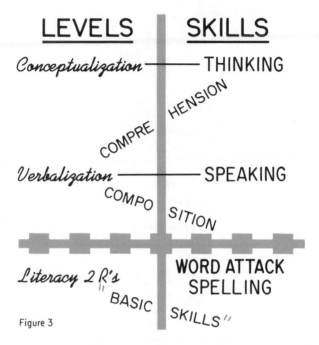

Figure 3

So I have written across Fig. 3 *comprehension* and *composition* to indicate that those first two levels cover a tremendous amount that is truly basic.

I want to continue translating those levels into other terms. Let's take just the literacy level for a while because teaching the basic skills, so-called, the two R's, tends to be such a tremendous problem in this country. I don't think it should be, but it is, and I hope I can indicate some of the reasons why it is when it should not be. So let me translate those levels now for purposes of getting just literacy for the moment into reading methods as they are practiced or could be practiced in school. In other words, we are getting into professional terms here. I say that any reading method is one or some combination of the four main reading methods listed in Fig. 4. I don't think this is my own invention, but it's my own way of codifying, if you like, what is done or talked about professionally in the field of reading, and there's a purpose to the order here.

Let me preface this first by saying that at the literacy level the learning task is essentially a paired association, as they say in psychology; that is, the learner is matching off vocal sounds he already knows with something new, which is the sights of the language—right?—the spelling. So, what we're into with the teaching of literacy is an audio-visual shift, a shift from an oral-aural medium to a visual medium, and that media shift is essentially what is called the two R's, or literacy. Anything that allows the learner to see and hear English at the same time, in some synchronized fashion, will teach reading in the basic sense of literacy. And anything

The Four Main Reading Methods

① Matching single sound with letter (s).

② Matching single spoken word with its written equivalent.

③ Watching one's oral sentences being written down.

④ Watching a text while hearing it read. Figure 4

that does not will not. I don't think this is true because I say so; I think you should test it for yourself, but, if literacy is basically a media shift, then you have to have both media represented. The student is going to have to hear the sounds of the language, which he knows already, at the same time he sees how those sounds are written or spelled and, if he has enough of that, he will learn to read. So the methods, in a sense, necessarily, logically, must break down into something like what follows here.

One way of providing this audio-visual matching is matching single sounds with letters; that is, match each of the forty-odd phonemes of English, the basic sounds, with its spellings, and most have more than one spelling. For example, as the learner is presented with a letter or spelling, he is told how to pronounce it, or he is given the sound and shown how it is spelled. But we are below the word level. This is like subatomic physics here, particles. The second method focuses on a larger unit. This method matches a single spoken word with its written equivalent. Here we deal with single whole words rather than with word particles. The third focuses on a larger language unit and consists of the learner watching his oral sentences being written down, so that he can see how what he says looks like when it's spelled. The last method also involves whole sentences and the continuity of whole sentences. It consists of watching a text while hearing it read. What I'm saying is that any way of success-fully teaching reading, in the sense of literacy, is bound to be one or more of these methods. This is my way of breaking it down. You'll have to test the truth of it yourself.

To translate these four methods into more or less traditional profes-sional school terms, the first one would be "phonics," the level of word particles. (See Fig. 5, which moves from small unit to large unit.) Match-ing a single spoken word with its written equivalent has gone by the name of "look-say" or "sight word." The classic example would be flash cards. A card having one word written on it is flashed and then someone says the word so that the learner can see and hear the word at the same time. That is a larger learning unit, the whole word.

The third goes under the name of "language experience approach," done generally in primary school; no reason not to do it at later ages. It consists of the learner dictating, in effect, a story of some sort to someone who is literate, who writes down what he says—again, so that the learner can see his own speech written down and thus make the paired associ-

The Four Main Reading Methods

(1) *Matching single sound with letter (s).*

"PHONICS"——————— Word Particles

(2) *Matching single spoken word with its written equivalent.*

"LOOK-SAY," "SIGHT-WORD"——— Words

(3) *Watching one's oral sentences being written down.*

"LANGUAGE EXPERIENCE"——— Phrases, Sentences

(4) *Watching a text while hearing it read.*

"READ-ALONG," "LAP METHOD"— Sentences

Figure 5

ation. The last one, interestingly enough, has not been dignified as a reading method, and thereby hangs a long tale and tremendous difficulties. Most reading research will not include it, and therefore I think most reading research having to do with methodology is perhaps for that reason alone not very valid. Watching a text while hearing it read aloud, to the extent it is now beginning to be recognized as a reading method in the field, is often called "read-along." I prefer my own term, the "lap method." I deliberately make it folksy to indicate that it has been done at home and not in school. The prototype of that is a bedtime situation in which the child is sitting on the parent's lap, looking at and perhaps holding the book himself and getting the audio in his ear from the parent. The child is seeing the text while hearing it read aloud. For a number of interesting reasons, schools have virtually ignored this, have never considered this a reading method. Anyway, these are the four.

Today there's a tendency to be somewhat eclectic and mix approaches. I doubt if anyone is so diehard as to say she can do it with phonics alone or look-say alone and absolutely nothing else. In any case, if there's anything at all going on realistically in the classroom, the last two methods are bound to be represented to some extent. A person is going to be hearing something read aloud while he's watching the text.

O.K., these are in a progression going, as I said, from the smallest unit of language to the largest. The issue here is what size shall the learning unit be? What language unit shall be the learning unit? Phonics focuses on the particles that make up words. Look-say, or sight word, focuses on single, isolated, whole words, and three and four focus on sentences and sentence continuity.

The other issue is who or what supplies the audio. Given that literacy is a media shift and both media have to be present simultaneously in a synchronized fashion, where does the audio come from? Does it come from the teacher? If so, the teacher is tied up with the whole class at once, and there is no opportunity to individualize. Shall the voice be recorded? Shall the voice be the learner's own voice, as it is in number three, the language experience approach, where individual learners or a small group of kids, let's say, who have been on a trip or following a project, dictate and the teacher writes this down? The audio is then supplied by the learner himself. Students might supply the audio for each other in group exchanges. These are the main issues I think we should think about—who supplies the audio and how large shall the learning unit be.

Now, I think that covered in this scale are the kinds of controversies that have ripped apart the field of reading with arguing about one or another of these things, and I think the fights are unnecessary. What we should do is think of these as an array or progression and understand the differences among them and try to exploit those differences. Properly individualized programs, for example, would help each student find which of these or which combinations he needs. We know, for example, that many, many students have learned to read and write extremely well without any phonics at all. Other students, we know from experience, seem to have difficulty without some explicit instruction by the first method, but it's hard to judge because there has not been enough emphasis on three and four in schools, for the most part, to know what the real power and impact of that would be, whether those students who seemed to have needed phonics, because they never quite generalized the phonetic relationships and therefore were memorizing words and could not attack new words, would have been able to attack new words had they had some of three and four. Do you see what I mean? The only way you're really going to know is to have all of these in play and find out.

I think I would say generally that we should emphasize the larger units more, put most of our force, and our faith, behind them on the principle, which I think is sound, that the wholes teach the parts, not the other way around, because the whole is larger and contains the parts, and in general the larger the context, the safer you are. Just for one example, there's no way to teach the reading and writing of punctuation if you don't have whole sentences, so that rules out methods one and two. Think about that for a moment. Without whole sentences, there's no way to deal with punctuation.

Much more important, I believe, is that the larger the context, the larger the unit you're working with, the more opportunity there is for meaning and, therefore, for motivation. How much motivation or meaning is there in the syllable "ap", A–P, or "tee", or just a single consonant, the K sound, for example? No meaning and, therefore, no motivation. When you get to the whole-word level, O.K., there is *some* more meaning. You know, single words have meaning, like the word "poison" on a medicine bottle and environmental writing, signs, and captions, and so on, that deal with single words. You may know the Sylvia Ashton-Warner approach, which she described in the book *Teacher.* She tells of working with Maori children in New Zealand, of having them ask for words that were of great emotional interest to them and then writing these down on a piece of tagboard so they would build up a little word-card collection of words they were motivated to learn. O.K., that's a very creative way to work with what is not a very powerful level, that is, the isolated-word level.

Then you move on up to three and four, where kids are dictating high-interest material because it's coming from them, whole sentences, a whole story, and then listening to a text while watching it, number four; you're in again to whole pieces of real writing, real reading. Therefore, you have more meaning and motivation. Generally, as you go from one to four, you increase the amount of meaning and you decrease the problem of how to motivate. So, strictly as a strategy, I would say the safest thing to do, the most powerful approach, is to work as much as possible with the larger units and bring in the smaller units only to the extent that you feel they are warranted by practical experience. That is, phonics is only a means. Working with whole words and whole sentences . . . those are, to some extent, ends, goals—to be able to read those—but it's not a learning goal, I think, to be able to read "ap" or "tee" or anything like that. It's strictly a means. Logically, you want to focus on the goals, and when something is a means only, like phonics, then use it as little as possible and only when it justifies itself.

I'd like to use now a passage I picked from a comic strip as an example of what I think actually happens in the reading process, let's say, of a learner who knows, who has generalized for himself or had taught explicitly to him, some phonics, some of the phonetic regularities of English, but is still a very shaky or weak reader or perhaps, left to his own motivation, a nonreader. Here is what I think happens and why it is that the larger context can teach the particles, the wholes teach the parts. Figure 6 is from the comic strip, *Miss Peach.* I don't know, I guess I picked that unconsciously, being a teacher; it often focuses on the classroom. A boy there had set up a little booth as a psychiatrist, and he hung out his headshrinker's shingle and was giving advice on one thing or another, counseling, and some girl had come back to complain to him. I guess he was acting as data mates, too. She said, "That boy you sent me is a real dud, and you told me our relationship would rapidly grow and blossom into something beautiful." I picked this really very much at random, but it seemed to me the sort of reading matter that would appeal to a kid in upper elementary or junior high who is having trouble and that might provide us with a very good sample to work with. Incidentally, his response to her complaint was, "Did you water it?" It threw a little of the responsibility back to her.

I have underlined those spellings that would pose problems for many shaky or weak readers—the OY ending, the *oi* sound—that diphthong—when it has a Y instead of an I at the end of the word; or notice the OU in *you, our,* and *would.* Again, I just picked this at random, but it's typical of English that you can have three different sounds for the same spelling

"That boy you sent me is a real dud, and you told me our relationship would rapidly grow and blossom into something beautiful."

Figure 6   MISS PEACH

in a passage as short as that. The *sh* sound in *relationship,* spelled with TI rather than SH or CH. The word *beautiful,* very irregular because of its French derivation, *beau;* and *grow,* the long *o* sound, is one of many spellings with the long *o* sound—O, OE, OUGH, OW, right? The long-vowel spellings are particularly difficult. *Real*—again, the long *e* is spelled many, many ways—E, EE, EA, EI, et cetera. O.K., what I think happens is this: let's say we have a . . . O.K., now, a learner, a blooming reader who is very weak, but he knows some of the sound-spelling relationships. What happens is that he does use context to figure out those phonic relationships he does not know yet, that is, has not been taught or has not generalized for himself. Now, if these were isolated, he would not be able to do it. Do you see what I mean? Even the isolated word perhaps he would not get, not to mention the OU all by itself—simply no context. You don't know how to sound OU by itself or even OUGH without the rest of the word.

What the context supplies are cues or clues of essentially three sorts. Any native speakers of English, by the time they enter school, really know the basic grammar, the syntax; that is, they know the proper order of words. Of course, they have no idea what the names are, the nomenclature about nouns and adverbial clauses and determiners and modifiers. But never mind. They know how to use these. They know those slots in the sentence. No child says, "Hat blue my." He says, "My blue hat." Whether he knows a possessive adjective from a doorknob doesn't make any difference. He knows the syntax of those words, and he decodes sentences he has never heard before, and he invents or formulates sentences he has never heard before. So, the psycholinguists are quite right in praising the tremendous learning that has already gone on before children get to school in generalizing for themselves the syntactic rules of the language. They know their grammar. When we speak of teaching grammar in school, again it is kind of a misnomer. We mean we are now going to ticket, to label, all the things that they already know in a functional, operational way. O.K., drawing on that knowledge, which goes with the *oral* language skills, a reader, an incipient or weak reader, can figure out what certain words must be; that is, there are only certain things that can go after "a" in "is a real dud." After the article, you know there's going to have to be a noun coming somewhere in there, or let's say, after "real," after the modifier, there's got to be a noun. Now, he doesn't formulate that for himself, but his experience of the language tells him that. Certain slots in the sentence can be filled only with certain types of words, so that narrows down which words come up there. If winter comes, can spring be far behind? If you get a determiner, can the noun be far behind? Or predicates: "Our relationship would rapidly grow." Now, any speaker of the language who hits the word "would" knows, in most situations, that the other shoe is going to fall soon, the other part of the predicate. They don't know anything about auxiliaries in an intellectual way, but they know that there has to be the other part of the predicate coming along, so they are waiting for it. Again, that reduces the possibilities for the "grow" slot. See what I mean? The use of syntactic cues—and any proficient reader, of course, is doing this very successfully. This all goes on at computer speed, in the old biocomputer here, as John Lilly calls it. That's one set of cues.

Another is the sense, the meaning, the ongoing meaning. Now, if there isn't any meaning, of course, that rules these cues out, just as, if you don't have whole sentences, syntactic cues are ruled out. Terrible losses, because even the proficient reader requires them, and the less proficient a reader is, the more he is going to rely on those clues. All right, following the meaning, that is, the drift, of what is being said here, you can guess, you can predict what certain words will be. For example, "beautiful," isolated by itself, might be a difficult word to figure out, but, given the context, if the kid has been following the sentence so far, he can make a good guess about "beautiful." He is apt to know B; the B sound-spelling is one of the earlier ones and easier ones to learn, and the T and perhaps the L. In other words, the consonants are generally fairly easy and, knowing those, knowing that that has to be an adjective in that slot, knowing what the sense of the whole passage is, "beautiful" . . . he can figure it out. This is going on all the time in any authentic instance of someone reading or trying to read. Of course, if they do not care, none of this will work. The will must be behind the old biocomputer or you get nothing, and this is why the motivation is absolutely essential. Without it you don't even have a basis on which to think about the problem.

The third source of cues is, of course, the actual spellings, the letter knowledge that the student does have so far, whether from explicit phonics or from his own generalization. Sense, syntax, and sound-spellings are, in compact form, the three main sources of cues with which to figure out a passage (see Fig. 7). Two of these are the ideas or the ongoing sense and the vocabulary/grammar, syntax having to do with the word endings, the word order, the relationships among words. Vocabulary/grammar goes with the syntax . . . is the second source; and then comes the final one, the sound-spellings or the phonics, the phonetic relationships, how all the forty-odd phonemes in English are actually spelled in various situations.

Now, again to speak just of the literacy level, we do best, I think, to bank heavily on the larger context. The larger the language unit that is used as the learning unit, the better off we are. Count on the wholes to teach the parts, that is, the ongoing meaning, the sense, the syntax, and so on, to bring along the sound-spellings. This is how a kid who has been presented only a few of the sound-spellings, through phonics, can learn the rest on his own . . . because he can use the little letter knowledge he

KINDS OF CUES

- SENSE — *Ideas*

  —NON-VERBAL—

  Conceptualization

- SYNTAX — *Vocabulary, grammar*

  —ORAL—

  Verbalization

- SOUND — *Phonics*

  —WRITTEN—

  Literacy

Figure 7

has. He can get a lot of mileage out of the little visual knowledge he has so far accumulated by using the oral knowledge he already has, preschool and out of school, the oral knowledge being the meanings that attach to the words and his knowledge of the grammar and oral vocabulary.

I have been dwelling just on the decoding aspect. I want to shift now to comprehension. If literacy is concerned only with the overlay, the last level of coding, in Fig. 1, then what about those first two levels? They are also part of the definition of reading. Remember, I began by saying that it's a word that has a double meaning. The person who is listening to something being read aloud is doing all the comprehending, in the case, let's say, of the Hebrew being read aloud, and the person who is reading it but does not understand it is doing the decoding. What *about* the comprehending? One of the main things, it seems to me, that this kind of analysis shows is that two-thirds, at least, of learning to read does not necessarily have anything to do with books or letters, print. In other words, the audio-visual shift, from the medium of the ear to the medium of the eye, is only the tip of the iceberg. Before that can have any meaning, utility, or motivational force, we have to have developed and continue to develop in students the thinking and speaking skills represented in Fig. 1 by "conceptualization" and "verbalization."

What teaches those things? Well, a million things teach them, right? All of the accumulating experience that a learner acquires from many, many sources, through many, many media, methods, and materials, is teaching reading. Part of our difficulty, I believe, is in considering reading as a kind of isolated specialty and as a sort of technical problem concerning books. I think often a student's difficulty with reading does not have to do with the speech-to-print shift, or, at least, that in order to handle that, they have to develop the others. In other words, you learn to read from talking, from getting the kinds of experience that develop the intellect, that develop concepts, logic, much of which can be done orally.

Comprehension, in other words, is not simply connected with reading. In nonliterate or preliterate cultures, everybody is comprehending all the time. You read the environment, you read other people, you listen to what other people say. There is oral comprehension and, if this is highly developed, I think there'll be no problem of reading comprehension, given, of course, that students do make the media shift. We have to think of the teaching of reading as comprising—I think this is the only realistic way to consider it—as comprising the whole mental and verbal life of the student, so that anything that develops thinking and speaking is going to have big payoffs for reading, as well as motivating the desire to read. It's possible to teach, I think, all levels at once to some extent, and this is highly desirable for reasons that I've been suggesting and that have to do with banking more heavily on methods three and four—the whole-sentence, whole-continuity methods that teach the parts through the wholes.

Let me describe a little more fully the method I call the lap method, number four or read-along, the one that has not been generally recognized as a method. Now, never mind that you may be interested in older students—this applies at any level. You say, well, how can they really learn the basic skills, word attack and spelling, by just listening to whole texts like that without isolating particular phonemes. How are they ever going to learn those details . . . really nitty-gritty details? I will try to explain how I think that happens; it has to do with the whole issue of wholes teaching parts.

Traditionally, what happens with preschool children and the bedtime story? They are following the text with their eyes, let's say, and they hear the parent reading in their ear. There's not too much text on a page, and often the typography is such that certain words stand out—end positions, different type, enlarged, and so on . . . often they are connected with pictures, a lot of picture cues. And there's a lot of repetition—the format of the stories has repetition—so that the children recognize certain words coming up again and again and, at the same time, they hear the sound of the word. Well, what happens at first is that they memorize whole pages. If you've read many bedtime stories to children, you know that they memorize the story after a while and, if you get anything the least bit out of order, they really raise hell about it. They won't let you omit anything and get things out of order, and they can turn the pages for you after a while. Okay, you say, well, that's not really reading, and it's true, because if you took the same words on that page and wrote another text with them, the children would not be able to read that yet. Fine. They have begun the reading process in this sense, though: they are turning pages, they have the whole idea that there are ideas in the book, locked into the pages, that you open the book, you turn the pages, the ideas unfold, the story ideas, the images, that there is *pleasure* connected with this, that there are goodies locked in the book, that it's very positive, it's unthreatening, it's something one wants to do. Furthermore, they've got the synchronization to some extent. They're now synchronizing large blocks, by memorizing the pages, let's say.

O.K., to pursue this, though, what happens if they're read to very regularly—and it takes a lot of it—the same text sometimes, a new text sometimes, so that there is some old, some new? What happens eventually is that their focus gets finer and finer and finer and, instead of just the gross blocks of whole pages, it gets down to certain sentences, phrases, certain words they recognize, the number two level there of sight words—again, the repeated words, the words that are made to stand out and so on—but also they're getting down to the phonics level of number one. With enough quantity, they begin to recognize that the WH, for example, that little configuration there, appears wherever they hear the "wh—" sound—*which, what, why, where* sounds; it's in the initial position. So, after a while, they generalize for themselves that WH spells that sound, and that is learning to read, to become literate. They do this gradually—no doubt, with the easier things first, the consonants, then the short vowels and so on, then long vowels—and they begin, in other words, to infer for themselves the regularities of English spelling in exactly the same way they did this for the grammar of the language in learning to speak. The old biocomputer that does this sort of thing, that is part of human functioning, is doing this generalizing in there, and it got well exercised before the children came to school. They have already learned some of the basic concepts and vocabulary so that all they are trying to do now is to attach those things that they already know to the new medium of print, using all of these cues.

I think this is what happens, then, in the read-along or lap method, seeing and hearing language at the same time. It gradually refines down, down, down, and the children get very specific and they learn phonics from that, and this is how many, many students have learned word attack beautifully, and spelling, without any phonics. But this has not been considered a school method, and I'm obviously making a very strong pitch for it, partly because of the problem of righting an imbalance; it has been virtually omitted so far.

Practically speaking, of course, you do not have to have a lap and, if you are teaching secondary students, a little face-saving has got to go on. You use other students perhaps who are more advanced, who are able to decode well. They might even rehearse a little first and then read to the weaker readers. Older students with younger . . . I have been involved in experiments in elementary school where fifth and sixth graders come in and pair off with primary or first grade kids. Both like their relationship and, with just a little coaching, the older kids can do this very well. It does not take a teacher, it only takes someone who is literate and who is interested in doing it. So, parents, aides, older students all could do this, provide a live voice, a live audio, for the beginning or weak reader.

In addition to a live voice of this sort, you can, of course, have a recorded voice. In the *Interaction* program I referred to earlier, we recorded eighty hours of the texts. You don't have to buy the recordings. You could make the recordings yourself, have other people do it, have students do it after they have rehearsed, but I would suggest recording a lot of the texts you are using in the classroom, or if you're working with other people in the classroom, you might recommend this to them. I have even recommended this at the college level. An economics professor says that his students cannot read or do not understand the text. And I say, "Well, if you read it to them, do they get it?" And he says, "Well, it goes a lot better that way." I say, "Okay, then record it." So, they go get the recording *and* the book. The illiteracy problem is so bad in this country that it's rising through the grades and is now a serious problem in many colleges. For older students, at any rate, a recording of the text so they can do read-along or the equivalent of lap method is an excellent way, I think, for taking a person who is dependent and not proficient and helping him to become independent and proficient without loss of face, without a tremendous sort of ego ordeal, of putting self-esteem on the line, because it's really fairly easy.

To get on to other recommendations I would make for creative programs in reading, I think it's essential to integrate reading with the other language arts. This is implied in what I've been saying so far. The larger the context, the easier the learning is. The more you isolate reading from the other language arts, the harder it is to teach, just as the more you isolate phonemes from the normal language context, the harder it is actually to teach them. We have a technical approach; we think if you isolate something out and drill on that, students will learn that and then they'll put it back together with the rest. That doesn't happen. Reading itself includes that hidden part of the iceberg that doesn't have to do with books, the thinking and speaking skills. For this reason, it develops better if it's connected with all the content areas. Fortunately, there's an emphasis today on reading in the content areas, I think partly because students read so badly that the problem of literacy has spread across the board now in schools as well as up the grades. At any rate, a positive effect has been to help integrate reading with the other language arts. By "integrate," I mean that reading tasks or assignments should be, I think, tied in to little series of activities, such, for example, that a student writes something, discusses, reads, acts out, and so on . . . various interweaving of the language arts with each other and with the graphic arts, the combining of reading with photos in the forms of captions and labels, maps, charts, graphs, where words are combined with graphics. This does a number of things at once. It teaches students to use one of the language arts or one of the graphic arts to get a leverage on reading, but it also *interests* them in reading. It has a motivational payoff. The larger the context, the more meaning, the more motivation.

Now for some of the kinds of reading matter that I think it would help to introduce into the classroom. I mentioned charts, graphs, maps, and captioned photographs—graphics combined with words. In the *Interaction* program, we put out whole booklets of nothing but those, so that they'd be legitimized as reading matter. We didn't care about whether this was language arts, social studies, science, because when you get into things like that, they cut scross the different disciplines. The use of transcripts . . . a tremendous amount of really interesting material covering any kind of subject matter students might be interested in is purveyed or appears in our society in the form of transcripts. Interviews, talk shows, hearings, court trials—a lot of this really interests students and, because it's oral transcription, the speech sounds natural, not so foreign to them. Yet, in these interviews or talk shows or trials, the content can be quite deep and can cover any kind of interest.

Again, the problem with meaning is in a way the biggest one. If you do integrate reading with the language arts and with the other arts so that reading has warm-ups and follow-ups, you'll find that it's tremendously powerful. For example, students reading a few fables together . . . a small group reading a few fables together, then writing their own, discussing fables without the moral until they try to agree on what the moral of the fable is and then looking to see what the moral is and then maybe writing some more fables of their own, and distributing these to other students who would then use that as reading material. Do you see what I mean? Interweaving the language arts.

I would recommend partner reading. This presupposes a system of small groups reading different kinds of reading material at the same time. I think it's self-defeating—and almost too negative to work with—to have an entire class read the same thing at the same time. I know this is standard procedure in most U.S. schools, but it's also one of the main reasons why we are having trouble with literacy. It's a gamble that you're bound to lose. The spread within any grade—third grade, tenth grade, it doesn't make any difference—the spread of interest, subject matter, content, of reading difficulty, of style, of individual and ethnic variation is so great, even in a so-called homogeneous classroom that, in effect, you have a spread of grades anywhere from four, six, eight to ten years within any one year, so that to assign the same text to a class at the same time is very self-defeating. I think there's no way to win that one. I realize this indicates a different kind of classroom organization, but that is precisely what I'm recommending. If we're serious about beating the reading problems in this country now, I think it means we have to individualize the reading from first grade on, but by "individualize" I don't mean programmed materials, that's for certain. I do mean students choosing their own reading material, given a very wide array of subject matter and difficulty, but this doesn't mean working alone. I think, on the contrary, most students, particularly if they're weak readers, will prefer to read something in company with a few partners. So what I recommend is a small-group process where students choose their reading material in combination with a few partners who are also interested in the same content, let's say, the same form, or read at about the same level of difficulty, enough to get along anyway.

So there are a number of things that go along with this approach. One is that you have to have a far wider array of reading materials in any one classroom than is customary; otherwise, individualizing is just a hollow slogan, as, indeed, it usually is. If there's no opportunity for the individual to find something of his own level to really interest him, then nothing else will work, and learning to read will seem the technical matter that you have to solve with a lot of expensive gear in a language lab, a reading lab, when actually it isn't. But the small groups choosing together the reading materials—this means, for one thing, you don't need whole-class sets of any text. What you need is to trade off the number of copies for the number of titles, get more titles in a classroom, but only a handful of copies for each, in some cases maybe only one or two. So an individual with a partner, or maybe in a small group of four, five, or six, can get both the advantages of individualization—that is, finding something that's really matched to them—and at the same time the advantages of cooperation and socializing. This is very, very powerful—different groups reading different things at the same time. I would recommend this also in a high school social studies or science course. We're rapidly losing students in the content areas in secondary school because the textbooks are just so hard for them to read or so uninteresting that we don't know how much is reading difficulty or how much is just indifference. The new math textbooks are virtually unreadable for most students. Again, we don't know how much the problem is simply motivational, because math is a dehumanized subject as it is generally presented in textbooks. So we have to get off the gold standard of the uniform textbook and, I think, get into something else, into what I'm describing.

Now, a way to facilitate this is to have a very varied, wide classroom library and to have the books cross-referenced to recordings of those texts, when you have recorded them, so the students can get the text and the recording and, as a group or alone, go off and play those. Have the books also cross-referenced to other materials that might be used in connection with them, such as graphic materials, or to activity cards that give the students follow-up activities to do in the way I was describing earlier, the interweaving.

So solving the problem of reading, I think, very much involves fairly drastic changes in reading materials and in classroom management to allow more powerful methods to operate. The same for number three, the language-experience approach of the learner dictating his own content and having somebody else write it down. That is usually done in primary school, but there's no reason not to do it in secondary. Although the teacher cannot, as with the read-along method, employ a machine, I recommend a kind of buddy system of more proficient students taking down the speech of the less proficient or—this may be most appropriate for secondary—having students talk into a tape recorder (again, maybe as a small group) or improvise a scene with a tape recorder going and then, together, transcribe their own words. This is very popular with many secondary students. It does not look babyish. It's really a language-experience method done in a more practical way for secondary. Together, with the teacher's help and with each other's help, collectively, they can transcribe their own speech and then read this back, read it to other people, or pass it on for someone else to read. It's a good use of the tape recorder, I think.

In general, I think the voice has to act as an intermediary for the beginning or weak reader between his oral language, his nonverbal experience, and books. The voice has to be the intermediary, in a progression somewhat like this: First, he has to hear some literate person sound the language while he sees it, to get the pairing of language sounds with spellings, or his own voice in the case of language experience; but there has to be an external voice to provide that intermediary in the beginning. Then what happens is that he internalizes gradually the aide's role so that he begins to be able to read solo silent more, and he is subvocalizing. The progression is: somebody else reads to you, then you begin to read out loud with partners taking turns reading the same book to each other in a small group, and then you shift the voice inside and subvocalize. The final stage—and this involves speed reading for those who are very proficient already—is that the voice disappears completely, even the inner voice, so there is a direct connection between *thought* and *sight* that bypasses the intermediary of vocalization, even subvocalization. At that point we are not talking about the kind of learners that most of us are involved with; we are talking about someone who has learned literacy so well that he can now read at the speed of sight rather than at the speed at which he can read a text aloud, and that is where you get into the Evelyn Wood type of speed reading for those for whom it works.[1]

This dissolving of the intermediary is equivalent to how, I am told, the Balinese teach their children to do their traditional dances. The adult stands behind the child and moves his body in the way the dance is made to move, and the child just moves with him by being receptive. They continue to move together like this until eventually the adult simply steps back and the child continues to move on his own. The supplying of the audio is like that, of live or recorded voice. It has to supply that kind of intermediary until the student can take off on his own. Solo silent reading may be the goal, but it's not the means. The means are social, interactive, and external until the process is learned, and then they can go on internally.

The final point I want to make is that I think the teaching of reading today, the main trends of it, are negative and going in the wrong direction, for some reasons that have to do with orientation of the whole culture, which at the moment is, in its materialism, directed toward the analytic and the particle, to breakdowns, to disintegration. The computer—which is not in itself anything bad—the computer can, in a way, symbolize this, in the way we have used it. The computer needs fine breakdowns. Programmed materials need fine breakdowns. Managerial technocrats, who want finely sliced instructional objectives, want fine breakdowns. The whole of the educational–industrial complex in this country now is pushing hard toward breaking reading and all other learning into very fine units, which is disintegrative.

As I say, it's part and parcel of a general materialistic trend that follows the lead of the federal government, which has had an extremely negative influence through its funding programs. State legislatures have followed in turn, and now it's very difficult to get support for a realistic kind of approach to reading because the trends in political and economic and legislative circles are going the other way. I say this not as a matter merely of complaint but in a positive sense. I think if as people involved in the teaching of reading you believe some of what I'm saying—you have similar insights, or this makes sense to you, or you want to test it out for yourself—you're going to have to lobby for it. I think corrective action is very much needed. The diverting of huge numbers of secondary students into labs of programmed materials where they're run through

---

[1] I did not mean to imply by this pragmatic line of reasoning for schools that people cannot in some circumstances connect thought to sight directly or initially. Deaf people frequently bypass oral speech in learning literacy, and to learn an oral symbol system before a visual symbol system is only a cultural convention, not a biological necessity. Preschool children's drawings and much of the world's graphic art also connect sight directly to thought.

phonic sequences they had over and over again in elementary school where it did not work the first time—this is a tremendously negative thing.

In this connection, standardized tests, I think, have been misleading us greatly, because they have no audio component. The use of cheap standardized paper and pencil tests—and that characterizes all of the ones we go by—misleads us because, without a vocal, audio component, there is no way to distinguish between decoding and comprehension problems. If a student scores low on a standardized test, *we do not know what it means.* It's generally assumed that because the test is called a reading test it's in the decoding sense that the student is failing. Most often, I would say, that is not the case. The older the student, the less true it is. More true, I think, is that his problem is in the oral language realm of thinking and speaking—what I have called the real basics. He simply doesn't know the vocabulary, he can't use the cues of sentences, the meaning, to figure out a text. But it's assumed he has a decoding problem, so he's shunted into some government-funded reading laboratory that has a lot of expensive material that isn't going to help him. If it worked, we would know by now. So I think the drift is the other way and we are engaged in trying to right that imbalance and we may have to fight for it.

6

Going with Growth: Fitting Schools to the Facts of Language Life

Background

This talk sketches some connections among cognitive growth, holistic learning, and vocal interaction. It has never been easy for me to explain how peer talk can further the most serious kinds of mental and verbal development. Few people believe it, even some who profess to, because very rarely, if ever, has a wave of students had a chance to benefit from even a whole year, much less several years' running, of good, sustained small-group vocal interaction in school. Most teachers who try it are quickly put off by such initial problems as kids fooling around and are discouraged from developing it by district insistence on teaching to tests on other things (usually language particles). So the evidence to convince is scarce. Without evidence, no conviction; without conviction, no evidence. This vicious circle makes it necessary, I feel, to combine any discussion of actual growth processes and suitable methods with remarks that bring out into the open this conflict between the political facts of life and the learning facts of life.

I doubt that I succeeded any more on this occasion than on others, but I was provided an excellent setting by another high-quality gathering, the Third Annual Conference on Language Arts Education, sponsored by the Department of Elementary and Remedial Education of the State University of New York at Buffalo in 1977. The topic helped—*Facilitating Language Development, Preschool through Adolescence*—and the emphasis that many of the following speakers gave to the *learner's* production of language, oral and written, supported well what I had to say. In 1978, the University published a report of the conference (bearing the title above and edited by Patrick Finn and Walter Petty) that produced the talks, including a transcription of mine with some following questions and answers. I was speaking from a brief outline.

A word about what is not in this talk but perhaps should be, at least in the future. In it I refer tangentially to Rudolph Steiner while mentioning developmentalists Piaget, Werner, and Erickson. Though the founder of a still-thriving international chain of Waldorf Schools, Steiner is virtually unknown among U.S. educators, most of whom would probably be

Reprinted with permission from *Facilitating Language Development, Preschool through Adolescence*, SUNY Buffalo, 1978.

astonished to read some of his statements on human growth. (See Steiner's *The Kingdom of Childhood*, Rudolph Steiner Press, London, 1974, and *The Recovery of Man in Childhood*, A.C. Harwood, Hodder and Stoughton, London and Toronto, 1958.) Though not necessarily an advocate of what Waldorf Schools do, I feel almost guilty to speak, as I did here, as if I think human growth comprises only what these excellent material scientists describe. My English comperes often say that I base my work on Piaget, whereas I have always worked much more intuitively than that. As with notions of inner speech, which came to me before reading Piaget or Vygotsky or Mead, I cite these figures to gain credibility with a society that believes only authorities in white lab jackets. Piaget was the most useful for getting a curriculum across because his concepts of egocentricity, logical development, and inner speech all certified, and extended, perceptions I was operating on but needed sanctioning of.

Steiner's ideas do not so much conflict with the developmental models of Piaget, Werner, Bruner, and Erickson as they subsume them. It is, in fact, fascinating to see how, although he died in 1925, he had already described mental growth very much as they did later (and also very much as Whitehead did in *The Aims of Education*):

> . . . the child up to its ninth or tenth year is really demanding that the whole world of external nature shall be made alive, because he does not yet see himself as separate from this external nature; therefore we shall tell the child fairy tales, myths, and legends.
>
> . . .
>
> It is only toward the twelfth year that the child is ready to hear causes and effects spoken of.

—pp. 63 and 65, *The Kingdom of Childhood*

Fine, that won't jar anyone today, but look further into *The Kingdom of Childhood* for a perspective far broader than that of contemporary psychology. In addition to having a strong scientific and mathematical bent and demonstrating a very accomplished intellectual scholarship (he was entrusted as a young man with the editing of Goethe's scientific writings), he was also spiritually gifted and employed these gifts in his researches. This extraordinary combination of faculties places his work, in my mind, above that of Piaget, Bruner, and Werner, who are indeed perceptive themselves but whose professional framework and affiliations would prevent them from saying what Steiner said even if they were seeing as he did (a problem of staying respectable that I think Jung and even Freud had, Freud having said in a letter that if he had it all to do over, he would go into parapsychology, and Jung having openly gone into it as well as having described an "out-of-body" experience in his autobiography).

I believe we'll soon have to expand our ideas of human growth beyond the ordinarily visible world until they embrace the full evolution of consciousness that we're really involved in. But so far I haven't felt free in such talks to do more than hint at spiritual growth, because many people turn off at what seems to them spooky or religious, especially when earning their daily bread means getting kids to score well on tests of meaningless fragments. I have tried to keep credibility so that an already difficult job of convincing will not become hopeless, while at the same time testing the upper edges of the audience to keep my own sense of integrity.

<hr />

The title of my presentation, "Going with Growth: Fitting Schools to the Facts of Language Life," does imply a discrepancy. That is, learning goes one way—the real authentic organic facts of learning—and institutionalism has a way of going its own way; so it's a perennial problem to get the two matched up and to *keep* the two matched up. I think we are in an era where they are particularly divergent, for a number of reasons.

We don't have a lot of time and I want to leave some time for questioning because this is a very mixed audience with different backgrounds and different concerns—I guess you go from nursery to college—so what I will say will be very sketchy and very suggestive and not very detailed or documented. I'll leave some of that to questioning.

Let me try to describe the growth of thought and speech in a general way as I see it. I think what can depict growth of thought and speech rather effectively is the series of pictures or photos that depict stages of growth of the embryo (or the human fetus). They used to draw these; now they have actual photographs of the embryo in different stages at several weeks, several months, and so on, *in utero*. What you see in these depictions is a whole. This whole begins with a very simple single cell that begins to divide and to differentiate into parts within itself. So if you look at depictions of the embryo at different stages you will see this whole becomes complicated within and yet—and this is my main point— it never ceases being a whole no matter what stage of development it is at. You will see the development of a cardiovascular system and a network of veins, of nerves, of various organs forming, and the limbs, but at no point is any of this separated. It is always a whole. In other words, it does not follow the industrial model of the assembly line, where the carburetor is sent in from Toledo to Detroit, and this sub-assembly is attached to other assemblies, and finally something plops off the end of the assembly line. This kind of model has been brought into education, rather inappropriately, and I think it misleads us in many ways. The growth of thought and speech does not proceed by the assembling of sub-assemblies. The teaching of tiny parts in the hopes that some day these will all get put together in the mind of a learner doesn't work. What happens is students go out of school and somehow the parts—isolated phonemes, isolated words, isolated sentences and isolated paragraphs—never get put together.

The main movement of growth is differentiation within an integrated whole. The whole is always there. Humpty Dumpty was an egg, you know, and he fell down and broke himself up, which is a kind of metaphor for the differentiating process that goes on in growth. The reason all the king's horses and all the king's men couldn't put him back together is that they couldn't put him back together as an *egg*. He is going to be something else after that, something more complex. You don't go back to being simple. There is a double process then of differentiation within a constant reintegrating. You have to keep both of those to maintain balance, and if we go too far one way or the other, growth is going to go very badly. These processes correspond to analysis and synthesis. To break the wholes down into parts corresponds to what was just described in the biological levels—differentiating the organs and the limbs, etc. within the embryo. Putting parts back into a whole corresponds to the biological integrating. As we become more complex within, the pulmonary, cardiac, intestinal systems, and so on have to be integrated. This corresponds to synthesis in the mental life.

You are probably familiar now with the research of the two hemispheres of the brain, which was actually done in the '60s but is only now being disseminated to the public and to education. The right and left hemispheres of the brain, it is now known, specialize, at least after a certain age. One half specializes in what we can call the intellectual, the verbal, the linear, the seriating part, the analytical; and the other in the intuitive, the holistic, the global, the synthesizing, the metaphoric. So this kind of double growth that characterizes the whole of human growth also characterizes the mental life very specifically, very concretely, with the two hemispheres of the brain.

Some critics of our education today in this culture say that we are emphasizing far too much one half, that we have a verbal/analytic or left-hemisphere education, a left-hemisphere culture, and this is one reason we are spinning very drastically out of balance. This is a point certainly, I think, to keep in mind. Reading is usually associated with the left half, but I think that is not the whole story. I think reading cannot get along very well, nor can any language growth, without the collaboration of the two hemispheres, of the metaphoric, holistic, spatially oriented right hemisphere, which incidentally is associated with the arts, sports, crafts.

So this dual aspect of growth is very graphically presented, if you want to think of it that way, dramatized by the physical separation of the brain into two specializing halves.

I think you can characterize the growth of thought and speech partly as a movement toward elaboration—that is, away from lumping things together globally, and toward separating things out, distinguishing, discriminating, differentiating, refining. This is a very, very general movement of growth which has been described not only by Piaget and Inhelder but very well by Heinz Werner and others. You can see it for yourself. For example, a small child will say in one word what really is a whole sentence, but he is not able yet to parcel out his thought, for one thing, to break it down into pieces and to assign to those pieces parts of speech. So this parceling-out process is precisely the direction in which he is going to grow. A very small child might say one word. He might say "coat." What he means is a sentence, but it is globally lumped together into one word. What he really means is, "I see my coat over there," or "I want my coat," or "What has happened to my coat?" But he says the one word "coat," and that *stands* for the whole sentence. So the direction of growth will be toward breaking his own thought down to fit the way in which his material and social world breaks things down.

Being incarnated on this material plane means we have to learn the laws by which the material plane is being run. Things are broken down; you have to know the difference between one thing and another, or one person and another, or else you get into trouble. You have to learn what the differences are, and in a sense this direction of growth is divisive and perhaps in some ways negative. It's a growth toward the natural, material breakdown of the physical and social world. In the beginning the child does not distinguish himself from the things around him but finally he must. In this first separation of self from world, his first breakdown, first analysis, is the model for all the breakdown analysis that is to follow. He learns that the ongoing panorama around him breaks down into pieces, and he has to know one piece from another and the names of the pieces, and so on.

Elaboration literally means, "working out," so one direction of growth is from the inside out. Since everything is already inside, latently—like genetic coding—it's just a matter of how it's going to be worked out, well or badly, and this depends on the other half of growth, the interaction of the organism and the environment.

Elaboration in language terms works out in vocabulary, in sentence structure, in composition and comprehension in very, very specific, concrete ways that teachers deal with all the time. The growth of vocabulary again is from the global to the finely differentiated. A child will at first use the word "boat" for every water-plying vessel, whether it goes on

oceans or rivers, whether it is sail- or motor-powered, whether it is pas-
senger or freight. You see what I mean. And these break down more and
more finely, as sailors all know, into catamarans and schooners and all
sorts of things that I don't know much about. It is a very, very fine breakdown, and the vocabulary follows the breakdown of reality, of boats into
superordinate and subordinate classes, and subordinate classes ramify in
turn on down into a million kinds of sailing vessels. So the process of
growth is getting into these systems of superordinate/subordinate classes.
But in the beginning, *boat* does for all. It's global.

The same thing happens with sentence structure. Sentences at first
are called kernel sentences, and this is an evolution itself out of the sin-
gle-word sentence I mentioned a moment ago with the example of "coat."
Finally we get into phrases and then into whole sentences and, of course,
the sentences again elaborate. But for teaching purposes what is important is how things get elaborated. I mean what teases or tempts the growing mind to elaborate? Why doesn't it stay global? You *can* stay more or
less global. This is what we mean by differences in development; some
kids are more advanced, and others seem retarded, verbally, or cognitively. This has to do with how much they have been teased out—this eliciting process from the environment.

Let's put it this way. You can try artificially to stimulate the growth
of sentence structure by lots of drills and exercises and by trying to teach
kids directly to analyze the sentence and the parts and to ticket all the
parts and so on. I think this has nothing to do with really effective growth
and may have a retarding effect. What makes people complicate their
sentences, essentially, is questioning by other people. Assuming authentic
speaking and writing situations where there is a real reason to be communicating, the elaboration of sentence structure into adverbial and ad-
jectival modifiers depends upon the eliciting action of questions (direct or
implied) of other people. *Where* did it happen? *When* did it happen?

Now the egocentric, naive speaker just blurts out things and leaves
it there, as kids typically do in show-and-tell if this activity is left in the
rudimentary state. We go around the class one kid after another, and each
kid shows something, he blurts out something, and then stops, and that's
the end of it. What needs to happen is to put show-and-tell into small
groups, often without the teacher, in very small groups, three or four, and
let the kids question each other about the object. This makes a tremendous difference. They can get in the habit of questioning if you model
for them. The teacher models a questioning stance so that the speaker
finds out that it's not obvious to the listener where this happened, or
when, or how he got something—the object he has—or what you do with
it, or how it was made. A million possible questions inhere in any kind
of initial statement like that. But the global, subjective-minded learner
has to find this out. This implies a very active social process that has not

yet got going in school nearly as much as it should because, I think, it's harder to manage, or seems harder to manage, the way most of us have been trained as educators.

A movement of growth that goes along with elaboration from within and the eliciting from without is what I call going from *co-operations* to *operations.* The use of the term "operation" obviously suggests Piaget. It can be very well exemplified in, let's say, the transition between kids hanging weights on a physical pair of balance scales and their later working with equations. The whole notion of balancing from a physical operation becomes internalized as a mental operation. We speak of balancing equations. That typifies this shift from outside operations to internal ones.

But what I want to talk about is the social operations, which I'll call co-operation as it becomes internalized. It has to do with proper ways of talking together so that a process of expatiation gets going. This can occur at any age. I'm using a fancy term here, but it can happen from preschool on. This is where people listen to each other and pick up on what each other has said and take it a little bit farther, and it includes the questioning that I was mentioning a moment ago that stimulates elaboration. But it has to do with creating ideas together, with exchanging vocabulary, with building on each other's sentence structures as well as on each other's ideas, on each other's comparisons and metaphors, wit, and so on. It's social, collaborative development. If this occurs in small groups, all the time, consistently, this will become internalized and become a part of the inner mental operations of the individuals in the groups.

Now, this can go well or badly. For example, if what happens when people converse is that they all sit around and heap abuse on some outsiders, this will be internalized, and people will think that way. And when everybody simply gives instances of the same thing, for example, how awful Kate is—"Oh yeah, I remember the time she did this" and "Yeah, well, the time I was with her she did that"—it's a very simple additive process that doesn't do very much for mental development. That's what I call the and-and-and model.

There's another kind of model—the but-but-but model, which is just constant contradiction, no matter what is said or what the subject is. The topic may change, but the altercation goes on. It's for its own sake, has its own dynamic. This is often, I'm afraid, encouraged by formal debate. I used to coach debate some in prep school, but I'm not an advocate of it really. I think it's better to have more spontaneous give-and-take and not have people invested in positions they *have* to defend and maintain. That gets ego involvement going and interferes with more useful intellectual work.

You can imagine other kinds of *co*-operation—that is, verbal collaboration—that can be internalized for good or evil, but the kind I'm suggesting is the expatiation type, whereby people listen to each other, pick up on what each other has to say, and together elaborate and discover what the implications are of each other's ideas. Humor and wit come into this; people pick up on each other's remarks, their humor, and carry it a little bit further, or their metaphors, and so on, and find where things go. If this is done in groups, at all ages, it does become internalized, and individuals all alone begin to think in these very salutary, positive ways.

This is a very sketchy kind of description of growth which I think can be applied to vocabulary, to sentence structure and to compositional forms, to reading comprehension problems, and so on. It has very much to do with what, again, Piaget has called decentering and egocentricity. This in turn relates to the global thinking. That is, I think most of our problems in composing our own ideas, whether we're talking or writing, concern our difficulty in separating ourselves from our audience and from our subject, so that we assume too much; and most of our problems in comprehending what others say and write concern trouble in tuning in on an individual who is separate from ourselves.

Many, many kids, I think, have reading comprehension problems because they can't really tune in on the author, for a lot of reasons. And it takes a lot of maturity to do this, and it takes role playing. You have to put yourself in the shoes of the author. That's the best way to read. People at Stanford who were doing research in hypnosis and who weren't really particularly interested in reading have accidentally come across a correlation between reading proficiency, great interest in reading—let's say, avid reading—and susceptibility to hypnosis. Some people really are willing to go along with somebody else's line of thought, and so on. This willingness correlates very highly with reading and liking to read.

I think that tuning in or role playing is really important. From the standpoint of writing you certainly have to role-play the listener or the audience; you have to sort of guess what they are going to need. Most of the things that school teachers remark about kids' writing have to do with problems of egocentricity. I think it would be much more helpful if we could think of it this way. The problem is knowing what the reader needs or how the reader is going to respond to this or that, as to word choice, the way sentences are arranged, the things you choose to mention, the things you leave out. It's very, very hard to know what to include and what to leave out in talking or writing. You can't say everything, you want to say enough and not too much. All of this requires very close attunement with the audience and being able to role-play him, and it's a movement away from egocentricity.

Well, what breaks egocentricity? Again, it doesn't happen alone. It's a social operation. It's constant comparison, I think. Kids reading together, talking about what they read, trying to act their stories out and discovering in the process of acting them out that they didn't interpret the characters or the plot or the action in the same way. They need to find all this out; they need to compare their *incomprehension, talk* about their incomprehension, openly, not try to *hide* it, and *work out* problems of comprehension—to raise consciousness. You can summarize, I think, so much growth of thought and speech as consciousness raising, whether it's Piaget's decentering—that is, losing your egocentricity—or whether it's moving away from the merely global to the finely discriminated whole.

Now the final part of the growth movement is spiraling around. One comes back over points but at different levels of consciousness so that if kids learn only to break down and analyze, to separate, to divide, this is going to be a negative movement. They have at the same time to learn how to put everything back together again. Our schools, following the general drift of the culture, are somewhat trapped into the one-sidedness that goes with the overemphasis on the left hemisphere of the brain, of being overly analytic, dealing too much with the pieces. Everybody is lost among the splinters of language. It's the drills and rules approach. This has gone on for some time—this isn't new. But I think recent trends in the culture have unfortunately reinforced the worst of the past, and sometimes it wears the guise of being new.

For example, the back-to-basics movement is a double misnomer. For one thing it isn't back to anywhere; we've never been anywhere else in this country. During my childhood or during my adulthood we have followed mainly a drills and rules approach. There was an effort to get away from this in the '60s that *Newsweek* magazine and other various organs have blamed our current ills on. The other part of the misnomer is that it's not back to *basics*, it's back to some people's notion of how you teach literacy. Some people say, "I'm for basic skills," which implies that other people are not. Now I don't know anybody—parent or teacher—who is against reading and writing, do you? So it's kind of a hoax to speak of some people as being for back-to-basics and others as being against reading and writing. This unnecessarily splits us up and creates tremendous problems, and it creates an artificial skills/frills division that we certainly don't need.

The best way to teach the skills, I think, is through other things that are not verbal, that have to do with the right hemisphere functions—crafts, sports, arts. There are many connections with language that should be used. I think that there is no great mystery about how kids learn to read and write. I know we have conferences and we feel that we need them to find out more about how children learn. I think we know a lot more now than we're acting on. I consult all over the country with schools and teachers in very different situations and regions, and I get the same thing constantly, which is that they know a lot more than they're acting on. And they are doing a lot of things they do not believe in. I don't think the problem is that we lack knowledge about child development. I don't think the problem is that we lack sophisticated notions about curriculum and methods and materials. We have more than we are using. The difficulty in fitting schools to the facts of language life has to do partly with the tendency of any large institution (not just schools) to get lost in its own institutionalism. And in our case, in this culture right now, this has got caught up in some political, economic movements that have been very negative, I think, and I hope we are going to work our way out of them.

Standardized testing is really dictating the curriculum with tremendous tyranny. These national standardized tests don't even test very well the things they are supposed to test—for example, reading and writing. Writing is construed as a lot of skills like formal grammatical analysis, or making dry runs on dummy sentences or correcting dummy paragraphs. No one has ever proved these add up to writing. Do you realize that there isn't any standardized test of writing where people really write, and, therefore, there is a very little instruction in schools in real writing? There are a lot of things alleged to teach writing. They are called composition, but they are various word and sentence and paragraph drills—what I call working with the pieces. I think we are going to have to acknowledge that this is so before we start talking about why writing has gone down, or why literacy has gone down.

The curriculum that is dictated by these very narrow standardized tests comes to us through commercial corporations which, frankly, cannot be trusted. They operate, as most large commercial corporations do, on very selfish principles that make it really impossible to get a worthwhile curriculum into schools through commercial processes. Educational manufacturers, I would say, cannot offer to schools the kind of materials that the curriculum in schools really needs at this point. I think they find it too hard to produce and too hard to sell. Schools, I think, have to take cognizance of this. Teachers have to teach what they know how to teach and not what comes through to them from commercial corporations.

A good model for school learning is home learning of speech; this is very organic, very spontaneous, very interactive, and it works really well. And learning to talk is much harder than learning to read and write. Cognitively speaking, in pure learning terms, it is much easier to learn to read and write than to learn to talk. It doesn't look that way, because there seem to be so many problems with learning to read and write. These problems arise from learning to read and write *in school,* in large groups and mass institutions. I think if we look at it that way we'll make a lot more progress. The problems are not learning problems essentially. They are institutional problems that are being governed by such things as the specific objectives and the accountability movement, which is tied in with standardized testing, which is tied in with commercial programmed materials. We must do our own consciousness raising about the whole educational–industrial complex that is really determining the materials, methods, and curriculum way outside the classroom. I think that the difficulty is that the people who know most about how kids learn, the ones in the classroom, today have not nearly enough to say about what they can do in the classrooms. One of the aspects of accountability that isn't brought out enough is that you can't tell people how to do their job and then hold them accountable for the results.

If you applaud that, be sure you applaud too some active lobbying by teachers to assert this. Too often teachers go limp and passive. The forces are big. The teachers have to make known what they think the facts of language learning are and try to get their own environment to fit that and not let everything be determined by state legislators, by school boards, who are too far from the classroom to really know how children learn, or by various national movements or commercial corporations. You have to take things back in your own hands a little more or else there won't be much worth in coming to conferences to learn more about how children learn or what the latest methods are. You have to be able to do something about it, and I think this means putting emphasis back on wholes, on the fact that the parts are taught *through* the wholes. *Via* the wholes. By means of the wholes. Not the other way around. You can't teach the wholes by trying to add up all the little parts. So we needn't get into any conflict about who's for basics and who isn't. I think we're all for the literacy skills, along with everything else. It's just a question of whether the small things are going to be taught in the thrust of whole growth or whether they're going to be isolated out very ineffectually into the old drills and rules approach.

Let me stop at this point and leave a few minutes for questions. What would you like for me to elaborate a little bit more on in the few minutes that we have? This is very sketchy, I realize. As I say, more suggestive than documented.

QUESTION: Is development within the whole a hierarchical or sequential process?

ANSWER: Only in a very long-range sense. I think this is sometimes a frustration to educators and curriculum developers, who would like a sequence, let's say, for a year, that holds true for all kids. I don't think you are going to find it, and it's a frustration because we plan by the year. But the kind of growth patterns, or movements, that Piaget, Werner, Eric Erickson, and a lot of other people have been working on are very long-range and these stages are more like blocks of *several* years. Rudolph Steiner says every seven years there is a major turnover in development. Unfortunately, it doesn't fit the school year, and I don't think we can try to wrench it to fit. We have to accept the fact that the growth patterns are very long-range, and it's an argument for much greater collaboration among teachers over spans of several years. This is one of the main things

I find missing when I consult with schools. There is very little connection between one year and the next. Not a rigid lock step between grades 7, 8, 9, 10, and so on but some way of keeping track of individual students over a span of several years so the kids come to you, you know what they have been working on, what emphasis they need now, and you can continue to individualize even though somebody else has been working with the kids for the last few years. We need something like that very much. A kind of bookkeeping system spanning several years so we can keep track of individual kids and not feel that the only way to get growth sequence is to make all kids do the same this year and then next year. Also, the accountability movement has tended to make kids do the same things year after year. And the whole movement toward minimal criteria reinforces a very negative thing, which in this instance is covering—that each teacher has to cover herself or himself for the same minimal learning standards for each child, and what you tend to do is make the kids study the same thing year after year so that each teacher can cover himself, or herself. Let's make sure that doesn't happen.

QUESTION: Would you elaborate on some of the activities which expand the right hemisphere of the brain?

ANSWER: Again, it's an argument for not stripping off the so-called frills in this phony frills/skills split. For example, there is a lot less art and music in grade school than there used to be when I was a kid myself. I think some of the main points of entry into the whole verbal world, into reading and writing, are through other arts and through other media, many of them nonverbal, or through sports or crafts. Not only things to talk and write about but specific ways of getting into writing. For example, from photographs, or from working with physical things and then talking about them. For example, we had kids in the fifth grade making things with toothpicks and paste and so on, and then writing directions for these to other kids and then making how-to-do-it books. They worked out the best way to do it and then put the directions down. Sort of like a recipe book. But the thing is there has to be a reason. Young kids don't particularly like to talk much about the physical operations they are doing; they don't see that much of a need for it. You have to set up a situation where there is a need to verbalize the nonverbal. Well, if you want to relay your directions on to someone else for making what you've made, that's a very well-motivated reason for verbalizing.

QUESTION: Can you say more about reading and hypnosis?

ANSWER: Ernest Hilgard, Department of Psychology at Stanford—I think he is recently retired—has advanced what I said. He and his wife, who is an M.D., worked with hypnosis in a very serious way in the Department of Psychology, and they were working on a scale for measuring how susceptible various people were to hypnosis, not to any Svengali treatment. They had graduate students and others learning how to talk people into this. So it is independent of the personality of the one giving the instruction. *Experience in Hypnosis* I think is the title of the book—of one book. The matter of reading came up very incidentally—practically accidentally.

I did cover a lot too fast, and when I do that I'm always aware of many, many unexplained things or many overstatements, and so on. So I would welcome a chance to elaborate some.

QUESTION: What's a writing sample?

ANSWER: Well, there was a writing sample, so-called, on college boards—which was removed in the '60s. It's too big a nuisance, you know. It's too hard processing students' writing. So expensive. So they dropped it. Now people are complaining about why kids can't write.

Now, there are many reasons that may account for this fairly drastic falling off in writing skills. But one of the main reasons is that the one thing that really tested writing by having kids write—it may have been under fairly artificial circumstances, but at least they really wrote a whole piece of something—was removed in the '60s. Now, all this influences teachers tremendously because to save their own necks teachers have to teach more or less directly to the tests—particularly in an era of accountability. It puts everybody's job on the line more and more in conformity with test scores. But there is nothing now, no standardized test that I know of, that requires kids to do some honest writing.[1] What is supposed to test writing is correcting a dummy sentence here, tinkering with a dummy paragraph there with multiple-choice answers or vocabulary work, or questions having to do with formal grammatical analysis. None of these will tell you anything about how well a kid can write. A token twenty-minute writing sample is tentatively being restored to the CEEB composition test the Fall of 1978 in recognition, perhaps, of the exam's negative influence.

To some extent there is the same situation with standardized tests in reading. If the scores are negative, you don't know what to make of it. In other words, if kids do well on them—O.K., you can assume they read. But you're really worried about kids who don't do well on them, and about them you don't know anything because there is no oral component to standardize reading tests. And without an oral component you cannot really separate the decoding, word-attack aspect (so-called phonics or whatever) from comprehension. Many kids score very low on reading tests because they simply don't know the vocabulary, or the concepts, and if you *read* the passages to them they would do very badly. But, you

---

[1]Fortunately, some states and districts are now instituting real samples of writing as part of their standardized testing program.

see, nobody reads them to them. Because again, that's too expensive. Our standardized tests are cheap quickies. That's what they are. And we are paying the price for a cheap quicky; it's ruining the national curriculum, and it has been for years. And it's not *cheap*. It's very expensive.

Setting up shallow, standardized tests that then determine the curriculum, which shrinks to fit them—that's very expensive. You don't save money that way. If you really want to know if a kid can decode, have him read aloud to you—sight unseen—sight-read to you while you follow the text with your eyes and notice the discrepancies, if any, that he makes, the way in which he reads, and so on. If you want to know his *comprehension, you* read to *him*. And then talk with him about what he understood. This is what alternative schools did, for example, in Berkeley, where there are a lot of poor minority students with lots of low scores. They just finally dropped standardized tests and went to their own way of testing to try to find out what kids really could do and what they couldn't. These schools had to introduce an oral component. Have the kids read to you, you read to them, and without that, as far as I'm concerned, the standardized reading tests are not worth very much at all because they don't tell you what you really want to know—*why* the students do so badly on them. You don't know why.

QUESTION: I would like to raise the question of teaching the parts of speech to facilitate foreign language teaching.

ANSWER: I taught French for three years and at that time there was a big controversy among foreign language teachers. The audio-lingual approach was just coming in, with language laboratories and so on, so that when you say, "I'm teaching formal grammar to help the French and Spanish teachers," you may be taking part in a very heated controversy about whether they should use a grammar-translation approach or a more oral-aural, direct-method approach. My feeling is that if foreign language teachers feel it is important—and I can see an argument there—then let them teach it. Most of them want to do it their own way anyway—in a way they figure that fits the target language better. If you're teaching German you might want to go about it a little bit differently from French or Spanish or Russian.

Actually, my own feeling is that the teaching of formal, grammatical analysis, the ticketing of parts of speech in this country, is really a hangover from the nineteenth century, when English was in a very large measure taught as a second language in American public schools because of the waves of immigrants coming in—wave after wave in the nineteenth century. And it made more sense then; it makes more sense to teach formal, grammatical analysis if you are teaching a second language, because the person is older, they don't learn language the same way even by age ten or twelve that they did when they were three or four or one or two. It makes more sense maybe to codify and use their generalizing ability to teach them some of the truths about the language. But I think it is a hangover from the days when teaching English as a second language was very widespread in the public schools. Now we have special programs as, for example, in California, which has a large Mexican/American population, and so on. Bilingual programs. So it has no point any more in regular classes.

QUESTION: What about grades?

ANSWER: She is asking about grades. I think you can cook up a grade for a kid regardless of what curriculum you are working under. I taught at a very grade-conscious school for a while; those kids had their slide rules out come marking period and they were figuring up. But even so the English Department there finally decided to quit putting individual letter grades on all kids' themes and just to make a general assessment of the writing for a marking period and to come up with a letter grade for the whole marking period rather than for individual papers. And I found that if I did this, I understood students' writing better anyway. I could spot the traits and the trends by looking over all the writing and making a blanket judgment.

7

Bajan Bestiary

Background

For a shift of brain hemisphere and mode of discourse, I insert here a suite of poems that may serve as mid-book interlude. Having vowed that I would write no more utilitarian prose while recharging myself in Barbados from the two methods books, I began writing for fun little sketches of some of the critters I saw almost daily around the converted sugarmill house where we were living or down at the sea nearby, where I spearfished with a native.

Writing these poems was a different process for me, and the immediate pleasure was very different from the long-range satisfaction of the writing I was more used to. I tinkered. I lingered over single words and phrases, toyed over and over with lines, experimenting with sound play other than rhyme and with the juxtaposition of images. It was all a luxury. I sat on a patio surrounded by the old coral-stone boiling house and conical mill and tall cane fields. I watched and wrote, watched and wrote.

Three of the four animals comprising the bestiary had folk names, as I indicate in the poems, by which the natives call them and which gave me mythic, metaphorical departure points. I wanted to imagine what was in Bajan[1] minds when they invented these names. I tried to share their metaphors. But then images of my own came to me, and the poems took more personal turns. Obviously, the folk names were only "story starters" to get me going, but I liked the feeling of immersing myself first in external terms and surroundings. The outward focus made expressing myself easier and more creative. I suspect most literary writers employ some such indirection to tease out and flesh out their insides.

Whatever the worth of these poems, making them showed me a great deal about the underground working of intuition in writing. Searching within the constraints of a given image, rhythm, phrasing, you surprise yourself as these constraints force verbal felicities or turns of idea that you would not have arrived at by common pondering. When finished, I was astonished to find that I had created a progression from air to land to sea, corresponding to an increasing descent into unconscious material and to a deepening of several themes that I had unintentionally carried over from poem to poem. One such theme touched on writing itself.

[1]Barbadian, of Barbados

The first poem was published in the *English Journal* of May 1974. I had thought the whole suite was being printed, but the other poems somehow got detached and lost in the editorial offices.

Hummingbird

1

Barbados' "doctor bird" is making rounds,
Innoculating flowers, tapping samples,
Hemming the blossomed hedge a pause a stitch
As doctors moving room to room suture
Up the corridors (he drops who stops),
So curtly prodding tendered guts he leaves
An aftermath of open-mouthed patients,
Zips off to query the next expectant
Corolla, flight a rapid riffling fillip,
Then sticks in space and tucks his tail, upheld
By focus only, wings a thicker air,
Doomed to higher metabolic rate,
Like surgeon freezing speed, for who else
Staying steady operates so fleet?

2

Still, sip-supping belles, he's tip-tupping
A whole blooming harem by himself.
Have they been drained or plenished, healed or had?
That sheen of golden green suffusing black
Betrays a garb of greenhead flies rippling
In iridescent Baudelarian evil
Perhaps, or just a sober-coated servant,
Depending which reflection winks the mind.
A blurring-motored airship takes a station
To kill or succor—*some* exquisite coupling.
A tiny vampire drinks the liquid life
Away but, incubus, pollinates the sleep.

Lizard

1

Black-eyed chartreuse lizards blink the heat,
Tautly menace flies, or scout the court
And stop to tilt a head and roll an eye.
Called a "cock," the male's a thrusting intent,
A footed phallus arousing housewives,
Who call him cute and feed him bacon scraps
But think: The charming little carnivore
Lumbers exactly like an alligator.
(A reptile's a reptile and, warm clime or not,
They're cold-blooded and don't feel the way we do.
Or at least don't think the way we do.
Or at any rate don't know they're thinking.)
Tumid emotion balloons his throat, conveys
To males a threat to overwhelm with choler,
To mates a promise to overwhelm with lust:
    I'm about to pop
    With something that has to do with you.
    Get out of my sight
    Or deal with what you make me feel.

2

Across stone-coral walls they scroll their length
In florid arabesquing signatures:
Scrawled on chalky hall a green graffito;
Embossed on door a hieroglyph; on bell
Of clarinet a clef in bas relief;
A cursive monogram subscribes a painting.
At every turn a flourish of self, and that's
How a body writes his autograph.

Crab

The inland crab is solid, red and black;
The seaside crab is weightless, washed of color,
Or sandy rather, as though beach showed through shell.
He scuttles ghostly over tiny dunes

To sky-reflecting flats that make him pause
To contemplate the waves. A fit of folly:
He cocks his elbows, gets a running start, and
Like a maniac pianist's treble hand
Scribbling wild arpeggios down the keys
He sideways sprints the stretch and bams the sea
As if to bounce that wave right back to France.
He's lost to sight, a foamed-over beau geste
Hissed by seething surf. Then drifting with
The froth, two black knobs on stems pop up,
Fix on you, bespeak a shrug (you can't win
Them all) and make the mute schlemiel's appeal.

One night a tiny Saxon helmet thresh-
Holds between patio and parlor, gleaming,
Borne upon six clustered legs and peering
Eyeless at us, some local crab who'd found
A metal cone to play the hermit in,
Substituting navy gear for shell
(Quite logically, given the goal of each).
A teutonic opera extra missing spear,
Unsure of cue, helmet blocking eyes,
He stumbles toward the onstage light and sound
But, unprojecting, lingers near the wings.

Another night a bigger bumbler finds
Himself clutching my daughter's coral wall,
Witlessly weighing his pointless position,
A trophy lobster lacking varnished plaque.
Waving monstrous claws, it beetles the pillow
At just the ritual hour of nightly tale
When dad and daughter put the beasts to peace,
Fêting the safety of drapes and counterpane.
I knock him clacking down and we square off:
That crustacean's itching to pinch my flesh
And I expect to crunch his exoskeleton.
He readies curving pincers like a wrestler
Aping a ballerina rounding arms.
His straight-edged mandible lifts and drops
As wooden as a puppet's clopping chin.
They're funny all right, but that's one clown I killed.

Octopus

"Sea cats" have a feline grace and trace the
Ocean floor in muscular liquefaction.
Small, and prized as food, they're stalked in shallows
With crook or spear. You poke a pocket of rock
That seems too small for even a junior cat
But you hook and pull until the hole
Explodes as flailing star several times
The size of where it hid and webbed around
From stretching tendrils every way at once.
The skewered center ripples out in spasms
To tips encoiling nothing but open sea.
You grasp the pulsing terror about the head
And feel at once the slimy tight adhesion
Of eight mucoused whips astounding your arm
And sucking with ringed holes of piccolos.
A tighter embrace one could not dread or hope
(From man amok or virgin just delivered).
So you palp the hump of grafted viscera
Then stick two fingers up a slippery sheath
While underwater nimbus clouds are rolling
About your hands to roil the deed from view
(Some defense! to hide from what you hug)
And, pressing thumb to dome, turn the insides
Out. Faint like lovers sinking back, you
Both subside, it to die a-languishing
(For instant death you bite between the eyes)
And you to wonder whether any critter
That lumps its brains and guts together deserves
The rape it gets, or whether thus to kill
A mollusk—evict, eviscerate—may not
Evince demented need to twice expose,
By entering in while looking at, instead
Of alternating. To see by feel you kill.
Such disclosing confuses thought with touch
Even more than mollusks do and causes
Lunatics to disembowel women
For secrets never learned if brought to light.
Of course I don't undo an octopus
To understand the universe but just
To sport with feeling in deeps behind the ink,
Despite the lashing of a cat o' eight tails.

8

Integrity in the Teaching of Writing

Background

The most positive development in English education during the '70s—indeed, during the whole period since World War II—originated with teachers, not with government, and spread in grassroots fashion from the bottom up instead of from the top down. The Bay Area Writing Project, now the National Writing Project, set an in-service model that has swept the country and accomplished far more good than all of the U.S. Office of Education Project English curriculum centers of the '60s put together. The astonishing success of the one and the monumental failures of the other constitute a valuable object lesson. But the success and national institutionalization bring on dangers that the Project must watch out for.

Since the mid-1960s, when I still lived in the East, I have worked off and on with the handful of devoted, veteran educators who began and developed BAWP: Jim Gray, a supervisor of English teachers at the Berkeley campus of the University of California; Albert (Cap) Lavin, a high school English department head and textbook author (and fellow participant at the Dartmouth Seminar); Miles Myers, head of the Oakland High School English department and a politically astute lobbyist and vice-president of the California Federation of Teachers; and Keith Caldwell and Mary K. Healy, two very experienced in-service leaders as well as teachers of young people. These people really know schools and really know writing. They obtained support from the University, local systems, the California Department of Education, Carnegie Corporation of New York, and—their main funding source—the National Endowment for the Humanities. They said, "If teachers are ever going to teach writing more and teach it better, they will have to practice writing more themselves." Bravo! This is how I learned to teach writing myself. Surely, a major reason that many teachers ignore, slight, or mangle the teaching of writing is that they lack direct experience with the learning issues entailed in writing. The BAWP originators said also, "The best people to teach teachers are other teachers."

They set up a summer course in which teachers wrote, talked shop about writing, and worked up a presentation they could make as consultants for other teachers during the following school year. So in the BAWP model a higher institution and local districts collaborate to set up a seeding system whereby those who have benefited from extra learning can pass on that understanding. Leslie Whipp wrote in the November 1979 issue of the *Network Newsletter* (the Project organ, published at U.C. Berkeley): "One astonishing feature of the National Writing Project model, and the major source of its strength, is that it is teacher-centered, and in two chief ways: teachers are teaching teachers, and teachers are writing for other teachers and reading and discussing the writing of other teachers."

I have taught for several years at BAWP summer institutes in Berkeley, Chicago, and Long Island, and have consulted with other projects following the model in North Carolina, Michigan, Minnesota, New Mexico, and several areas of California. Every summer new projects start up. I feel that this wonderful burgeoning shows some pent-up spirit finally finding release from the repressive environment of today. Teaching teachers to write has touched me deeply. The booklets of their writings collected after a summer session always make very interesting reading matter, because of their individual reality, and show an artfulness, depth, and personal force that are surprising only because most classrooms don't reflect these assets—surprising not least to the authors, and that is part of what touches me every time.

I place the participants in groups of three or four for the whole institute (four to six weeks). Learning to write with these partners is undoubtedly the best part of the session. They help each other get and settle on ideas during prewriting activities, think out and talk out their ideas during mid-composition, and reflect usefully on their final drafts. They learn as they never could otherwise what are the most useful ways to respond to others' writing. A remarkable relationship usually develops in these groups as they go about balancing honesty with delicacy, task effectiveness with intimacy, difference with empathy. The difficulty comes when the groups have to break up. Only through these writing workshop groups have I ever succeeded in convincing teachers of the tremendous power of small-group process.

BAWP has attempted to be eclectic, but it's never really possible to embrace all ideas and practices, if only because of practical limitations, so selection and emphasis will always occur. Project staff or invitees give presentations or assign readings on certain methods or approaches they prefer, omitting others, and when participant teachers are asked to choose early in the institute a topic to present later, they naturally come up often with pet lessons, faddish exercises, or bad conventional practices. Besides unwittingly misleading itself and others, by adopting this open-arms pose BAWP appears to endorse or push certain methods in violation of its own "eclectic" policy. The more influential it becomes, the more everyone involved in the Project's inspiring national network should work to keep the movement universal in nature, to determine what is most fundamental, not merely widespread or fashionable. My own approach is never to recommend activities with sentences or paragraphs that are not part of an authentic discourse or that don't constitute an authentic discourse. What is universal are the kinds of utilitarian, literary, and scientific discourse practiced in our culture; the general processes for composing and revising alone and with others; and the elements of any language acquired through speaking and reading.

The following article grew rather directly out of experiences helping teachers write and think about how to help others write. It seemed to me that in order to focus on the actual writing processes themselves, it was necessary to clear up, if possible, some confusion in traditional thinking about what activities constitute writing. This led to a scale of various definitions of writing that I would put on the board and discuss with BAWP classes and with my similar summer course in writing for teachers given in 1978 at the Bread Loaf School of English (Middlebury College, VT). (I seem to think in scales; there are three in this book and several key ones scattered in other writing.)

Phi Delta Kappan published this piece in its December 1979 issue. It will serve as an introduction to the final article in this book, of which it was once a portion.

———————◄●►———————

A phalanx of educators from out of state recently visited the Bay Area Writing Project in Berkeley expecting to be shown how to teach handwriting. If these people work with primary school, as I suspect, they have a better excuse than the rest of us for construing "writing" overconcretely, because the age of their pupils forces them to deal with writing as drawing—and, indeed, drawing is one aspect of writing. Because it bridges between the invisible world of spirit and the visible world of matter, writing has so many aspects, covering such a broad spectrum of physical and mental activities, that it may be defined at whatever level of depth suits the profession, public, or other stakeholders such as governments, foundations, and commercial companies. And, as always, ambiguity lends itself to political, economic, and cultural biasing. At the moment, a very materialistic definition of writing pegs the teaching of it at such a low level of meaning that a dramatic expansion of the educational view of it seems in order.

At the lowest level, writing is drawing letters, but for the sake of perspective it may be worth backing down a little before going up. That is, drawing letters itself culminates a long history of using other material media, beginning with the body when used for signaling and symbolizing. But real writing began with message-leaving and mnemonic devices. One had to "say" something to someone not present, perhaps not born yet, and one had to remind oneself of something or keep track of some tally. For storing and transmitting information across time, beyond personal memory and face-to-face communication, the body will no longer serve, and external media then come into play. This kind of long-range communication or message-leaving is the essence of writing, which must have begun as one form of tool-using. Some of the first writing consisted of knots and notches for keeping score in business transactions. (A main advantage of writing still remains that the thinker can "take stock" of what he has got so far before proceeding.) But for concepts going beyond mere quantity, into the astronomical, geodetic, mathematical, historical, zoological, botanical, and metallurgical knowledge that we now know ancient civilizations possessed, a medium admitting of more complex symbolization was required.

The "prehistoric" form of writing was building. Modern archaeology tends increasingly to interpret ancient monuments such as megaliths, ziggurats, steles, obelisks, temples, and pyramids as *embodiments* of information, as repositories like today's libraries or, at least, like our time capsules. For this reason, the term "prehistoric," which means pre-writing, should strike us now as a misnomer and a prejudice, since building-in as a way of writing-in not only left records (for those who knew how to read) but evolved to very high levels of sophistication in the Nile, Indus, and Tigris–Euphrates valleys. But this sort of message-leaving was of course not the sole function of these monuments, which seem also to have served as observatories, tombs, surveying markers, initiation sites, places of worship, and other things, often all at once. One of the reasons, no doubt, why modern people have not credited ancient people with writing is that for a long time the ancients did not *single out* writing as a specialized activity but rather, in their typically syncretic way, fused multiple functions in each activity. (Millennia later, we have still not reintegrated writing into the rest of the curriculum!)[1]

The sequence from then to now probably followed a path of increasing specialization and abstractness in symbolizing. Some part of a building or monument depicted a story of past events, schematized the zodiac, or laid out steps in how to make something. Earlier, these ideas might materialize as effigies, bas-reliefs, or even key features of architectural layout, then later as pictures incised or drawn on walls or steles. Two-dimensionality is a higher abstraction than three-dimensionality, the symbols being farther removed from what they symbolize. As message-leaving specialized, it became more portable: tablets and scrolls supplanted murals and inscriptions. Then direct pictorialization yielded to ideography, wherein pictures become standardized and systematized into a consistent spatial order and lexicon and take on less concrete meanings associated with the pictures but (eventually) not themselves depictable.

[1]See, for example, Francis Hitching, *Earth Magic* (New York: Simon and Schuster, 1978); Peter Tompkins, *Secrets of the Great Pyramid* (New York: Harper and Row, 1971); and Louis Charpentier, *The Mysteries of Chartres Cathedral* (New York: Avon, 1975).

Petroglyphs thus become hieroglyphs. Incision and cuneiform, the holdovers from monumental writing, give way to drawing and painting, less substantial but faster and more flexible for writing as a special activity. Cuneiform, the printing of a single wedge shape in different positions and numbers, no doubt led, however, to the acceptance of arbitrary, imageless symbols such as characterize the alphabet.

So although children today may be regarded as starting to write by drawing graphic symbols for sound symbols, this historical summary reminds us that just as early man worked his way up to the alphabet, so may the child—and for good reason. Most psychologists, even of variant schools, would probably accept the capsulized form in which Jerome Bruner once characterized stages of children's mental development as enactive, iconic, and symbolic—the respective acting out, depicting, and abstract representing of thought. Just as "prehistoric" man began to write before we give him credit for it, so children start writing some time before we think of some of their activities as writing. Learning to symbolize begins with mimicry and pantomime and the other signifying behavior that we call "body language"; accumulates the external, three-dimensional media of collaging and modeling and constructing; refines these to the two-dimensional media of stamping, imprinting, drawing, and painting; then proceeds to ordering pictures into a story and to drawing and sequencing the geometric shapes that comprise letters. All this sets the stage for the stunning moment when two independently evolving symbol systems come into conjunction—one vocal and auditory, the other manual and visual.

Rising on now through the spectrum of writing definitions, the next level above letter-drawing or *handwriting,* to use the school term, is the *transcribing* of speech sounds. Transcription comprises spelling and punctuation, which respectively render vocalization and intonation (stress, pitch, and juncture). They shift speech from an oral to a visual medium, and because they are basic to literacy are misleadingly called "basic skills."

From here on up the scale the issue is how much real authoring is occurring. We may start with direct *copying* of a text, a teaching method practiced in some times and places in Europe on grounds that it imprints spellings, punctuation, vocabulary, and sentence structures. We have only to reread Melville's story "Bartleby the Scrivener" to appreciate the practical importance of the amanuensis before the invention of the typewriter and the ensuing technology of copying. Perhaps we should place stenography a shade above copying on the writing scale, since the interpretation and translation of speech sounds requires more thought. Both result in writing, but in neither case does the "writer" create the content or necessarily even understand it. As a former French teacher I can attest to the value of the dictée, however, for second-language learning, where the literacy issue of matching written symbols with spoken words naturally looms as large for the learner of any age as it does for the small child with his native language.

Paraphrasing seems to mark the point of shifting from copying or transcribing toward some degree of authoring. It can range from barely changed quotation to significant shift in vocabulary and sentence structure that indicates much interpretation. But to the extent that a second party summarizes a text as well as rewords it, we are into précis or résumé and hence into the more extensive interpretation that selection and reduction entail. These French terms betray the origin of the same old-world pedagogy that underlies the copying method. Actually, the précis is intended to elicit comprehension, not interpretation, and reflects the frank avowal of traditional French schooling that a youngster should only take in until age eighteen because he or she is not ready before then to do original thinking. Though unavowed in this country, this attitude clearly operates powerfully throughout the entire curriculum.

It is impossible to understand the teaching of writing in America if one does not realize that, in one form or another, from first grade through graduate school, it serves mostly to test reading. In elementary school the main form of writing is the book report, which becomes dignified in high school and college as the "research paper" or "critical paper," then deified in graduate school as the "survey of the literature" in the doctoral dissertation. The real goal of writing instruction in the United States is to prepare for term papers and essay questions (although secondary and college teachers increasingly fall back today on multiple-choice "objective" tests, partly because "the kids can't write"). We have always been far more interested in reading than in writing, so much so that writing in schools has hardly existed except as a means to demonstrate either reading comprehension or the comprehensiveness of one's reading. Because writing produces an external result, it is a natural testing instrument if one wishes to regard it so, whereas the receptive activity of reading leaves no traces outside. Using writing to test reading, then, seems the perfect solution to an institution so bedeviled by managing and monitoring problems that it resists student productivity tooth and nail and regards testing as the solution to everything. Writing about reading quite effectively kills two birds with one stone.

So we have geared the teaching of writing in this country to the level of quotation and paraphrase, précis and book report. Students are to be told to, not to tell. Since even regurgitation entails some interpretation and synthesis by the reader, it is fair to accord to this level of "writing" some degree of authorship. But surely school practices of writing about the reading represent minimal authorship. In any case, wouldn't educators do well to ask constantly how much authoring their writing program honestly calls for and how much it truly aims to teach writing for the sake of writing? It is certainly very true that the degree of authorship is relative in *any* kind of writing. Even great professional writers usually incorporate into their thought and work, at some level of assimilation, the thoughts and works of others. But their kind of taking in and giving out exists for them to have more to say, not to prove to others' satisfaction that they have done their homework. Authoring ought to be construed, it seems to me, on a rather tough criterion of originality if only because the less a learner imitates or borrows, the more he has to do his own thinking, regardless of how much he may read.

The next-highest conception of writing emphasizes *craft*—how to construct good sentences, paragraphs, and overall organizations. Everyone respects craftsmanship, no less in writing, surely, than anywhere else, but if the question of genuine authorship is finessed, then such an approach results in a mere carpentry course. For the very reason that they are assuming that content will be supplied by books or lectures, schools have taken it for granted. The only problem is how to cut and fit. Naturally allied to the emphasis on reading and general student passivity, formalism dominates the teaching of writing, by which I mean forming the language only without nearly sufficient concern for developing the thought. This level of writing instruction does deserve the name of "composition" for the very reason that it features construction—selecting and arranging for maximum effect—but it fastens almost hypnotically on the surface level of language, at which thought *manifests* itself, and blandly stops short of the long internal processing that must go on to engender something to manifest.

At its best the crafting approach to writing can help a student see alternative and better ways to say what he has in mind, but without at least an equal emphasis on finding and developing subjects of his own, and the clear primacy of purpose over form, the "writer" ends by carpentering clichés to make the sentence or the paragraph or essay form come out right. At its worst, the approach loads a student with prescriptions and proscriptions that no serious writer could ever follow and still keep his mind on his business, and even degenerates into what I call decomposition—manipulating grammatical facts and labels as information, memorizing vocabulary lists, and doing exercises with isolated dummy sentences. Language parts are tools of the craft, right? But they must not, of course, be mistaken for the craft itself.

Well-meaning teachers try hard to make the crafting approach work by assigning "provocative" or "open" topics for the content and "creative" exercises in sentence-combining or in rear-loading of sentence modification. These valiant efforts can look successful within the narrow notion of authorship taken for granted in our schools today. But when writing on demand for a grade in an institution, how provocative and open really is "We have met the enemy and he is us," the topic of the 1978 College Board's English Achievement Test and a fair sample of topics that teachers of the craft tradition might assign (and might think appropriate because it comes from a comic strip, *Pogo*). Reporting as a reader for this exam, James Gray, head of the Bay Area Writing Project, found "mechanical paragraphs masquerading as organized essays" and "overgeneralizing, posturing, and earnest moralizing."[2] Since the crafting approach represents about the highest point on our spectrum that the teaching of writing would have attained in the schools from which these college-bound students derived, Gray's description seems a fair indication of the most we can expect from a concept of writing so unbalanced between language and technique, on the one hand, and thought and purpose, on the other. After all, how much does being allowed to make up your own sentence combinations or sentence modifications amount to in the bigger picture of rendering thought into writing, even though the exercises may seem like fun compared to grimmer alternatives? For a final commentary on the crafting emphasis, I invoke the greatest thinker of our century, who said in the preface to his *Relativity: The Special and General Theory* that when the intent is to get ideas across, "matters of elegance ought to be left to the tailor and the cobbler."[3] Einstein's ability to communicate clearly to the layman the most difficult ideas of our time certainly ranks high among his achievements.

The notions of "writing" so far reviewed, none of which honor full authoring, smack suspiciously not only, as I have suggested, of institutional convenience (usually beyond the control of teachers themselves) but also of a materialistic framework that inevitably biases schooling and anchors the teaching of writing at inferior levels of any scale aspiring to excellence. In fact, it is the materialism that places the institution over the individual, form over content. Specifically, it shows in a favoring of more *concrete* definitions of writing, as transcription or carpentry; in the *superficial* view that spelling and punctuating are basic skills, instead of thinking and speaking; and in the *analytic* isolation of language units as curriculum units (the phoneme, the word, the sentence, the paragraph). Generally, the materialistic bias of our culture practically forces us to prefer the visible domain of language forms, which linguistic science has so well delineated, to the invisible domain of thought, which is still a scary can of worms. But teachers have no business preferring either and have no choice but to work *in the gap* between thought and speech. Writing is a

---

[2] James Gray, "Twenty Minutes of Fluency—A Test," *The National Writing Project Network Newsletter,* volume 2, number 2, March 1979, p. 12.
[3] Albert Einstein, *Relativity: The Special and General Theory* (New York: Crown, 1961), Preface, p. v.

manifestation of thought, but, however tempting, we cannot deal with it only as it finally manifests itself visually in writing or even audibly as speech. Too much precedes the physical sounds or sights for teachers to take up only at these forms.

But how can we get at the writing process before it materializes in these forms? Answering this teaching question brings us to the top of the spectrum of writing definitions, where schools should be operating. Educators would do best, I submit, to conceive of writing, first of all, as full-fledged authoring, by which I mean authentic expression of an individual's own ideas, original in the sense that he or she has synthesized them for himself or herself. True authoring occurs naturally to the extent that the writer is composing with raw material, that is, source content not previously abstracted and formulated by others. Teaching aimed this way would emphasize subject matter lying easily at hand within and around the writer—firsthand content like feelings, fantasies, sensations, memories, and reflections, and secondhand content as drawn from interviews, stored information, and the writings of others to the extent that the writer truly re-abstracts these in his own synthesis. Insisting on maximum authorship should stave off the construing or treating of writing as only some sort of transcription or paraphrasing or verbal tailoring from ready-made cloth. (Behind the basic meaning of "author" as "adder" lies the assumption that a writer has something unique enough to add to the communal store of knowledge.)

Presupposing true authorship, the highest definition acknowledges that *any* writing, about whatever personal or impersonal subject, for whatever audience and purpose, can never comprise anything but some focused and edited version of inner speech. When writing, one writes down what one is thinking—but not everything one is thinking at that moment and not necessarily in the form that first comes to mind. What the writer transcribes is some ongoing *revision* of inner speech, which is itself some verbalized or at least verbalizable distillation of the continually flowing mixture of inner life that psychologist William James long ago named the "stream of consciousness." The writer intent on his subject presumably tries to narrow down drastically for the moment his total field of consciousness—shuts out most things and concentrates on one train which he has set in motion at will and tries to sustain. This means that to write one must control inner speech and not simply let it run at the behest of normally interplaying stimuli. We could say that composition begins with this attentional selectivity except that, at the time of writing down thoughts, a writer stands at the mercy of prior rumination about the subject as it will surface in the inner speech that spontaneously presents itself for further composition. We had best include as composition the whole continuum of inner processing that determines what will occur to the writer about the subject focused on. A person cannot write something he cannot say at least to himself—think—but he also keeps recasting a subject in his inner speech, perhaps long before he knows he will write about it.

The chief reason for defining writing as revision of inner speech is to ensure that writing be acknowledged as nothing less than thinking, manifested a certain way, and to make sure that it is taught accordingly. In addition to the more commonly accepted possibilities of revising what one has already written down, two less familiar teaching issues emerge—the immediate one of how best to set conditions for tapping and focusing inner speech at the moment of writing down, and the long-range one of how best to develop the highest quality of inner speech so that when one sits down to write, the thought that spontaneously presents itself offers the best wherewithal for the more visible and audible composition that will follow.

Compactly recapitulated, the ways in which writing may be defined array themselves in this way, reading upward from most material and external to most authorial. Lower definitions are lower not because false but because insufficient.

- Revising inner speech—starts with inchoate thought.
- Crafting conventional or given subject matter—starts with given topics and language forms.
- Paraphrasing, summarizing, plagiarizing—starts with other writers' material and ideas.
- Transcribing and copying—starts verbatim with others' speech and texts.
- Drawing and handwriting—starts with imagery for sensorimotor activities.

Writing consists of not just one of these activities but of all of them at once. All definitions are correct. When people write, they are simultaneously *drawing* letters, *transcribing* their inner voice, *plagiarizing* concepts and frameworks from their culture, *crafting* their thoughts into language forms, and *revising* the inchoate thought of their inner speech. None are wrong, but failing to include all is wrong. Nor is it true that the learner begins at the bottom and works his way up. From the outset, lettering needs to be connected to meaning, to the symbolizing of inner speech, as when the small child watches while a helper writes down his story for him or her as the child dictates it and then literally retraces the writing. All these definitions apply all at once at all stages of growth. Older students who say they have nothing to write have simply spent all their school days copying, paraphrasing, and fitting given content into given

forms and never have had a chance to see themselves as authors composing their inner speech toward a creation of their own. The scale does correspond to an order of increasing difficulty for both the writer and the
teacher of writing. Small wonder we're tempted to lop off the top!

Teachers with whom I have used this scale of definitions in workshops have said that they found it very useful. It should help a teacher
place his or her approach and to decide if change seems called for. In
which sense or senses am I teaching writing? Is that what I mean to do?
If not, why am I teaching this way? If not, how would I have to change
my classroom practices to teach writing as I think I should? The scale
should help also to think about that old bugaboo, evaluation. For each
definition here there correspond criteria mostly irrelevant to the other definitions. Do the standardized tests by which my students' "writing" or
"composition" ability is judged do justice to all these definitions, to writing as a whole? Am I teaching writing by one definition and assessing it
by another? Am I operating by certain definitions and my colleagues or
superiors or constituency assuming others? And—where do "basic skills"
and "minimal standards" fall on this array?

The ambiguity of the word "writing" not only creates tremendous
confusion about teaching methods but makes it possible to plug in any
meaning that suits any motive. Prevalently, most schools are teaching
something else and calling it writing, in a version of "let's don't and say
we did," which receives perfect support from tests that measure something else and call it writing. Nearly all the stakeholders in the teaching
of writing have reasons for wanting to interpret it as "mechanics" or decomposition or book-reporting or carpentry. All of us, in and out of
school, have tacitly conspired to lobotomize writing, precisely because, if
undertaken seriously, it threatens to be dangerous, unmanageable, and
untestable by current cheap instruments. Everyone senses, quite rightly,
that real authoring would require radical changes in student role, classroom management and methods, parents' and administrators' heads, evaluation, and the whole atmosphere of schooling.

And yet the public is now claiming to want improvement in the
teaching of writing. Since this interest and the ensuing funding were inspired by low test scores, college complaints, and popular reportage, we
needn't wonder long about where on the scale just sketched the notion
of writing in question falls. Never mind. Some interest and funds have
appeared, and this should be taken positively. But it is important that
educators try to hold this trend to the highest conception of writing, the
one that has the most educational value, and the one that works because
it stems from meaning and motive. Otherwise the current support could,
like most of the title money of the Great Society programs, end by locking in even more tightly the errors of the past.

The processes of writing cannot be realistically perceived and taught so long as we try to work from the outside in. The most fundamental and effective way to improve compositional "decisions" about word choice, phrasing, sentence structure, and overall organization is to clarify, enrich, and harmonize the thinking that predetermines the student's initial choices of these. We must never forget, no matter how much a technocratic mentality and an uncontrolled educational–industrial complex bully us the other way, that the heart of writing beats deep within a subjective inner life that, while neither audible nor visible at the time the most important action is occurring, governs all those choices that a composition course tries belatedly to straighten out.

What teaching methodology does this highest definition imply? As regards the immediate circumstances of actually getting something on paper, the definition indicates: the providing of audiences and of opportunities to grasp the various purposes of writing; individual choice of subject, form, and time; the arraying and illustrating of the entire range of kinds of writing in the diverse modes of discourse; the use of partners and coaches with whom to talk over and try out ideas before and during written composition, in order to aerate and revise inner speech across successive versions; the teaching of meditational techniques for knowing, focusing, and controlling inner speech;[4] and the interweaving of writing with other media, arts, and disciplines so that all these forms of knowing remain in natural relations with each other, providing warm-ups and follow-ups for writing and offering it as one among alternative ways to discover, develop, and render the mind.

As regards the long-range development of inner speech, the highest definition implies any means that will exercise thought itself. Enriching, refining, sharpening inner speech require, throughout all the school years: various and plentiful thinking activities as embodied in many games, practical problems to solve, imagining, and dialectic with others; much experience in small-group process where all sorts of good conversing can be practiced—task talk, topic talk, improvisation—that when internalized will become part of individual thinking; copious and wide-ranging reading as can occur only when students can individually select their own reading matter from a huge array of all sorts; rich physical and social experience with the things of this world, so that inner speech has much to reflect from the outside. The more that thought benefits from the cyclic turning over of outer and inner experience, outer and inner speech, the less revision will the actual writing phase of composition require. Deepening and clearing thought undercuts the familiar writing problems.

If we concentrate our forces on fostering the highest development of inner speech, we will automatically not only teach excellence in writing

---

4See "Writing, Inner Speech, and Meditation," pp. 133–181.

but lift other subjects along with it into a new learning integration, for the quality and qualities of inner speech determine and are determined by all mental activities. Reading or writing "across the curriculum," the "core curriculum," "teaching the humanities," and so on will all take care of themselves. We have to consider writing in relation to the rest of the curriculum. Because inner speech is the matrix of spontaneous discourse that can be composed in any direction and that reflects any externalities, it allows us to integrate all discursive learning.

9

Instructional Television for Language Learning in the '80s

Background

In 1977, a nonprofit consortium of departments of education in American states and Canadian provinces, called the Agency for Instructional Television, asked me to write a paper on "the role of instructional television in enhancing primary language arts/communication skills instruction in the 1980s." As part of their Skills Essential to Learning Project, their staff was starting to plan a primary school series for the '80s and wanted to know what I thought they ought to do with it. Operating on contributions from its constituents and on large grants from the Corporation for Public Broadcasting, AIT was already deep into writing and initial production of some series of programs for elementary and junior high school aimed at fostering "essential skills" but not aimed at raising standardized test scores. In a press release CPB President Henry Loomis said that this AIT project "permits us to put significant money into instructional broadcasting without any possibility of influencing the curriculum, which is a situation that is absolutely essential for us."

AIT gave me a budget for travel and consultation, so I set up two meetings, one on each coast, of teachers and of people experienced in filming, writing, or analyzing educational television. Thus well informed and advised—and perhaps even programmed—I wrote the following paper. Since part of my commission was to prophesy the situation of language learning in the '80s, the first half of the essay summarizes the recent past, then gives a capsule forecast of a possible educational future. That portion was published as "Language Learning in the '80s" in the *McGill Journal of Education,* Winter, 1979. The remainder has not been published before now, and since it was privately commissioned by AIT I am especially grateful for their generous permission to print it here. A list of my consultants follows the text.

Background

In planning programs for the 1980s we have to make a special effort at the outset to shake off the limiting mood of the present. Along with the rest of our culture, education is going through a spell of depression and repression. It is most important that negative tendencies now reigning should not be assumed for the future as well. Hard times can push people to an extremity that engenders better times—just as good times can dupe people into worse.

The inversion of the "Great Society" programs

Accounting for the no-account. As an example of the good-to-worse, and as a starting point for a summary of current trends *not* to be assumed for the '80s, let's recall the large funds and great expectations that went with the Great Society programs inaugurated in the mid-'60s. The catch in all these programs was that the federal government wanted their funds accounted for in ways fetched up from Detroit and the Pentagon—cost-benefit, "systems" approaches such as the Planning, Programming, and Budgeting System that required making aims and budget categories one and the same and both strictly quantifiable. Such accountability not only did not fit human education but didn't, as it turned out, work well even for gross stuff like autos and heavy weapons (or at any rate, worked well only for special-interest groups, not for the public).

The computerizable fiscal accounting systems of heavy industry joined in unholy wedlock with two other trends, one in psychology, one in education. The behaviorism of Pavlov, Hull, Skinner, and, in education, Edward Thorndike, lent itself well to the industrial model of schools as factories turning out products from inert materials (students). It followed that such products (learning results) would be easily measurable, i.e., countable. At about the same time, programmed materials were making a big splash. This was perfect. They inched the learner from one tiny measurable bit of behavior to another, in steps so small they ensured a right answer to keep the learner moving but never added up to the big goals of education. "Specific" or "performance" or "behavioral" objectives became the order of the day. And that *was* an order. To get federal money, you cut learning into pieces small enough to fit programming procedures and the standardized tests they plugged into. The testing industry had, of course, long since perfected the art of redefining learning to fit its bite-sized computer-scorable questions (and had eliminated the writing sample from College Boards as too expensive and bothersome). Then schools could buy commercial materials that did it for you—taught and tested out the pieces, organized your classroom (even boasting "individualized instruction"), and made you accountable so you could get federal money. State legislatures and district governing boards got the point and followed the lead of Washington. So by the '70s the emphasis on easily measurable, fractionated pieces of overt behavior was locked into schools with the force of law and money at all levels of government. Today, in an era of tight money, these programs have been eliminated or severely curtailed, leaving the field of education stuck with a materialistic approach it cannot warrant in learning terms. What made the wave is gone, but the wave is just now cresting across the continent!

Reinforcing the worst of the past. Two other painful ironies arose from this state of affairs. First, the idealism behind the Great Society thrust for improvement ended by reinforcing the worst of the past—the ineffectual drills-and-rules method of teaching that was itself what needed to be reformed. Ticketing parts of speech, picking synonyms, pairing words beginning with the same sound, doctoring dummy sentence structures, underlining the simile—all got defined as "cognitive" and "basic" and took over the curriculum while few people noticed that the real basics— speaking, listening, reading, and writing—were not getting taught. They were *assumed* to be taught by the drills on the parts. "Reading instruction" was taught, but not reading; "composition," but not writing. Why should the wholes be taught if the test, which merely replicates the drills, is only about the pieces?

"Back to basics" as double misnomer. This very unfortunate perfecting of the errors of the past contributed substantially to the now-notorious rise of illiteracy and the fall of scores even on the standardized tests to which the drills-and-rules approach was teaching. At this point we hear the hue and cry to go "back to basics." Where else have we ever *been?* No one opposes the teaching of reading and writing, of literacy. But those who fly banners of "back to basics" appear to champion the two R's against some adversary who is opposed to them. Since the opponent doesn't exist, the movement is a hoax. What the movement really supports is a certain way, or *method,* of teaching reading and writing—namely, the drills-and-rules method that, if it were to work, would have done so decades ago. Actually it *cannot* work because it assumes that parts can teach wholes, or add up mechanically into wholes the way subassemblies are assembled into machines, whereas the parts—the spellings, the individual words, the various sentence structures, the similes—can be learned only as functions of the wholes of which they partake. The more they are isolated out, the harder they are to learn—and the less motivation the learner can find to *want* to learn them.

The "back to basics" movement attributes the decline of skills in thought and language to la-de-da liberal experiments of the Great Society's heyday. Some of those innovations were bound to have been ill conceived and executed, as is expected for experimentation, some never got off the ground for lack of support, and some went well but were discontinued when Nixon began cutting funds for education and decrying change. Actually, the decline owes as much, or more, to sociological changes and the impact of TV as to school performance one way or the other. To the extent that school performance is indeed responsible, the dominant method of the '70s, the '60s, and before is and has been the drills-and-rules particle approach. So "back to basics" is a double misnomer. Not only is the movement not back, it is not toward the basics, which are the whole, authentic acts we call thinking, conversing, reading, and writing. The standardized tests that generate the scores cited in the outcries do not, in fact, *measure* the basics; they measure the bits and splinters that some people for years have erroneously *assumed* to add up to the basics. Actually, the *productive* activities, like speaking and writing, are not measured at all on current standardized tests. Problem solving and critical thinking are also finessed, and even the receptive "basic" of reading is measured so unscientifically—there being no oral component on paper-and-pencil tests to separate variables—that low scores are uninterpretable.

The teacher defrocked. The second irony of the Great Society's well-intentioned program is that its brand of accountability made it impossible to hold teachers accountable! The situation still obtains today. Taking over the old fractionated learning and dressing it up in performance objectives, programmed learning materials, and criterion-referenced tests, all designed to compare costs with benefits, took decision-making away from teachers and placed it in the hands of federal agencies, state legislatures, and school board officials. This occurred because these parties had to cover (account for) themselves and hence dictated, through mandated objectives and tests, the sort of curriculum and methods they would tolerate from teachers. Stipulating specific behavioral results (observable by computer scoring) acts backwards, as all required tests do, to determine what is taught and how it is taught. To the extent that federal agencies, legislators, school boards, and district administrators force teachers to teach a certain way, they, not the teachers, must assume responsibility for the results.

Had teachers cleaned house before all this, however, they would not be forced to teach in futile ways now that they know better. And many do know better; far more people outside than inside the classroom want to pour the old wine into new bottles. But the imposition of centralized, standardized specifications of teaching and testing units has thoroughly confused the natural perceptions teachers have of how children learn.

In sum, as the people's will, expressed in Great Society programs, was processed through government and industry, it became distorted and eventually even inverted, so that reform ended in the triumphant enshrinement, via the "back to basics" movement, of what was to have been reformed, it having long since been tried and found untrue.

Independent curriculum creation

This review may not only help us avoid projecting into the '80s a historical flip-flop better left, indeed, as history, but may also show how valuable a role a nonprofit organization may play. Government and industry are very hard to control and keep on target, as many forces may pull them off course. *Any* organization may go awry of course, but a consortium not organized for profit and specialized in intent has a better chance to accomplish a certain mission if it resists the infections set abroad by government and industry.

Sesame Street—a cautionary tale. The example of *Sesame Street,* however, serves to show the dangers that even the nonprofit organization faces. The profit motive and public bureaucracy may be ruled out, but both federal and foundation funding can exert influence, and popular cultural trends may be very hard to resist. *Sesame Street* was conceived and executed by an elitist operation enjoying many benefits. Its sponsor, the Children's Theater Workshop, was well heeled and well connected. Despite these advantages, between the original conception and the first production the aims of *Sesame Street* were narrowed and lowered considerably.[1] The well-chosen experts who stated the program's aims, in the summer of 1968, seemed constrained to the form and content of the objectives-writing trends already current in funding circles. Then came production. The program's initial emphasis (since much corrected) lay on memorizing letters and numbers. Much program time and media wizardry were spent teaching the alphabet. Now, some old "reading research" supposedly shows a correlation between reading achievement and knowing the alphabet early, but it was professionally very naive in 1969 to take this or any other isolated statistical correlation at face value. Obviously, what correlates with reading achievement is a *middle-class home setting,* in which children are (were?) not only taught the alphabet but talked with, read to, and given adult models for reading and writing. Such children probably learn to read well *despite* learning the alphabet early, since alphabetical pronunciation of letters conflicts considerably with the actual spelling of English sounds. Learning the alphabet can be dignified as "cognitive" and "basic" (i.e., very serious and worth funding) whereas in fact it is neither.

If the logic of *Sesame Street* was "Middle-class children learn to read; therefore we'll give poor minority children what those kids get," then it should have afforded poor children what middle-class kids were getting that really *counted:* it should have shown illustrated pages of good children's books while sounding the texts in a good storyreader's voice—that is, should have read to them in "lap method" style. But stating the objectives and the testing for this programming would have been much harder than for the learning of the alphabet. Educational Testing Service announced authoritatively that *Sesame Street* was accomplishing its objectives—at least those objectives which ETS chose to measure, the easier ones. Children *did* learn the alphabet. ETS accepted the objectives themselves at face value and hence would never discover whether learning the

[1]See *Getting to Sesame Street: Origins of the Children's Television Workshop,* Richard M. Polsky, Aspen Institute, Praeger, New York, 1974.

alphabet aided reading or not. So long as measurement tests particle activities, teaching.can appear successful and still not teach the real goals, which are broader.

At any rate, *Sesame Street* partook too much—at least until criticized—of the regular commercial and educational worlds. Its mistaken focus on the alphabet stemmed from the same payoff anxiety that caused the commercial world to develop in the first place not only performance objectives and numbers games in assessment (like Nielsen ratings) but also the zoom-flash, overexcited programming techniques that *Sesame Street* also borrowed. But the decision to feature the alphabet also showed too little autonomy from the educational momentum toward teaching isolated parts (in this case not even the relevant parts!) according, precisely, to what we have been describing as the major misdirection of the whole educational establishment.

Still, keeping in mind this cautionary tale, and granting to any pioneer its right to some mistakes, we return to the point that education needs badly a curriculum agency of at least some degree of independence. Such an agency must *foster* this independence and recognize it as its greatest asset. Perhaps the most pertinent question that an independent agency can ask itself is, "What can we do that government and industry don't or can't do for education?

Problems of the medium itself

A final negative element of the present that future plans should take into account concerns the very medium itself. Both formal research and native perception indicate clearly that television has had bad effects on children that go beyond either the content or the quality of programming. No matter how good a program is, it still tends to induce passivity and to replace interaction with other people and the environment. Reading and listening to the radio are relatively passive too, but reading requires far more inferring and imagining, and even radio leaves it to the audience to fill in the visuals. TV is no worse, of course, than movies, which also supply a video and immobilize the viewer. It is only TV's presence in the home and the consequent large quantity of viewing that make it more dangerous. Schools can control both the quantity and quality of ITV fare, but they still have to face the fact that they are adding more viewing time to an already crippling amount of it. Many of the recommendations in this paper aim not only to teach language but to do so in ways that may offset the damage inherent in the medium.

Future Educational Trends Affecting Language Learning

In order to describe the current educational situation that will be changing during the '80s, I have had to touch on politics, economics, and technology because these have determined education more than have pure learning factors. Likewise it is impossible to envision future language arts in isolation from other aspects of education and social change with which they will become increasingly enmeshed. But fortunately, what language learning will be mixed with or determined by will be increasingly benevolent and relevant. Inevitably also, prophesying mixes what *will* be with what *ought* to be, and the issue becomes not just how to *fit* ITV programming into the future but how to help *create* the future with it.

Toward pluralism and holism

During the '80s the technocratic approach and the "back to basics" bandwagon will deadend in ineffectuality because they are inorganic and unrealistic, and the humanistic forces will gain ascendance. Temporarily buried during the '70s by fearful reaction to change, the innovative impulses of the '60s to reform society and education will resurge but with greater knowledge, effectiveness, and balance. Standardization will give way to pluralism; the particle approach to holism. Drills-and-rules will give way to realistic, well-motivated activities found outside of school, as people become aware that human ends cannot be achieved by mechanistic means.

So one hallmark of education in the '80s will be *alternatives,* to accommodate the plurality of differences in personal makeup and development, of familial and ethnic background. But these differences will be constantly reintegrated on the basis of human *universals,* the other hallmark. Students of different age, capacity, and temperament, for example, will be accommodated by flexible subgrouping within a heterogeneous group or "class"; special-education and English-as-a-second-language students will get some special treatment while remaining mainstreamed. Restating our description, we feel that perhaps it makes more sense to say that pluralism will replace the particle approach, since both share an emphasis on differences and breakdowns, while holism will replace standardization, since both of these share an emphasis on similarity and unity. In reality, then, trends may not be reversing but rising, rather, to a higher plane. Instead of putting analysis and synthesis in the service of rationalizing institutionalism, people will be putting them to "the human use of human beings" (mathematician Norbert Wiener). School "subjects" are not objects, foreign and outside. This elevation will play a part in the ongoing evolution of human consciousness.

Individualized instruction, alternative schooling, student contracts, special education, classroom learning stations, multi-ethnic curriculum, electives, and the open classroom will coalesce into a fully developed practical management of student-centered learning accommodating every significant sort of individual variation. Parallel to this, such trends as team teaching, cross-grade grouping, pod arrangements, racial integration, older students teaching younger, school resource centers, community aides, work-study courses, interdisciplinary studies, and flexible scheduling will coalesce into the instituting of larger, more mixed pools of learners. Any such pool will give an individual daily opportunity to work with different adults, older and younger students, and a variety of materials, methods, media, and environments. This tandem coalescence will not only allow for differences but put these differences into useful interactions by flexible subgrouping within a pool not too large to cohere or too small to afford variety and a sense of community.

Alternatives. Alternative *means* to the same general goals will be accepted and facilitated. Children will learn to read and write, for example, by different combinations of the four possible approaches to literacy—phonics, sight word, "language experience" (the pupil watching his stories being written down), and read-along (following a text with the eyes while hearing it read). They will practice reading by reading different selections and practice writing by doing different assignments, all in a personal order but often with partners. One sequence for all for each year and one lesson plan for all each day will phase out and become a thing of the past. These variant routings to the same goals will be logged for each learner, and this logging will accumulate in records, along with learners' products, and be passed on from year to year so that students can start where they left off the year before.

Children will be taught from primary on how to render experience into *alternative media and alternative symbolizations*—to dramatize, depict, or narrate stories, for example; to express feeling through mime, dance, song, music, poetry, photography, or plastic arts; or to cast information quantitatively as mathematical relations, qualitatively as verbal description, or combining these with graphics, as maps, charts, diagrams, slide-tapes, captioned photos or drawings, or moving pictures with voice-over. This will fulfill the theme of logician/epistemologist Susanne Langer that human beings have various alternative "semantics" to express "feeling" (thought/emotion).[2]

Balancing the brain. Powerfully supporting this "equal time" offering of the modes of communicating and informing is the recently disseminated research finding that the human brain cognizes in two main modes. One is analytical, intellectual, verbal, and literal and processes data serially. The other is synthesizing or holistic, intuitive, nonverbal, and metaphorical and processes data simultaneously. One strikes a note at a time; the other, a resonant chord. They are different but equally valid and should collaborate on many tasks (such as reading, which combines linear processing with the metaphorical nature of words).

[2]*Mind: An Essay on Human Feeling,* Johns Hopkins Press, Baltimore, 1967.

Until around eight or so years old, people cognize both ways in both hemispheres of the brain, but then, perhaps because socialization and acculturation begin to threaten with extinction the holistic mode, the hemispheres specialize so that, in most right-handed people, the left takes charge of the analytical and linear, associated with the "academic curriculum," while the right takes charge of the mode associated with metaphor, arts, crafts, and sports.[3] It is around this time, during or after third grade, that a notorious slump occurs in many if not most school children. We may have a clue here to ways it can be avoided. The influential work of Joseph Chilton Pearce strongly asserts that stereotyping and premature stress on verbal/conceptual learning during primary schooling account for the slump and seriously cripple the astonishing native learning capacity of the small child.[4]

A growing number of psychologists and educators are arguing very convincingly that our culture currently favors the left hemisphere so much as to create a dangerous imbalance and that school must make deliberate efforts to educate for the right hemisphere by restoring the arts to elementary school—now scorned as frills impeding the skills—and by letting children's intelligence fully explore imagistic, metaphoric, fantastic ways of symbolizing.[5] One of the giants of child psychology, Bruno Bettelheim, has recently made a penetrating and eloquent case for the profound emotional and conceptual value of fairytales.[6] Ironically, it is holistic cognition, so undervalued today, that best copes with the interrelational intricacies of inner and outer life that characterize our epoch.

Alternative realities. The ultimate set of alternatives for which the '80s will eduate is *alternative realities*[7] in the sense that Carlos Castaneda has now made a part of our modern heritage—i.e., fundamentally different experiences of what is real. Carl Rogers, one of the most influential of living psychologists and therapists, said precisely this at a conference in 1974 at Stanford called "Readin', Writin', and Reality." The title itself, yoking the humble literacy skills directly to one's level of consciousness, serves as signpost to the educational changes we can expect. Up to now it has always seemed natural that schooling should perpetuate a single public reality to fit routine acculturation processes going on outside of school. But at our present stage of evolution this may destroy rather than preserve society, for if we do not encourage variant perspectives and a range of levels of consciousness, society will fail to solve its complex problems for lack of creativity. One notion of reality is not enough, es-

---

[3]See *The Psychology of Consciousness,* Robert Ornstein, W. H. Freeman & Co., San Francisco, 1972.
[4]See his *Magical Child,* E. P. Dutton, New York, 1977.
[5]See *The Metaphoric Mind,* Robert Samples, Addison-Wesley, 1976.
[6]*The Uses of Enchantment: The Meaning and Importance of Fairytales,* Vintage paperback, Random House, New York, 1977.
[7]*A Separate Reality* and other books of his tetrology of conversations with the Yaqui Indian shaman, Don Juan, Simon & Schuster, New York, 1971.

pecially if it represents the conventional, common-denominator, center-of-gravity stance. Exactly parallel to the danger of teaching a single reality is the peril of suppressing the right-hemisphere functioning, so badly needed to deal with today's intricacies and to restore the balance of the mind. Fostering alternative realities really means letting the mind entertain all possibilities and find its most expanded state of consciousness. The alternatives in means, methods, materials, and media, and especially symbolizations mentioned above, will allow different learners to utilize each other's partialities to forge impartiality, wholeness.

The shift in psychologies

The reign of behaviorism is clearly over. It lingers only as embalmed in some commercial and administrative circles. For some time it has been losing ground to the deeper insights of child development (Jean Piaget, Jerome Bruner, Heinz Werner), psycholinguistics (Roger Brown, Noam Chomsky), neurophysiology (Wilder Penfield),[8] Gestalt or holistic psychology, the psychologies called humanistic or transpersonal that focus on the highest human capacities and follow such exponents as Carl Rogers and Abraham Maslow, and finally the various dynamic and interactive psychotherapies aiming beyond mere coping to liberation and even bliss. Checked momentarily during the '70s, these psychologies are becoming irresistible because they are obviously more accurate and fruitful than the simplistic stimulus–response psychology so dominant in this century. As a bloc these emphasize *innate capacity* and the possibility of indefinite evolution.

What these experts say runs counter to conventional education. To survive, schools will convert in the light of this new knowledge and in the light of old failures. This better understanding of how people learn makes clear that constant prodding, provoking, and manipulating are unnecessary (appearing so because students can find no motivation to work with particles) and retard learning. People are born learners. The greatest learning occurs spontaneously before school,[9] and before heavy acculturation and institutionalizing. Schools will improve in the '80s by deinstitutionalizing.

Reading readiness. Government has clearly "bought" the evidence that preschool children are sensational learners and has espoused Early Childhood Education. Funding in this area may run counter, however, to another insight from these same psychologies, which is that forcing a certain *kind* of learning, before readiness, retards that learning. Forced instruction may even seem to succeed, as reading scores often appear to indicate for a while, but scores usually crumple. Or scores may hold but at a cost in

---

[8] *The Mystery of the Mind,* Wilder Penfield, Princeton University Press, Princeton, 1975.
[9] See *The First Three Years of Life,* Burton White, Prentice Hall, Englewood Cliffs, NJ, 1975.

total growth not worth the price. Piaget has always felt that Americans try too hard to speed up development that will occur anyway. Virtually all of the psychologies above would agree that verbal learning is pushed too soon in our schools, a condition that accounts in large measure for the swelling ranks of "remedial readers."

There seems little question that all youngsters would learn to read without stress if given time. It's not that hard, requires little intelligence, and can happen quickly when circumstances are personally right. But a first grade teacher today is considered negligent if she allows a child to pass to the second grade illiterate—or she may be accused of racial discrimination or of depriving the child of his "right to read." Many primary teachers will admit they force children, against their better judgment, but they have to cover themselves. An entrenched aspect of current education requires "grade-level" reading scores, a denial of individual differences.

By the '80s, this self-defeating pressure will perforce yield to the realities of learning. Primary teachers then will have to allow for some children becoming literate before entering school or early in school and for others becoming literate only by third or fifth grade. Now being rediscovered, Rudolph Steiner, founder of the international network of Waldorf schools based on his clairvoyant views of growth, recommended fifty years ago that literacy be deferred until around nine when, he said, the child's full consciousness of having an ego separate from the world readies him for the degree of conceptual objectification necessary for literacy to take well. Children build abstract conceptualization out of imagery based on physical experience. The proper and well-established order is from bodily enactment to pictures to abstract symbols. Pairing spoken words with written words is hardly developmental and *may* be learned early, but the *point* of it, meaning, is developmental.

Chanting while jumping rope, or singing words to music, represent excellent extensions of the nonverbal into the verbal. The Carl Orff and Shinichi Suzuki methods of teaching music to children claim to prepare for or foster other kinds of learning, including verbal/conceptual, and will increasingly influence primary education, along with Steiner, who emphasized not only a whole-soul approach but specific utilization of rhythms, music, and body movement to help teach language and math. We can expect music, rhythm, song, and dance to play a serious role in all of primary and elementary education in the future, not merely restoring the arts but undergirding more abstract learning.

Regulating one's own mind and body

Allied to these ascending psychologies, the "human potential" movement begun in the '60s will flower in the '80s, having in the interim picked up tremendous momentum from Eastern spiritual/physical disciplines, biofeedback, and autogenic techniques of self-regulation, and the acceptance by growing numbers of scientific and medical communities of the validity of psychic phenomena. All of these are already making their way into schools. With stunning force and rapidity, Eastern and Western methods of increasing mental and physical capacity beyond conventional norms are fusing into a major cultural force, as Alan Watts presaged a decade ago.[10] From the oriental martial arts; from Western physical and mental therapeutic techniques; from the practices of yoga, zen, sufism, and Amerindian shamanism; from commercial self-improvement courses like EST, Arica, and Silva Mind Control that synthesize the preceding techniques; and from scientific research in self-hypnosis, parapsychology, and neurophysiology has emerged an increasingly coherent methodology for teaching people of all ages how to live at their highest capacity—not merely personal capacity but even transpersonal. This teaching methodology begs for introduction into schools, and many public school teachers now are teaching forms of meditation and related exercises for relaxation, internal awareness, concentration, centering, balancing, and energizing.[11] These fundamental controls of mind and body underlie other learning, however academic. Consider just the role of attention in reading and math.

Psychic powers. For millennia yoga has calmly asserted that advanced practitioners achieve "supernatural" powers as a by-product of their spiritual discipline. Now the recent letting out of psychic phenomena from the closet, reduplicating tremendous interest in the subject by leading minds in the late nineteenth century, seems destined to convince people of the near future that they can learn to do far more with the mind and body than modern humankind has ever conceived. America's foremost psychic healer, Olga Worrell, has been published in the *Journal of the American Medical Association,* and the flourishing organizations for holistic healing or medicine, such as the Academy of Parapsychology and Medicine, are founded usually by physicians and assume invisible energy fields moving in and out of our bodies that mind can influence. The Stanford Research Institute research by Targ and Puthoff on psychics Uri Geller and Ingo Swann has been published in *Nature, the* journal for announcing scientific discovery. The reality of psychic phenomena such as telepathy, clairvoyance, and psychokinesis has been acknowledged by many of the best minds of today, many of them scientists and other establishment figures.[12] Parapsychology has been gathered into the fold of the American Psychological Association—finally—after Gardiner Mur-

[10]*Psychotherapy East and West,* Pantheon Books, Random House, New York, 1969.

[11]A pioneering handbook for such teachers by two education professors is *The Centering Book,* Gay Hendricks and Russell Wills, Prentice Hall, Englewood Cliffs, N.J., 1975. George Leonard in *Education and Ecstasy,* Delacorte Press, New York, 1968, first pulled together these movements for education.

[12]See *Psychic Exploration,* edited by astronaut Edgar Mitchell, G. P. Putnam's Sons, New York, 1974.

phy had been proving in labs at Duke the existence of these phenomena for thirty or forty years. (As Einstein said, pursuing the physical always leads into the metaphysical.)

So-called *extra*sensory perception and *super*natural powers are being accepted as potentialities that everyone might manifest if the single reality of acculturation does not suppress the small child's belief that anything is possible, and if academic schooling does not break his initial attunement with the force fields in which he lives.[13] The years between the shedding of the teeth and the onset of puberty constitute the period of greatest susceptibility to hypnosis and of spontaneous psychic powers, of absorption in reading and of concrete intuition. Some children may well be seeing the auras or energy fields around other people.[14] Instead of being a slump period, ages 8 to 12 should see great spurts in adult-modeled competencies. The real job of primary schools may be to set this up.

Changing priorities. We know now that human beings can learn to regulate their own heart beat, respiration, brain waves, metabolism, skin temperature, mood, state of health, level of energy, state of mind, focus of mind, and state of consciousness. The real revolution in education, due for the '80s, will focus on the extension of the personal capacity to control one's own mind and body in relation to other people and force fields of our natural and manmade environment. The senior policy analyst of the U.S. Office of Education made a step in this direction in 1978 by promoting a series of papers and conferences on precisely the human-potential trends I have just described, including the exploration of extraordinary and "psychic" powers.[15] The value of such learning is obviously so great, approximating as it does the basic intent of all learning, that matters now held of great importance will be dropped, deferred, or played down. In this reordering of priorities we can well expect that literacy may not be an important objective of primary school, especially since it can be deferred with more chance of gain than loss. Most likely, instead of enjoying the spotlight, as now, language generally will play no more a role during primary school time than it does outside of school at that age of life.

An isomorphic alphabet

An important sociotechnical change that could come about during the '80s is worth mentioning, because, should it occur, it would also dras-

[13]In "Cosmic Consciousness," J. A. Christensen, *Media and Methods,* February 1975, the author suggests that educators take psychic power seriously and prepare to deal with it in schools.
[14]See James Peterson's article, "Extrasensory Abilities of Children, An Ignored Reality?" *Learning,* December 1976, and *The Boy Who Saw True,* Cyril Scott, A. Wheaton & Co., Exeter, England, 1953, 1961, a nineteenth-century diary by a child seeing auras.
[15]See "The Outer Limits of Human Educability—Proposed Research Program," an official paper presented by Jerry L. Fletcher, Senior Policy Analyst, Office of the Deputy Assistant Secretary for Education, Department of Health, Education, and Welfare, 200 Independence Ave., S.W., Room 317, Washington, D.C. 20201.

tically alter schooling as we know it. Fulfilling George Bernard Shaw's old recommendation, the English-speaking world might adopt an isomorphic alphabet (one-to-one correspondence between sounds and their spellings) just as it is now shifting to the metric system. Such adoption would reduce the problem of "basic skills"—literacy skills—to insignificance, since English spelling makes word attack and writing far harder to learn than, say, Italian or Turkish. Most European children learn to read and write a couple of years sooner than English-speaking children.

An isomorphic alphabet would make literacy easy enough that children could pick it up incidentally, with far less stress. This would free schools to shift gears upward into precisely the higher sorts of learning just discussed, instead of being hung up on a merely mechanical difficulty for years on end. Much school time now has to be expended on what amounts to remedial literacy, whatever the subject or grade.

The Unifon Alphabet, invented by John Malone, comprises forty symbols closely resembling conventional letters, and each standing for one phoneme. It could be used only for initial literacy learning, as a transition into the intricacies of actual English spelling, but few teachers consider a special learning alphabet as worthwhile. (The old Initial Teaching Alphabet never caught on, and its inventor, John Downey, now backs Malone, who claims only a few days of transition are needed.) Unlikely as it might seem at first thought, the English-speaking world may start to move this way during the '80s, in response to two main forces.

For one thing, more and more of the world is speaking English; it has already become virtually the international language. As a second language for different nations, it serves admirably, being not only the language of a major literature, but being inextricably interwoven into the world's political and commercial transactions. Second, great incentive is growing to create machines for typing recorded speech and for electronically sounding out a text—that is, for machine translating between voice and print. Such machines would require almost certainly an isomorphic alphabet. Add to this the advantage itself of lifting a great burden from public schools, and you have reasons to take seriously the possibility of spelling reform. Even if only begun in the '80s, it would force educators and the public to support higher kinds of learning to fill the large vacuum so created.

Recommendations

First, consider how TV differs from other school media resources. How does it compare with sound films, for example? One difference is that films are usually made for large-screen viewing, whereas TV relies a lot on close-up shots for small-screen viewing. But, more important, TV is *broadcast,* that is, controlled from a center outside the classroom. Allied to this concept of broadcasting is that of *programs* or *series,* of creating sequence or other continuity (setting, format, characterization, serial story) from one "program" or film to another. But there is no exclusive connection between broadcasting and continuity across presentations, since movies as well as TV "programs" can be made in series. All that broadcasting accomplishes is to place the power to start and stop presentations outside the classroom. This does not ensure that programs will be utilized, because the teacher still retains the old right to switch sets off and on. In fact, by forcing on the classroom a time of viewing that may be unsuitable, broadcasting risks reducing viewership.

Recent technology

Recent technological advances make possible a flexible classroom control such that presentations could be not only started and stopped at the class's convenience, but also interrupted, resumed, and rerun at will. Video cassettes enable a classroom to manipulate TV programs as they would films. The only difference is that the programs are on videotape, played in the form of cassettes through a regular TV monitor of the same sort used for broadcasting. Any forecast of the '80s should assume that video cassette players will be available in schools and probably also that they and the monitors will accommodate color. One advantage of classroom control over broadcasting is that the staggered hours of viewing permit teachers to pass around a limited quantity of machines and hence render unnecessary a set for each classroom. Actually, a more likely and more attractive forecast would be to expect that video cassettes will be replaced in the '80s by disks played by laser beams (which Music Corporation of America and other companies already have). Laser disks are cheaper to produce, easier to stop and start, and better wearing than video cassettes.

Classroom control

Programs could be reproduced on either cassette or disk. What is essential is that programs so shown be conceived at the outset to utilize classroom control. No advantage would accrue if programs were not made to be interrupted, for example, so a class could do an activity in direct response to what it had just viewed. The key assumption underlying classroom control is that students will take action as an immediate result of what they see. Programming produced deliberately for variable interrupting and for optional replay or for ad hoc viewing by a subgroup of a class differs from programming for continuous, one-shot, whole-class, pre-scheduled viewing. Classroom control better implements the individualization, interaction, and integration required for an improved curriculum.

Reproducing and rebroadcasting. One difference between the cassette/disk and regular school films lies in how the master is reproduced. Although made for classroom control, future programs *might* be broadcast once throughout a district, say, in order to permit schools to record copies that henceforth could be used like any other AV materials. Or other local means of reproducing may well offer themselves as technology develops during the '80s. In any case, what the distributing agency distributes is a *master made for reproduction.* As it is currently, some school and district offices make illegal copies of commercial audio cassettes, videotapes, and films. Programs produced by a nonprofit organization can build into their whole design an arrangement for legal local reproduction.

The more TV resorts to reruns, as *Sesame Street* and *Electric Company* have understandably done, the more TV broadcasting resembles film rental. Rerunning takes distribution in the direction of local control, since after an initial broadcast some of the target audience will have seen the program and some will not. Within school districts, programs are often transferred to videotape to facilitate rerunning. Periodic rebroadcast helps to give classrooms more choice of viewing time but obviously limits choices far more than classroom control does and does not allow variable interrupting and instant replay. Well-made ITV programs should be made available for viewing many times over a year and over several years, but rebroadcasting cannot satisfactorily answer this need.

Programming for classroom control clearly furthers two significant trends gaining ground for good reasons—local reproduction of, and rebroadcasting of, remotely produced materials. Since classroom control furthers so well also the desirable traits of a good future curriculum, a sound conclusion seems to be that ITV should become materially like other AV resources stocked in the classroom or resource center.

Casting off broadcasting

It is very fitting that the *tele-* or broadcasting aspect of ITV should be eliminated. As we have pointed out, the most damaging criticism of the medium is that it renders viewers passive in a negative sense. This criticism hurts worst because high-quality programming cannot offset it and could in fact increase dependency and passivity. Doesn't the broadcasting of remotely produced programs risk contradicting the educational ideal of an active, questing intelligence, if we consider that it will be added to home viewing of commercial programming? Certainly, well-designed informative programs can supply food for thought and stimulate further questing, but *any* one-way transmission puts the learner in a receiving posture. Still, cannot "high quality" programming be defined, precisely, as that which stimulates viewers to interact with things or other people? It can probably—if broadcasting is eliminated and if remote programming offsets its disadvantages by building in flexible classroom usage.

Interaction in learning requires the other two i's—individualization and integration. The right stimulus has to be available at the right time for the right pupils. Let's say that improvisational dialogue is modeled on screen by peer performers for viewers to emulate. The program needs to be interrupted right then, resumed only when viewers have finished their own improvisations, rerun immediately if some viewers need that, and shown in the first place only to those members of the class ready for it. Local selection and timing need not conflict, however, with the concept of a *series* of presentations. The model improvisation, for example, could be one of a sequence of demonstrations by a group of children and a teacher who become known to the viewers and could be presented in a recurring setting with familiar sound effects, and so on.

The real value of ITV resides not in broadcasting but in the simultaneous presentation of sight and sound. It would influence education best at this point by showing through programming precedents how to produce school AV materials that will promote the most needed curriculum. As a medium TV fails precisely where schools do also. Both tend to be overbearing and induce inertia within. We do not need better ways of doing what is already overdone. One-way transmission naturally emphasizes the merely informational aspect of learning and hence imprinting or memorization, whereas more important learning consists of developing abilities to *do* things. What remote programming *can* do well is show viewers how to get into learning interactions not commonly practiced in schools for the very reason that their interactive nature makes them harder to demonstrate and direct through bookish media and harder also for school institutionalism generally to tolerate. Viewers should alternate watching and doing. If schools are to use TV wisely they must not merely accept it passively themselves, as employed commercially, but make it serve as needed. This means eliminating broadcasting so as to deepen programming potential.

Modular packaging

Disks/cassettes need not be of a uniform length when broadcasting and hence scheduling are not an issue. Furthermore, the variety of content that in traditional broadcasting has been placed on one videotape may as well be broken down and spread over separate disks/cassettes so that each portion can be most feasibly matched off with the appropriate students. The more modular, the more flexible.

What in the past was a variety show of, say, a half-hour, comprising some story, some animation of letters and words, and some documentary, would in the future be produced as separate materials, for the sake of individualization. Different learners might in this way view different portions of the former variety show, usually in small groups, or view the same portions but at different, more appropriate times. Some students, for example, might benefit from collaborative writing of limericks but not from choral reading aimed at literacy. Others might need the literacy reinforcement but not be ready for the collaborative writing. If physically separated, these and other portions could be used simultaneously, if desired, by the different working parties, or, playing another option, used in mixture with other materials at various times. Furthermore, some footage that might formerly have been locked into the entire variety show can now be produced by itself in a form for instant replaying so that any subgroup can rerun it—to listen and watch at first, read aloud or sing along a second time, turn off and replace the sound track with their own voices. Teaching literacy through animated letters and words can work wonders, but if this approach does not accommodate individualization and rerunning, it should not be included in programming because no classroom contains members coinciding so specifically in readiness for certain sound-spellings, and good use of the screen-as-page technique would have to include easy replay in film-loop fashion. Such animation goes too fast to absorb all on one viewing. Material could be repeated throughout a longer program, but it is cheaper and more interactive to let viewers do the repeating by rerunning.

Content of programming

For primary school language-learning, three domains of content are open. First, there is the world of things, the nonverbal world, about which people form concepts, ask questions, make statements—in short, think and talk. TV can be a very effective source of information to extend experience undersea and overseas, into nature, into town, and so on, to enlarge what can be thought and talked about. Much of so-called "reading readiness" consists of expanding children's world of experience. Without this base, speech means little.

Directly based on this nonverbal world, and immediately underlying reading and writing, is the world of people talking to each other, the uses of oral language, by means of which everyone learns not only the speech sounds and basic vocabulary but also the grammar for putting the sounds and words together into utterances and the most effective ways to express oneself. Children talk outside of school, true, but they usually learn today a very limited language and limited *uses* of language. (And they spend five to six hours a day before a TV set.) They especially need to learn *more ways of interacting vocally* that they may not learn outside of school on their own. They should practice language not only for play and for socializing but also for problem solving, for giving directions, for expressing themselves, for communicating ideas, and for collaborating to develop thought.

Finally there is the world of print. Besides literacy itself—the audiovisual matching of speech with print—there are all the things that can be found to read—labels and captions, stories, facts, games, signs, directions, etc. Undergirded by the nonverbal and vocal worlds, the world of print caps a rich layering of content possibilities.

A strategy for selecting. As a matter of strategy, ITV programming for the primary level should allow for what schools are likely to have and to do already in these areas of learning. ITV can serve most usefully by balancing existing school programs. What schools most readily provide on their own are factual things like the spellings of the language sounds (phonics), the names for things (vocabulary), a body of reading matter (mostly environmental labels and stories, in primary), and perhaps some stimuli for story telling and writing. What schools provide less readily are means for developing oral language in small groups (discussion and improvisation), peer collaboration in reading and writing, reading along with *shown-and-sounded* texts, a wide spectrum of reading and writing opportunities stimulated by interweaving the language arts with other arts, other media, and other subjects.

There seems no limit but maturity level and money to the amount of factual or fictional content that could be dramatized and depicted for children to think, talk, and write about. But again, ITV producers can select according to what schools lack most. Many fine films of stories and nature exist. What is rarer are programs specially designed to invite extension by the audience—the incomplete story to finish, for example, or the factual depiction that raises questions for discussion or further investigation.

A kind of in-service training. The strategy of emphasizing what schools tend to do least conveys an additional benefit: it affords teachers a subtle but very effective in-service training. While pupils are viewing a trio of peer demonstrators read and write puns or tongue twisters together, following instructions on an activity card or poster and only occasionally consulting with their teacher, the local classroom teacher can see not only that such an activity so managed is possible but how it can be set up by means of an activity card (perhaps supplied with the disk/cassette), small grouping, and a teacher role as roving consultant. *Why* tongue twisters are worth working with can also become clearer as the teacher witnesses children making the sound-spelling discriminations that phonics programs aim to teach. While a teacher on screen is talking viewers step-by-step through a dramatic exercise, the classroom teacher gains a model for his or her action.

Most teachers need such concrete demonstration of the *how* and *why* of small-group, interactive, oral-language, learning-game, or dramatic activities because spontaneous activity by pupils is hard to manage, justify, and evaluate within the confines of a conventional curriculum. There is no doubt, however, that such high participation teaches more. Whereas educational manufacturers and teacher training institutions generally partake too much of the conventional curriculum to revise it, independent ITV could break the cycle and get much-needed activities into the classroom, partly by getting them into the minds of teachers. So one important principle of selection in programming might well concern in-service by indirection.

Three suggested kinds of programming

Three general kinds of programs could be combined for primary school. Although several or all could be spliced together to form a variety-type show, if produced as physically separate disks/cassettes they would usually, as argued above, facilitate greater flexibility.

1. *Demonstrating desired activities.* Peers or elders model certain activities, usually interactive, that deserve greater currency in schools than is generally accorded them, such as small-group show-and-tell with peer questioning and without a leader[16]; task talk and topic talk in small groups, playing of cards and other games for learning phonics or vocabulary or sentence structure; enactment of familiar stories from memory; improvisation of dialogue and action from a bare story idea or situation; partner reading (taking turns in duos and trios reading aloud a common text without the teacher); collective writing with a scribe; dictating stories to a more advanced student or adult aide, then reading back the dictation; talking into a tape recorder with a partner and transcribing later; working up a rehearsed reading of a text to perform for others or a Story Theater performance; pantomiming; choral reading or group singing; and so on.

After watching these activities modeled on screen, viewers turn off the set and follow suit. Sometimes, however, the on-screen teacher may talk the viewers through an activity, such as guided fantasy, or tell a story for viewers to pantomime step by step or make a series of provocative sounds for viewers to move to. Sometimes the camera shows pupils demonstrating the activity, then focuses on the teacher directing viewers to do the same thing.

2. *The screen as page.* Letters, single words, sentences, tongue twisters, puns, whole stories, songs, appear on screen as they are vocalized on the sound track. Panning up or to the side, flashing, and a bouncing-ball type of indicator are used to help viewers synchronize spellings with sounds. Spellings of short and long vowels may be introduced in isolation but consonants only in combination with vowels. No alphabetical names. And any isolated phoneme spellings or syllables are soon blended into others to make words, which are ordered into sentences. Various animation techniques such as simulation of a slot machine can transform one word into another by substituting, adding, deleting, or reversing letters while the results of each transformation are sounded.

Machinery for easy replay by small children is important, for individuals vary in both absorption rate and sound-letter knowledge. Also, on a second or third viewing children might join with the sound track and

---

[16]For a clear example of this very activity as it might be modeled, at third grade, see "Do and Talk," one of eighteen such films constituting the *English through Interaction* series in the *Interaction* language arts and reading program, senior author James Moffett, Houghton Mifflin Co., Boston, 1973. Also in that series, "A Pupil-Centered Classroom" shows first-graders following a curriculum such as that proposed in this article.

practice read-along or sing-along. On later viewings, children can turn off the sound track and sound the on-screen words themselves.

Music can be well used to enliven such programs and to synchronize viewers' voices with each other and with the printed words. Notes and beats provide additional cues and bring out stress and syllabification. Songs make for a fine read-along, join-in activity. They may teach literacy better than anything else.

Since children vary a great deal in which sound-spellings they need introduction to or occasions to practice with, these disks/cassettes would most often be shown to subgroups of a class, as explained earlier, different pupils skipping or repeating as needed. Such programs could form a series less and less phonetically controlled and employing increasingly uncommon spellings and words and punctuations, but from the outset some balance should be kept between the showing of isolated spellings and words and of whole sentences and sentence continuities. Small focus should never last long. Fine material for whole continuities of words are jokes and puns, tongue twisters, jump-rope jingles, and nursery rhymes, in addition to short poems, songs, and stories.

It is not recommended to show on screen at once both animated letters and the competing action of human, puppet, or cartoon hosts, as *Electric Company* sometimes does. It seems better to focus attention without distraction on the adding, deleting, reversing, and replacing of letters and on the *meaning* of what is being spelled out in word strings and continuities of sentences. The mind should be directed to and *through* words to the referents of the words. Sometimes the referents—objects, characters, settings—may be illustrated motionless, at the same time the words appear, as in story books, but essentially viewers should become accustomed to picturing referents in the *mind*'s eye and to finding interest not in what they see around words but in what the words say. TV is accused, precisely, of robbing viewers of the incentive to imagine for themselves. Animate the words, not the illustrations, when presenting both at once, so that language does not get up-staged just when it is barely making it *on-stage*.[17]

3. *Material for viewers to extend*. Stories may be dramatized and information depicted in such ways that viewers can finish them, refashion them, or detail them themselves. This kind of programming furnishes fodder for children to think, talk, read, and write about; to act out; to cast into

[17]See Caleb Gattegno's *Toward a Visual Culture* for the full description and rationale of teaching literacy through sound films of animated letters and words, and see his film series *Pop Up* implementing his ideas, both from Educational Solutions, New York. *Pop Up* consists of eighteen one-minute lessons on super-8 cassette or 16 mm reel.

See also in the *Interaction* Literacy Kit the super-8 cassette series of thirty-four 2- to 3-minute films *Sound Out*, Bobby Seifert and James Moffett, Houghton Mifflin, Boston.

Both these series show animated letters and words, without other visuals. Emphasis is on using animation to show transformations of one word into another and to build syllables and words into sentences. *Sound Out* also teaches punctuation and capitalization.

other media; or to research further. It is a source, too, of concepts and vocabulary, providing proper pronunciation and contextual, pictorial definitions of new words, whether material is make-believe or scientific. The audio can carry voice-over, dialogue, or sound effects and can feed in mature sentence structure, happy phrasing, metaphors, and, in conjunction with the visuals, good rhetorical devices for narrative and exposition. These dramatizations and factual presentations employ live actors, puppets, cartoons, three-dimensional animation, or realistic photography of objects and nature. Viewers can stop a story to act out, tell, or write their own ending, or guess the next part then resume the show to compare their own version with the program's, or simply discuss what they understand or don't understand so far. The program itself could sometimes offer several versions of the same story, or alternative endings, to induce a sense of point of view and creative possibilities or to place what happened against the background of what might have happened. This open-endedness can in turn be related to oral storytelling and folk-type variations of well-known tales.

Not only different courses of action but different *styles* of storytelling can be offered and fostered. The same set of visuals can be reshown with different narration or dialogue that either changes the action or recasts the language into another dialect or style. Or the same narration or dialogue can be resounded with different visuals. The video channel can be blanked to allow viewers to visualize the action for themselves. Or the audio can be silenced to allow the audience to make up narration/dialogue. (Thus we use one channel to focus on another.) This will act as priming for children's own writing or telling of stories. A story may begin with live actors or a storyteller and continue with puppets or cartoons or clay animation, to encourage viewers to take a story and put it into another medium. Or it may consist of a series of stills held long enough to give viewers time to make up intervening action.

Interrupting factual presentations such as a documentary on a bee colony or a lapse-photography sequence on the growth of a plant allows viewers to ask questions about what they don't understand, to recapitulate collectively what they *do* understand, and to tease out implications from what *is* shown of what is *not* shown. As with stories, viewers can attempt to predict from what they *have* seen so far of an activity what they *will* see. Then the show can be resumed. For difficulties in comprehension, or to resolve some uncertain or disputed matter, footage can be rerun. When viewers' predictions differ from what they witness once the program is resumed, they can discuss what this difference means with factual material as compared with alternative endings to fictional stories.

Interrupting stories and documentaries should help make children more critical viewers of commercial television, especially if questioning and discussion occur. Merely calling them back to themselves from time to time during a presentation should induce some detachment. The value of interrupting and discussing will surely be enhanced by mixed-age viewing, because the multiplicity of viewpoints will be richer, and children of greater maturity can influence the younger. It is just such enriched possibilities that argue for heterogeneity in classes or pools.

Special techniques. Both #1 and #2 types of programming just listed can utilize such techniques as:

- Show sentence, then sound it, then show the action it states (vocalizing the sentence again as it is acted out).
- Show a "title card" before or after the action it states comes on the screen, as in old silent movies. Alternate title cards (or narration/dialogue) with action. Use audio for sound effects only.
- Move camera in and out of book pages to catch both text and illustration, then move over details of illustrations (but not often while text is being sounded).
- Show stills of illustrations, then animate the illustrations.
- Sometimes use children's own stories and illustrations.
- Use chorus sometimes to read texts on the sound track in order to demonstrate choral reading and invite viewers to join in, breaking chorus into subgroups for different voices, phases, moods, etc.
- Use voices of nonstandard dialects sometimes, not only when the text is in dialect but sometimes even when the text is in standard English, so that nonstandard speakers can identify with the texts and standard speakers can taste the variety of their language.

Accompanying software. Most of the recommended programming would yield best results if accompanied by software along these lines:

- For programming #1, illustrated activity cards bearing directions for the activities demonstrated, written and illustrated for pupils to follow collectively with some help from the teacher or an aide, one card per activity (i.e., per working party), including directions for making and playing in small groups the card and board games for phonics, vocabulary, sentence structure, and logic.
- For programming #1, a teacher's manual describing how to form and handle small working parties, how to set in motion an activity-card system cross-referenced to books and other materials, and how to keep records of what language experiences individuals are accumulating.[18] This manual might include sample verbatim scripts for tak-

[18]See the teacher's manual for *Interaction,* Houghton Mifflin, Boston, 1973, and for *Student-Centered Language Arts and Reading,* James Moffett and Betty Jane Wagner, Houghton Mifflin, Boston, 1976. Both contain detailed descriptions for setting up and operating a classroom incorporating all of the activities and approaches proposed in this chapter. Many of the activity cards in *Interaction* could serve, in effect, as "treatment outlines" for programs ("level one," for primary school).

ing children step by step through guided fantasy, concentration or relaxation experiences, or stories to be pantomimed by a group in unison.

- For #2, printed booklets (half a dozen only, enough for a working party) transferring texts from screen to paper, including musical notation so teacher can help children recall tunes if need be.
- For #3, activity cards and/or manual for making best use of unfinished or variant stories and extending of factual presentations through interrupting, rerunning, and following up. An issue here is how much the teacher and how much the pupils will control the program screening and the interim activities. This function could pass increasingly from teacher to pupils, with the help of activity cards to remind pupils of what they can do and how to go about it.

Final reminders

Some good footage exists already in all three categories of programming that might be sought before producing new. It would most likely have to be transferred to newer formats, but the modular disks/cassettes proposed herein would facilitate utilization of, say, animated-letter footage, footage of modeled activities, or footage of stories and documentaries that would serve for some of #3 when put into interruptible format. On the other hand, since most TV and film footage does not assume immediate audience interaction, much would have to be produced fresh.

Consistency and familiarity are important for children. They like to feel at home, to recognize elements recurring from one presentation to another. But this can be effected in many ways without always having a central locale or hosting character(s). The three programming types outlined above can have continuity of form and content, human and other, across programs: recurring teacher and pupils demonstrating model activities for #1; the same book cover opening to different texts within for the screen-as-book approach of #2 or to introduce stories in #2; repeated melodies with different lyrics for #2; recurring animation techniques such as slot machine or typewriter or clay coiling for #2; the open-ended or variant-version aspect of #3; perhaps a familiar marker in #3 programs to suggest useful or suspenseful interrupting places; recurring visual and auditory motifs such as theme songs and logos; and so on.

Finally, the very effort to plan around language as a singled-out subject, and especially to feature "essential skills" of language, can constitute a serious hazard. In practice, producers should probably expect (1) to allot substantial programming to nonverbal activities like art and music and drama that either accompany language during primary or that merely set up language-learning later; (2) to emphasize *oral* language, both for its own sake and for literacy readiness; and (3) to handle literacy only as a *possibility*, not a *necessity*, for primary pupils, keeping it in its place among other burgeoning learning. A strong emphasis on chanting and singing— sometimes while doing other physical action, sometimes while viewing the words—is most recommended.

Acknowledgments

This paper owes a great deal to the very helpful consultation of:

RICHARD ADLER, Aspen Institute, Program on Communications and Society, Palo Alto, CA.

YETIVE BRADLEY, Director of K–Follow Through and Early Childhood Education, Oakland (CA) Unified School District.

WERNER BUNDSHUH, filmmaker, WGBH, Boston, MA.

ROBIN CANO, third grade teacher, Pacheco Elementary School, Novato (CA) Unified School District.

COURTNEY CAZDEN, professor, Harvard Graduate School of Education, Cambridge, MA.

HENRY FELT, filmmaker, Educational Development Corporation, Watertown, MA.

JUANITA INGLE, first grade teacher, The Alternative School, Novato (CA) Unified School District.

HENRY OLDS, educational consultant, Other Ways, Cambridge, MA.

DAVID SOHN, coordinator of language arts, Evanston (IL) Elementary School District.

MURRAY SUID, educational writer, formerly of *Learning* magazine, Palo Alto, CA.

BETTY JANE WAGNER, professor, National College of Education, Evanston, IL.

JANE WALLEN, formerly TV director for Instructional Television, Portland (OR) Public Schools.

10

Yoga for Public School Teachers

Background

Throughout the latter '70s my wife and I taught yoga under Swami Sivalingam, along with others of his experienced students, and managed much of the practical operation of the Prana Yoga Ashram, which he had founded with our help as a nonprofit corporation based in Berkeley and having branches in other towns and countries. (*Prana* is the vital force, associated with the breath, and *pranayama* is breath-control practice.) The teaching and managing—the service—are an important part of studying under a spiritual master. Besides such valuable experience, this article reflects, above all, direct acquaintance with Swami Sivalingam and the benefits of his teachings. To him it is dedicated. The more schools could teach what we privileged ones learned from Swamiji, the better they would fulfill the real purposes of all learning.

With another educator working under Swamiji, I started teaching extension courses around the Bay Area in yoga just for teachers. To regular class time we added another half hour to talk about how we might apply yoga to our classroom and our teaching life. (One sign of the times was that school districts quit allowing credits to teachers who took these courses.) Much of this article is based on what I learned from teaching this course.

Part of the operation founded by Swamiji was publication of a journal called *Prana Yoga Life,* which published this article in its first issue, Fall, 1977 (Prana Yoga Ashram, Box 1037, Berkeley, CA 94701).

------◄•►------

Yoga can help teachers in four main ways that are independent of particular subject matter or age of students.

Self-Development of Teacher

The first way is by improving the personal capacity of the teacher. Staff development is self-development. Yoga practices—meditation, postures, and breathing exercises—relax, integrate, refine, and liberate the practitioner. The emphasis of prana yoga on breathing intensifies these practices. Through them a teacher gains, for one thing, some survival techniques to preserve sanity and serenity. Yoga affords also a spiritual perspective. Preserving the deeper self intact within a spiritual perspective allows the teacher to do new things with his mind and body and to discover how to help children do the same. Liberate yourself, then you can liberate others—from the artificial limits that biological and human conditioning place on the divine potentialities of the spirit, which is by definition limitless.

Teachers who practice yoga increase their energy, expand the range of their physical dexterity, stay steadier through classroom trials, think of more creative teaching ideas, get more insights about their students, deal more effectively with colleagues and administrators, enjoy their work more, and radiate a positive, heartening atmosphere for their students. The evidence for this comes from testimonials made by teachers in classes given by the Prana Yoga Ashram especially for educators.

People in the so-called helping professions have to help themselves if they are truly to serve others. We have to clear up our own physical ailments and mental problems. Otherwise we drain, instead of aid, students. We must feel good on our own. For several thousand years before the advent of psychiatry, yoga stressed knowing oneself, what we call today "consciousness-raising." Real learning starts at home. A good teacher should be self-aware and self-governing. If we have learned how to learn, we can transmit this capacity to those in our charge.

Putting Oneself in the Place of the Learner

Practicing yoga entails learning new things. This puts the teacher in the position of his students. Yoga's special emphasis on self-awareness enables a teacher to make use of his own new learning experiences to get insight about what is going on in his students as they attempt what he proposes.

Learning to control the breath can challenge the ego, raise issues of will, and draw on unused resources the same as learning to read and write. Getting into a new posture can stretch one over into a triumphant state of increased power the same as solving a hard math problem. Sticking to a daily discipline raises the same problems of procrastination and motivation as doing home work or following through on a course project. What do we feel, what do we do, when we can't accomplish the task as described or demonstrated? Do we give up, compare with others, put off, manage a compromise, accept the failing, ask for help, get angry, etc.? With what other aspects of our lives do the ups and downs of our practices seem to correlate? What seems to determine success and failure, good or bad feelings?

Practical teaching strategies can come out of this personal insight. We get a sense of what works and what doesn't, what student behavior means, what different students need for success. Above all, we learn how success depends on spotting negative thinking and converting it to positive. This is the key to learning. If we can become alert to how our own learning efforts relate continually to habits of mind, attitudes and turns of thought, we will understand what our students are doing wrong and how to set them right.

Relaying Yoga Practices to Students

Allowing for differences in stages of growth, we can teach to our students the same practices we learn ourselves. What is self-development for the teacher is basic education for youth—how to relax, focus, integrate, and refine. Children can learn some forms of meditation, breath control, and postures.

Yoga lays a base for all learning because it teaches control of mind and body. Without relaxing and concentrating, for example, no one can learn well either academic subjects or sports and artistic skills. The learner has to relax and let go useless motion so he can conserve and channel energy. He must concentrate his attention so he can focus selectively on some activity or subject. He must center himself so he can line his will up behind the activity (be "motivated"). He must balance and integrate himself so he can summon all his resources and can experience the learning activity throughout his whole organism. So learning requires a holistic state of full access to memory and feeling, to all sensory modalities, to both halves of the brain (intellectual and intuitive), to head and heart, mind and body. This enables the learner to draw on the past and to store for the future. "Yoga" means "union," after all, and it has stressed for millenia what is only now creeping into U.S. education—full, integrative functioning.

The body is a model for subtler planes of life. What one learns through the body transfers to mental, emotional, and spiritual levels of existence. Balance the body, steady the emotions. Stretch into a posture hitherto impossible, open up hope for willing other changes in behavior. Sensitize kinesthetic awareness, discriminate finer degrees of perception and thought. Isolate muscles, zero in on an idea. Because it is obvious and grossly perceptible, the body makes a good medium in which to work simultaneously on higher levels. Children intuitively understand the body as a metaphor for their invisible, intangible life of thought, feeling, and spirit. They master matter first through gaining control of their own bodies. This level of self-control implies for them the possibility of regulating all the aspects of their life—mood, health, social relations, state of consciousness—and hence of achieving happiness. Success with bodily skills sets off a chain reaction of power. Thus children learn the basic lesson of mastering matter by mind.

Applying Yogic Learning Strategies

Veteran teachers will recognize a practical shrewdness in yogic learning strategies once they perceive certain general principles emerging from
the practices. We can generalize a few here as instances that with a little
imagination can be applied to any sort of learning at any age.

The less you rely on other people and other things, the more you
learn. One strategy can be stated this way, as a matter of self-reliance or
independence. To the extent you depend on others, Swamiji says, you remain stupid and incompetent. Dependence and knowledge are in a direct
inverse relation. The overprotective mother and the "chivalrous," sexist
gentleman enslave the child or woman they purport to serve. This strategy is naturally nonsexist. Swamiji is a far better cook and shopper than
most housewives, and he insists that women disciples master machines
and finances. Endurance and skills belong to all.

Such an approach to learning implies great change in American classrooms, which tend to infantilize students and to prolong the dependence
already protracted by most parents. Letting children work out things for
themselves interferes with the standardized, technocratic systems of management currently in vogue in institutions today. Television induces a
crippling passivity. Adults themselves depend so much on technology
and complex social organization that when shortages of energy, water, or
food occur, or when delivery systems, transportation, communication,
and manufactured products fail, they cannot care for themselves. We
have a product or specialist for every need or desire, from stimulating
pleasure to relieving pain. Unable to control our own minds and bodies
we depend on someone or something outside. By contrast, yogis learn to
regulate their own temperature or temperature tolerance instead of using
outside energy to cool and heat their whole surroundings. Instead of taking vitamins, hormones, drugs, and other external chemicals, yogis tune
their endocrine system so that it produces these things itself. (Postures are
a kind of self-massage that increases, decreases, and balances glandular
secretions.)

Most often, outsiders do not understand how much the austerity of
yoga serves this learning strategy. Doing without things and other people
forces the yogi to learn more. Special trials build knowledge and power.
Most teachers and parents in our culture today do far too much for
youngsters—so much that children grow up relatively helpless and feeling powerless. Instead of putting activity directions in writing, for example, so that students will have to read (on posters or activity cards) most
teachers give directions orally. An education for real self-reliance will require schoolroom methodology based on tough independence—that is, on
peer collaboration in small working parties and on true individualization
of the open classroom sort whereby youngsters learn to do for themselves, make decisions, initiate projects, and use adults only as periodic
aides to finding ways and means.

This independence, fostered early, works well only if school learning tasks have obvious real-life value. This realism will become increasingly easy to bring into schools as technology continues to pull back in the face of energy shortages and economic crises and as such social systems as medical and health care continue to degenerate. Doing for oneself is rapidly shifting from an aristocratic philosophy, as it may have been in Ralph Waldo Emerson's time, to a stark matter of survival.

Another yogic learning strategy is to suspend some normal part of one's life to see what difference the loss makes. Fasting teaches what food really is, what one's relation to food is, what oneself is. The learner gains knowledge of subject and object by means of each other. Holding the breath teaches not only a lot about breath but about oneself. Like Christian monastics, yogis sometimes suspend speech (a practice called *mouná*). A fine way to learn the role of language in our lives is to do without it for a while. This suspension is the main rule of charades; limited to gesture, one fairly bursts to speak. Other folk games are in fact based on this strategy of withholding a familiar condition. Consider, for example, blindfolding games like Pin the Tail on the Donkey. Periodic solitude reveals one's social nature and interdependence. The meditator suspends inner speech, that is, the whole culturally acquired filter system of conceptualization/verbalization.

Suspending a familiar condition constitutes only a special case of playing with variables to see what happens. Children enjoy playing around this way with normality (which explains their love of novelty). This is the essential play of science. Experimental research consists of setting up unusual circumstances to see what happens. The aim is to understand better what is normally happening. Yogis are naturally scientific in this regard. Swamiji constantly urges his disciples to alter their routines and to do things differently from time to time. The spirit is playful, as with a child, but the aim is to keep learning all the time.

Sometimes this yogic playing with variables focuses the learner on fine contrasts, as in slight variations of a posture. Doing the cobra with elbows straight instead of bent, or the plow with one leg straight at a time (in half-lotus), amounts to systematically "controlling" for one variable at a time. What difference does each variation make in breathing, in organs affected, in balance, etc? The yogi may work with extreme contrast, as when he does the "trembling pose," deliberately tensing his body to the point of shuddering then completely relaxing. So we learn relaxation! Nuanced discriminations, on the other hand, subtilize the organism, creating a spiritual movement, like the shifting progression of sounds in the words and tunes of the God-songs called bhajans, where sometimes the words are held constant while the tunes change, and sometimes both keep varying in ways to tease attention. Playing the variables—suspending or altering—makes one attend and attune and gradually refine. This is the real alchemy. Child development as charted by Western scientists progresses from lumping to discriminating thence to simultaneous perception of similarity and difference, unity and multiplicity—as in mandalas. Moreover, suspending a normal condition gradually de-conditions—that is, liberates—the learner from his cage of physical and social incarnation.

The main yogic learning strategy is to assume ever and always the primacy of mind over matter. You become what you think, Swamiji insists, so it is critical to think positively and to quickly nip off negative thinking as soon as it starts to crop up. The "bad self-concept" of our educational circles is only one case. Yogic training constantly alerts the learner to the myriad subtle ways in which negative thinking insinuates itself into our behavior. If the mind rules, then life consists of endless possibility. Controlling the mind becomes extremely important. To control the mind, the self must assert the will. Concretely, the strategy is to remind the learner constantly of the power of the mind for good or evil and to help him affirm the will by leading him into challenging action that will temper it. He is told tales of "supernatural" power as truth, and given increasingly difficult tasks that imply limitless power. At the same time, all the practices combine to put him in touch with the transpersonal part of himself, the divinity within, that will in fact enable him to make this truth true.

Practice and study of yoga suggest an educational future founded on a curriculum of rhythm, on different vibration rates or frequencies. It would encompass arts, sports, and crafts as well as language, mathematics, and physics. Everything in this life comes down to pulsation and periodicity, ratio and rhythm, staying and changing. In such a curriculum the learner would ascend from grosser to subtler frequencies in various spectra, progress from simpler to more complex rhythms and measures. But that is an idea for another time.

11

On Essaying

Background

These are more thoughts prompted by working with teachers in writing. It happened that, at about the same time, the editor of the *National Writing Project Newsletter* and the editor of *fforum,* a newsletter of the English Composition Board at the University of Michigan, asked me to write a piece for them to publish. The occasion for the *fforum* piece was an issue devoted to the work of Jimmy Britton and myself. I wrote the short articles in such a way that they could later be joined back-to-back as a continuous essay on a subject I felt strongly about—the personal nature of all good writing even when content goes well beyond the individual. I had been rereading a lot of classic essays in English letters and appreciating again how well they spoke for us all by speaking so well for themselves.

The first half of what follows appeared as "Confessions of an Ex-College Freshman" in the *NWP Newsletter* of May 1980; the second half was printed in the October 1980 issue of *fforum.* As I hope is evident, I tried to make my own essay an example of what I was trying to say about essaying itself.

———————◄•►———————

I flunked my first theme in college. My composition instructor had said to write on "your home town." O.K., fine, I could choose one of three—where I grew up till adolescence, where I went to high school, or where my parents currently resided, which I knew only in summertime. Today, I naturally see in my lethal choice of number three a fine example of how composition begins with decisions about which raw material to use. But those were pre-prewriting days.

Below the grade of flat E the instructor declared, with terrible justice, "A mass of tourist-guide-propaganda clichés, FW [fine writing], and J [jargon]. Moreover, you really have no exact subject—your title gives you away ['My Home Town']. Quite below college demands." Here was I not only an untested freshman fearful of losing a full scholarship by not attaining a B average, but I was half convinced anyway that I didn't really belong at Harvard and had only got in by way of some back door carelessly left open. Furthermore, I figured to major in English!

Brittle grad-school bachelor that he was, toiling away in one of twenty-odd sections of English A, my teacher really acted charitably. He knew I was on a trolley headed utterly the wrong way, toward endless suffering, and that only a powerful jolt right at the start would derail me so that I could make it in that course and even perhaps in college generally. My first paragraph read:

> Los Angeles, while not exactly the city of angels as its Spanish name proclaims, has within its environs a multitude of entertainments to please natives and tourists alike. Regardless of what his individual tastes may be, deep-sea fishing or listening to a fugue by Handel, there is probably always something which will satisfy his whim.

Over this you can see already a *New Yorker* type of rubric, Themes I Never Finished Reading. But it was a perfect thesis paragraph, for it stated exactly what kind of bullshit the reader was expected to wallow through afterwards. We toured the beaches of Santa Monica, the Hollywood Bowl, where "an open sky of stars lends enchantment to the symphonic works," the nearby desert, where "the moonlight accentuates the unique charm of the quiet expanses," and the downtown L.A. theater district. One topic-sentenced paragraph was on sports, one on food, one on night-clubbing, and so on. No chance of the reader getting lost here. No problems of transition or organization or coherence. The signposts were all there, and the sentences scanned grammatically. But it was atrocious writing. In fact, it wasn't really writing; it was a paste-and-scissors job, only collaged inside the head instead of with physical clippings and splicings. My teacher rejected it out of hand because it was so borrowed and so unreal that he had no way even of assessing it as composition, nothing to come to grips with. It was ghost writing of an unconscious sort, very much like the great majority of papers English teachers waste time marking up.

I wrote that theme as I had written stuff all through school. An all-A student in all subjects through high school, I always did what teachers wanted. The teaching of writing, and of English generally, remains now about the same as then, in the '40s, some exceptions having occurred by dint of strenuous innovation, and many of those having been wiped out by the regressive movement that has prompted publishers to dust off and reissue the English textbooks of that time. Mostly, my classmates and I were asked to write about what we had read to make sure we *had* done the reading and to see if we had got the point. The teaching of writing in this country has for so long been harnessed to the testing of reading that few teachers I meet even today can grasp the enormity of this bias and the consequent mischief and fraudulence.

Whenever I was asked to write about something outside of books, the subject was so remote from me, such as national affairs, that I could know it mostly only secondhand and hence could hardly do anything but paraphrase the information and arguments that I got from newspapers, radio, and grown-up talk. But that's the point. *My teachers really just wanted familiar, adult-sounding prose.* This they equated with mature writing. They *wanted* phrasing they recognized, views they had heard aired around them, because this meant their students were joining the adult world. Isn't that the whole point of school? They loved and encouraged my five-dollar words, straight out of *Reader's Digest* vocabulary quizzes, because big words show learning and correlate with intelligence. They were nice people who didn't know much about composition as such at all. They too had never written anything besides the usual school and college testing stuff—book reports, term papers, and essay exams—and so they had never learned how to shape material not predigested for them by others. Anyway, a glittering travelog on a glossy town seemed O.K. to me.

After that first failure I got the point quickly. (No doubt I was also relieved to know that the institution I was going to spend the next four years at wasn't going to deal in that kind of bullshit.) My instructor advised me to do the assignment over—and knock it off this time. I did and got an A. Great, a happy ending, but what was the difference? Well, it was all the difference in the world, and yet I was pretty much the same person I had been the week before. I didn't know any more about organization or sentence structure, I didn't have a better vocabulary, and I hadn't acquired any new "writing skills." Nor was I a more logical thinker.

For my second chance I chose to tell about "My Boyhood in Jackson," a significant decision because that town really meant something to me. I told how my friends and I played out our adventure fantasies against the Mississippi background as Twain's characters had done in Missouri. In the dense foliage along the Pearl River we pretended to be buccaneers, explorers, and Stanley looking for Livingston. Or:

> I was a scientist—the sole survivor of an expedition sent up the Amazon on an important quest. After I staggered from the jungle into the clearing, my feverish body fell lifeless before those waiting for me. In my outstretched hand lay a small vial containing the juice of a rare plant—the cure for cancer.

I told how we dug niches for thrones in the steep white clay banks of the railroad cut, using tie spikes for tools, and lit discarded flares to stake out our thrones with. Then the train roared through the cut.

> The surging power of the locomotive was mine, for I felt it pass through me as the earth rumbled under the passing train. Besides, the engineer gave it to me by the friendly waving of his hand.

I concluded unpretentiously that although I might well have play-acted some of the same things had I lived somewhere else, the fact is that "I played and grew in Jackson, and that is what endears it to me."

In a way I was being myself in the first theme too: the glamor of Los Angeles and the emptiness masquerading as impersonality were true for me to the degree that I was attracted to the one and had learned to put on the other. So the difference between the themes was really in the level of the self. I just suddenly changed my whole orientation toward writing. My teacher had said, in effect, "No one wants to read what he knows already or could come out with himself. We read for something new. Write what only *you* know, or what you have put together for yourself. *Make* something, don't just *take* something." I had no problem with that. We all live on all planes of shallowness and depth all the time and so can shift planes at any moment if someone or something sets us straight. I thought, "Oh, I see. *That*'s how it is. Writing isn't what I've been led to believe. It's saying what you really think and feel or what you really want to put over." But, of course, I had known that before from reading great writers and from trying to write extracurricular stories. It was *curricular* writing I had a false notion of. And this dissociation of writing from reality afflicts most students in this country.

The main reasons for this are two. Traditional schooling has shown no respect for writing, exploiting composition instruction as a way to service its testing system and as a way to spawn the pencil-pushers required to stock all those clerical jobs in industry and government, where you do not want thinkers. You just want people who have passed minimal standards—can read just well enough to follow directions and write just well enough to take dictation. But I'm not talking about some conspiracy by *them*. All of us share through our culture and bear within us a deader, less evolved aspect of being that calcifies because it is still mineral or vegetates because it is still plant-like or preys because it is still animal, all while the human aspect of the self works toward its partly divined divinity. This sludgier element of individuals settles out in society as sedimentary attitudes and institutions that mire down efforts to better ourselves.

The other reason for the shallow tradition that has neutered the teaching of writing is that teachers themselves have practiced writing so little that they fall back on hopelessly irrelevant procedures. Many simply don't know how real writing takes place. It is patent to anyone who has worked much with teachers that the less practice they have had, the more they rationalize book reports, formal grammatical analysis, paragraph formulas, sentence exercises, vocabulary quizzes, and a prescriptive/proscriptive methodology. "You have to *teach* them," they say, never having learned how themselves. Compelled once to coach a sport I had never played, lacrosse, I too gravitated toward a simplistic rules–results approach that was an effort to distill experience I had never had.

The National Writing Project has succeeded and gained support precisely because it makes teachers practitioners instead of mere preachers.

When I am teaching teachers to write in summer institutes, I see the same thing happen to them that happened to me with that first freshman theme. They discover that if they write from the heart they not only have something to say, something that interests others, but that they can better order their thoughts and can actualize their latent talent. It is more than ordinarily moving to see *teachers* discover how writing really occurs, often after many years of frustrating themselves and their students. Maybe I identify with late bloomers, but I'm especially touched by the delicate transition from recalcitrance to confidence that takes place as they find out just how well they and their partners can, after all, write.

Before they have made this discovery, many teachers will call every kind of writing that is not term-paper or essay-question stuff "personal" or "creative" writing (the two terms being interchangeable) and hence put it in a big bag that goes up on the shelf. Priority goes, of course, to "exposition," which is equated with "essay," which is equated in turn with forced writing on given topics from books, lectures, or "current issues." In these institutes with teachers I break a class into trios in which members help each other for several weeks to develop subjects and techniques by hearing or reading partners' writing ideas at various stages of working up the material. Some of this material is gleaned from memory, some is information obtained fresh by interviewing or observing, and some is feeling, thought, or imagination elicited suddenly by a stimulus such as a tune or other in-class presentation. The material may take the form of stories, dialogues, essays, or songs and poems. It soon becomes obvious that ideas stem from all kinds of material and take all kinds of forms and that the very limited sort of exposition used for testing enjoys no monopoly on intellectual activity; participants can see, often with astonishment, how loaded with ideas is this rich variety of writing they have produced.

When schools narrow the notion of *essay* to fit it to testing, they are violating the whole tradition of the genre from its very inception to the present. College composition instructors and anthologists of essays have doted for years on George Orwell's "Shooting an Elephant," which they hold up to students as a model of essay or "expository writing." Please look closely at it even if you think you know it well; if a student had written it, it would be called "personal writing," that is, soft and nonintellectual. Orwell narrated in first person how as a British civil servant in Burma he was intimidated by villagers into shooting an elephant against his will. But so effectively does he say *what happens* by telling *what happened* that the force of his theme—about the individual's moral choice whether or not to conform to the group—leaves us with the *impression* that the memoir is "expository," that is, chiefly cast in the present tense of generalization and in third person. What we really want to help youngsters learn is how to express ideas of universal value in a personal voice. Fables, parables, poems and songs, fiction, and memoir may convey ideas as well as or better than editorials and critiques. Orwell does indeed provide a fine model, but teachers should not let prejudice fool them into misunderstanding the actual kind of discourse in which he wrote that and other excellent essays, for this leads to a terribly confusing double standard whereby we ask students to emulate a great writer but to do it in another form.

Orwell wrote deep in a tradition of English letters honoring the essay as a candid blend of personal and universal. It was resurrected if not invented during the Renaissance by Montaigne, who coined the term *essai* from *essayer,* to attempt. From his position of philosophical skepticism ("What do I know?") he saw his writing as personal attempts to discover truth, what he thought and what could be thought, in exactly the same sense that Donald Murray or Janet Emig or I might speak of writing as discovery. From Burton's *Anatomy of Melancholy* and Browne's *Urn Burial;* Addison's and Steele's *Spectator* articles; through the essays of Swift, Lamb, Hazlitt, and De Quincey to those of Orwell, Virginia Woolf, Joan Didion, and Norman Mailer, English literature has maintained a marvelous tradition, fusing personal experience, private vision, and downright eccentricity with intellectual vigor and verbal objectification. In color, depth, and stylistic orginality it rivals some of our best poetry. Look again at Hazlitt's "The Fight" (and compare it with Mailer's reportage of the Ali-Frazier fight in *King of the Hill*) or "On the Feeling of Immortality in Youth" or "On Familiar Style"; De Quincey's "Confessions of an English Opium-Eater" or "On the Knocking at the Gate in Macbeth," which begins, "From my boyish days I had always felt a great perplexity on one point in *Macbeth*"; or Lamb's "The Two Races of Men," "Poor Relations," "Sanity of True Genius." Consider, too, a book like Henry Adams's *The Education of Henry Adams* for its simultaneous treatment of personal and national or historical.

Some essayists, like Montaigne and Emerson, tend toward generality, as reflected in titles like "Friendship" or "Self-Reliance," but tone and source are personal, and we cannot doubt the clear kinship between essays featuring memoir or eyewitness reportage and those of generality, for the same writers do both, sometimes in a single essay, sometimes in separate pieces; and Lamb and Thoreau stand in the same relation to Montaigne and Emerson as fable to moral or parable to proverb. The difference lies not in the fundamental approach, which is in any case personal, but in the degree of explicitness of the theme. "I bear within me the exemplar of the human condition," said Montaigne. Descending deep enough within, the essayist links up personal with universal, self with Self.

These essayists frequently write about their reading, and they love reading. They set, in fact, a model for writing about reading that is very different from writing-as-testing, because *they* have selected what to read according to their own ongoing pursuits, and, second, they cite ideas and instances from books *in mixture with* ideas and instances drawn from everyday experience, thus fusing life with literature. Many openly framed assignments that I have long advocated will elicit from students exactly the kinds of essays that constitute our fine heritage in this flexible form. They call for the writer to crystallize memories, capture places, "write a narrative of any sort that makes a general point applying beyond the particular material," "put together three or four incidents drawn from life or reading that all seem to show the same thing, that are connected in your mind by some idea," or "make a general statement about something you have observed to be true, illustrating by referring to events and situations you know of or have read of." The point is to *leave subject matter to the writer, including reading selections.* Any student who has done such assignments will be better able, strictly as a bonus, to cough up some prose to show he has done his homework than if he has been especially trained to write about reading.[1]

Schools mistreat writing because the society suffers at the moment from drastic misunderstandings about the nature of knowledge. Applying "scientific" criteria that would be unacceptable to most real scientists making the breakthroughs out there on the frontier, many people have come to think that subtracting the self makes for objectivity and validity. But depersonalization is not impartiality. It is, quite literally, madness. Einstein said, "The observer is the essence of the situation." It is not by abandoning the self but by developing it that we achieve impartiality and validity. The deeper we go *consciously* into ourselves, the better chance we have of reaching universality, as Montaigne knew so well. Transpersonal, not impersonal. It is an undeterred faith in this that makes a great writer cultivate his individuality until we feel he utters us better than we do ourselves. Teachers should be the first to understand this misunderstanding and to start undoing it, so that schooling in general and writing in particular can offset rather than reinforce the problem.

Here are two examples of what we're up against—one from a famous current encyclopedia and one from a leading publisher, typical and telling symptoms. Most English majors probably have sampled or at least heard of Sir Thomas Browne, a very individualistic seventeenth-century master of an original prose style, a writer's writer much admired by successors. Of his *Pseudodoxia Epidemica* Funk and Wagnalls's *Standard Reference Encyclopedia* says, "Its unscientific approach and odd assemblage of obscure facts typify his haphazard erudition," and then concludes the entry: "Despite Browne's deficiencies as a thinker, his style entitles him to high rank among the masters of English prose." What this verdict tells me is that

---

[1]For these and other recommended writing assignments, see James Moffett, *Active Voice: A Writing Program Across the Curriculum*, Boynton/Cook Publishers, 1981.

the scholar who wrote that entry felt overwhelmed by all the books Browne had read that he had not and that our scholar knew far less than he should have about the enormously important and complex networks of thought and knowledge, called esoteric, that after several millenia of evolution still had great influence on Newton, Bacon, and Descartes (who displayed at times equally "irrational" intellectual behavior). Such a judgment on such a writer is nothing but smart-ass chauvinism; permitted to poison basic information sources, it makes "science" as deadly a censor as ever the Church was during its Inquisition.

We can avoid producing Brownes from our school system by having all youngsters read and write the same things—a goal we have closely approximated—and then their approach will not be unscientific, their assemblage odd, their facts obscure, or their erudition haphazard. And we will have ensured that no one will be able to emulate the great essayists we hold up as models (or even read them with any comprehension). Real essaying cannot thrive without cultivation of the individual. Who would have any reason to read anyone else? (And I want to know how Browne's style could be worth so much if he was not a good thinker.)

The second example is personal. When I received back from the publisher the edited manuscript of the original edition of *Student-Centered Language Arts and Reading, K–13,* I was aghast. "My" editor had rewritten sentences throughout the whole book to eliminate first-person references and other elements of the author's presence and voice. This included altering diction and sentence structure at times to get a more anonymous or distanced effect. Faced with the appalling labor of restoring all those sentences, I called up the editor, furious. She said righteously, "But we always do that—it's policy." It never occurred to her to exempt, or even to warn, an author who wouldn't be publishing the book in the first place if he weren't regarded as some kind of expert in writing.

You can't trust your encyclopedia, your publisher, your school administration. And you can't trust yourself until you learn to spot how you too may be spreading the plague, as Camus calls it. The double standard about "Look at the greats, but don't do what they did" naturally goes along with our era of Scientific Inquisition, which is really technocratic plague. Teachers stand in a fine position to spread infection. If you let yourself be convinced that "personal" or "creative" writing is merely narcissistic, self-indulgent, and weak-minded, then you have just removed your own first person.

12

Writing, Inner Speech, and Meditation

Background

I first became interested in inner speech while studying literature as an undergraduate. A natural tendency to introspection and a strong interest in fictional technique combined. Innovations toward interior monologue or stream-of-consciousness by Joyce, Woolf, Faulkner, and Eliot fascinated me. I ended by writing a senior honors thesis called "The Relation of the Inner and Outer Lives in the Works of Virginia Woolf," which won the Bowdoin essay prize, mostly, I suspect, because of boosting by Albert Guerard, Jr., a professor of comparative literature, now at Stanford but then at Harvard, who is a novelist himself and an unusually perceptive critic. In his lectures and articles he opened new doors for me to fictional process. Like most literature professors in the heyday of Hemingway, he preferred masculine action novels and wondered if Virginia Woolf was really readable, but his support of my weird preoccupation with her valiant and artful efforts to make inner events as dramatic as outer testified to the ability he had, which made him a real teacher, to subordinate his own attitudes to the education of his student.

As a teacher myself later, learning through trials and errors at Exeter, I gradually worked out a spectrum of fictional techniques scaled according to the point of view of the narrator, whether avowed ("first person") or anonymous ("third person"). With the help of colleague Kenneth McElheny, I embodied this spectrum in an anthology of short stories (*Points of View,* a Mentor book, New American Library). The matrix was interior monologue, the fictionalization of inner speech, the initial "narrative" point of view from which others are departures to varying removes in inner and outer space/time. An important concept from Guerard, which I've never properly acknowledged, is that of the "imperceptive narrator," who tells a different story from what he thinks he is telling, because he is not on top of the experience recounted. Guerard pointed out examples in Gide and Dostoevski and other modern novelists. Eudora Welty's "Why I Live at the P.O." is a fine instance, and, descending to burlesque, so also is the popular song of some twenty years ago, "I Saw Mommy Kissing Santa Claus underneath the Mistletoe Last

Night." Such a narrator stands somewhere between raw (unabstracted) inner speech and "objective" discourse.

Then matters got out of hand. I began to see such a scale not only in narration but in all discourse. Carried away, across the whole hierarchy of levels of abstraction, I tried to get rid of my obsession by writing it up, or out, as key chapters of *Teaching the Universe of Discourse.* Always it was from the amorphous, undifferentiated crucible of inner speech that these gradations of discourse were generated. (*Matrix, mother,* and *matter* all come from the same root.) By then I was reading scientific descriptions of what I had first known from my own introspection and from literature, and these helped me to formulate and support my theories.

Just as my old preoccupation was becoming perhaps too much of a head trip, and stagnating there, I began to practice meditation and then to undergo the inner disciplining of Swami Sivalingam. Then I saw inner speech very differently from the way I had through either psychology or literature, though perhaps I was only going back in a new way to where I had begun, in introspection. This career-long trip spiraled over into another dimension, and I had to start re-viewing and re-casting most of what I had ever thought about language and literature, as I am still doing. Some of us just seem to take a long time getting to the point—late bloomers I guess we're supposed to call us in education.

This essay went through three lecture versions in 1979—one delivered from detailed notes at the convention of the California Association of Teachers of English in San Diego, a much longer one read over three evening sessions from a written text at the Bread Loaf Summer School of English in Vermont, and a reduced form of that to the first annual conference on writing of the Independent School Association of Massachusetts in Cambridge. In 1980 I spoke on this subject at the Third International Conference on the Teaching of English at Sydney, Australia. The article is published here for the first time.

———————◄●►———————

Writing and meditating are naturally allied activities. Both are important for their own sake, and through each people can practice the other. Relating the two by means of a bridging concept, that of inner speech, brings out aspects of all three that can illuminate old educational goals and identify new ones. To work with this three-way interrelationship, we must construe writing in its highest sense—beyond copying and transcribing, paraphrasing and plagiarizing—as authentic *authoring,* because inner speech and meditation concern forms of thought, the composing of mind that constitutes the real art and worth of writing. Authoring is working up a final revision, for an audience and a purpose, of those thought forms that have surfaced to the realm of inner speech.

Inner and Outer Speech

Whatever eventuates as a piece of writing can begin only as some focusing on, narrowing of, tapping off of, and editing of that great ongoing inner panorama that William James dubbed the "stream of consciousness." What I will call here "inner speech" is a version of that stream which has been more verbally distilled and which can hence more directly serve as the wellspring of writing. We might ask someone suddenly to say what he is thinking and thereby learn the subject matter, the order or disorder of the thoughts and images, and perhaps some aura or vein characterizing this material, but until asked to tell us, the person may not even have been aware of his stream and, even if aware, may not have put it into words. And the selection, wording, and emphasis with which he verbalizes the material to us may not be the same as he did verbalize or would have verbalized it to himself. So we must understand "inner speech" as referring to an uncertain level of consciousness where material may not be so much verbalized as verbalizable, that is, at least potentially available to consciousness if some stimulus directs attention there, and potentially capable of being put into words because it is language-congenial thought (discursive).

When James Joyce and other fiction writers have simulated stream of consciousness, verbalization often shifts or wavers between that of the persona and that of the author, between the literal realism of speech that is "in character" and the poetic realism of language that cleaves to a truth beneath words. The two samples here from *Ulysses* may illustrate how the literary technique of "interior monologue" plays in between stream of consciousness as distilled for oneself into inner speech and stream of consciousness that might, without an author's intervention, remain as subverbal imagery and feeling. Strolling near Trinity in Dublin, Leopold Bloom watches the great Parnell pass by talking to a woman at his side:

> Her stockings are loose over her ankles. I detest that: so tasteless. Those literary ethereal people they are all. Dreamy, cloudy, symbolistic Esthetes they are. I wouldn't be surprised if it was that kind of food you see produces the like waves of the brain the poetical. For example one of those policemen sweating Irish stew into their shirts; you couldn't squeeze a line of poetry out of him. Don't know what poetry is even. Must be in a certain mood.
>
> > The dreamy cloudy gull
> > Waves o'er the waters dull.[1]

Now Stephen Dedalus, alone suddenly in the library:

> Coffined thoughts around me, in mummycases, embalmed in spice of

---

[1] James Joyce, *Ulysses* (New York: Random House, 1934), p. 163.

words. Thoth, god of libraries, a birdgod, moonycrowned. And I heard the voice of that Egyptian highpriest. *In painted chambers loaded with tilebooks.*

They are still. Once quick in the brains of men. Still: but an itch of death is in them, to tell me in my ear a maudlin tale, urge me to wreak their will.[2]

Inner speech distills not just *the* stream but a confluence of streams issuing from sensory receptors, memory, and a variety of more or less emotional or logical kinds of reflection. All the elements of this rich mixture trigger, interrupt, and reinforce each other. Sometimes they interplay rapidly, indicating perhaps that attention is free to skip more "randomly" or "spontaneously." Sometimes strong external influence or strong inner will sustains attention so steadily on one current that a clear continuity develops. Sword fighting, for example, holds consciousness to sensory information. An old person finished with striving may "dwell in the past," shutting out environmental stimulation and letting the memory current flow with little interruption—chronically, in some cases. Another person well into maturity may constantly see in everyday occurrences or news instances of generalizations that he is given to forging, so that reflection stands in high ratio to memories and sensations. A teenager may spend much time worrying about what will befall him in the future or making scenarios to help meet trying situations he is busy foreseeing. At any moment this heady stuff can be tapped off and converted to ink.

Clearly, numberless circumstances, inner and outer, determine what sort of mixture the stream consists of and hence what kind and qualities of discourse might ultimately be further distilled from the inner speech. Some of these circumstances are immediate, like what the person is doing at the moment, what his surroundings are, his mood, the state of his mind and organism, and so on. Other circumstances span a long time—personal traits, conditioning, habits, relations. Stephen's and Bloom's interior monologues are meant to contrast in this way, partly by holding time and place constant to some extent so that both react to the same external circumstances and thus differentiate character. Influences on the qualities of inner speech range then, in time, from immediate to long-term and, in space, from the most indwelling nature to the farthest-flung cultural and material environments.

If talking to oneself and hearing voices indicate insanity, then the whole culture is crazy. True, for most of us this does not happen "out loud," for we learned some time befor entering school that some things that come to the tongue you had jolly well better keep to yourself and let "come to mind" only. But the main reason the child splits off his ex-

[2]Ibid., p. 191.

ternal speech and shunts some of it inward to subvocalization or silent thought concerns not merely social disapproval but social irrelevance. What Piaget has called the "egocentric speech" of the small child comprises play prattle (often to objects), "task mediation" or guiding and planning talk accompanying an activity, self-reminders, and just a kind of rehearsing of verbal powers in the form of running observations cued by ongoing or surrounding stimuli. Speech that is egocentric does not distinguish speaker from listener or speaker from subject, in keeping with the general trend of cognitive development to begin in syncretism and move toward discrimination. As the child realizes that some speech is really for himself, he deflects it inward. Momentous indeed is this shift from thinking out loud to thinking silently, for the inner life that was constantly manifesting itself in external speech as well as action now becomes inaudible and invisible (expressive body action becoming more subdued also), so that henceforward we cannot regard the child as an open book but must expect him to manifest his mind by excerpting and editing his inner speech.

As fluency is confluency, so interior monologue is really interior dialogue. We can gain tremendous perception and perspective from regarding inner speech as colloquy among the individual's many personas—the roles, factions, viewpoints, and other divisions within himself and the culture he has incorporated. George Herbert Mead described some time ago with great justice this process of introjecting the "other" into one's inner life.[3] When the child shunts some of his outer speech inward, he is necessarily internalizing the voices of others whose language he or she learned.

The idea that most thinking, the discursive part, derives from internalized speech seems rather universally agreed on by specialists in cognition today, as shown by the enthusiasm of Piaget and Americans for the work of Lev Vygotsky and A. R. Luria, whose school has for decades insisted that the sociohistorical origins of thought have not been adequately emphasized.[4] Society peoples the head of the individual via speech, which is learned from and for others but in shifting inward merges with universal inborn logical faculties, biologically given, and with idiosyncratic penchants of mind to result in thinking that is at once personal and cultural. As Hans Furth reminds us from his work with the education of the deaf, not all thinking is verbal, and conceptual maturation may occur

---

[3]George Herbert Mead, "Self" in *On Social Psychology: Selected Papers*, ed. Anselm Strauss (Chicago: University of Chicago Press, 1964).

[4]First see Lev Vygotsky, *Thought and Language* (Cambridge, Mass.: The M.I.T. Press, 1962). Included in this volume is an insert, "Comments" by Jean Piaget, that gives Piaget's main views of inner speech, especially as related to Vygotsky's. Then see his *Mind and Society* (Cambridge, Mass.: Harvard University Press, 1978) and A. R. Luria, *Cognitive Development: Its Cultural and Social Foundations* (Cambridge, Mass.: Harvard University Press, 1976).

among people who cannot speak.[5] The Russian psycholinguists accept that thought and speech originate separately, but they play down the independence of innate mentation because they believe that human psychosocial evolution ("historical dialectic") determines individual thinking more than the biological givens.

Surely, we have here a serpent with its tail in its mouth: mind and society feed in and out of each other. Such biological givens as the faculties of analyzing and synthesizing can be neither given nor taken away by society, and idiosyncrasy asserts itself very powerfully not only among citizens sharing the same sociohistorical conditions but also among siblings sharing the same familial determinants.

Individuals influence history and language and are influenced by them. But the Russian emphasis does restore our balance and receives support not only from the too evident truth of McLuhan's (very Marxist) insight about technological shifts altering consciousness but also from recent findings about specialization of the brain hemispheres. This specialization into analytic and holistic does not occur in other mammals and occurs in humans only after around age seven, after inner speech has become established, that is, after the pristine thinking of the innate equipment has become thoroughly imbued with the culture's ways of perceiving and conceiving, embodied in the language and in the social relations in which it is learned. Joseph Chilton Pearce and others, including myself, believe that specialization of the hemispheres may occur to salvage holistic, nonverbal, metaphorical thinking from the heavy acculturation that makes the analytic dominate, even after the split, and that hits children at just about the time hemispheric specialization occurs (and when the notorious slump in school performance and attitude begins, toward the end of third grade).[6]

On the biological foundation, culture builds its own psychological structure, different from one epoch to another. Individuals are in a sense "bugged" by institutions, implanted with an invisible transmitter in the form of a discursive system that structures their own nervous system so that they are in some degree participating in group thinking whether they know it or not or like it or not. Language works by resonance, between sender and receiver, and this requires tuning all circuits to the same frequency. An insane person can no longer resonate with the society, but we note that the auditory hallucination so common to classic schizophrenia usually consists of hearing the voices of parents, God or the devil, or other authoritative voices from the near and far culture. Or to vary the comparison, it is as if acculturation hypnotizes us at the outset, when we are

---

[5]Hans Furth, *Thinking without Language: Psychological Implications of Deafness* (New York: Free Press, 1966).
[6]Joseph Chilton Pearce, *Exploring the Crack in the Cosmic Egg* (New York: Julian, 1974) and *The Magical Child* (New York: E. P. Dutton, 1977).

utterly open and undefensive, "suggests" by voice but by nonverbal means also that the world is so and so and not such and such, and thenceforward that is how we see and think about it. This is group hypnosis and, once built in, self-hypnosis—except to the extent that idiosyncrasy does indeed assert itself even to the point sometimes of affecting the very language and history that will in the future hypnotize subsequent generations.

Probably nothing is so important to education as this circularity of inner and outer speech, mind and society. By external speech, individuals communicate to each other, and by inner speech each informs himself. Aside from the broad matter of consonance or dissonance among individuals and between individuals and their shared institutions, this circularity of internal and external applies to other school activities such as listening, viewing, and reading, all of which entail wholesale introjection into one's stream of consciousness or someone else's stream. That is, in varying degree the auditor, viewer, or reader allows some interlocutor, performer, screen, or book to supplant his inner continuity with their or its own. Unless "entranced" or "spellbound" we probably never permit another to take over our consciousness completely, but pre-adolescent children are especially suggestible, and even much older people "lose themselves" in a book (if their ego is strong enough not to doubt regaining themselves). The effects of films and television may become clearer if we regard such programs as supplanting inner programs.

It may be helpful for teachers to regard listening or reading, say, as assimilating someone else's outer speech into one's ongoing inner speech, the effect being something like a garbled script or heavily annotated and superscribed text. Evidences of this hearing or reading may evince themselves minutes or years later when our receiver becomes sender in turn and synthesizes his own continuity for others to introject, naturally drawing on what he has heard and read along with other experience and his unique creativity. The circles keep turning over. People learn to talk and write by listening and reading as much as by anything else.

Educators need not feel that in staying especially mindful of the cultural inculcation of the individual, via such routes as the internalization of outer speech, they are subscribing to any school of psychology or political view. Growth means change, and educators have to concern themselves with the changeable aspects of people, which are not usually the biological givens but the cultural forces and, the individual willing, his idiosyncratic traits. Even to know if or how he wants to change, the individual has to be at least partly awakened from the hypnosis of acculturation. And education, finally, should foster human evolution. I am not interested in helping to teach young people to read just well enough to follow directions or write just well enough to take dictation.

Writing as Revised Inner Speech

However personal or impersonal the subject matter, *all* writing as authoring must be some revision of inner speech for a purpose and an audience. To say this is not at all to say that writing is solipsistic thinking about narcissistic content or even that it favors "personal experience." Because of the circularity just discussed, one's revised inner speech may reflect convention so much as to hardly bear a personal mark. "Off the top of the head," as we say. In Samuel Beckett's play *Waiting for Godot* a slavish character called Lucky gives a remarkable soliloquy that starts as a surface verbal stream full of stock stuff and familiar phrases straight out of ads and folk talk and official promulgations, then moves downward to poetic and original verbalization of the deeper self, à la Molly Bloom or Anna Livia Plurabelle. (Beckett was not Joyce's secretary for nothing.) I saw the Trinidad dancer, Geoffrey Holder, perform this soliloquy by dancing out this descent into the self at the same time he vocalized the deepening verbal stream, creating an unforgettable audio-visual emblem as he bucked and spluttered his way down through tensions into the grace of unconflicted fluency.

Egocentricity is merely a localization within the larger circles of ethnocentricity, biocentricity, and geocentricity that are concentric to it. This is why "subjectivity" is not so personal as it is usually made out to be and why it is not the only issue to consider in adapting inner speech to public communication. So much of the dullness, awkwardness, shallowness, and opacity that teachers object to in student writing owes to skimming along in the froth instead of plunging into the current, where intuition lines up with intelligence and particularities of experience correct for cliché. Seldom has anyone shown them how to work their way down, like Lucky. Most discourse in society today follows the now notorious circuit of the computer, "garbage in, garbage out." Something really significant has to happen inside—mediation by mind. If "output" differs from "input" mainly in being more amateurishly put together, then subjectivity has little meaning, and objectivity cannot be an authentic enough issue to be dealt with.

What really teaches composition—"putting together"—is disorder. Clarity and objectivity become learning challenges only when content and form are *not* given to the learner but when he must find and forge his own from his inchoate thought. Now, *that's* hard, not the glorified book-reporting or the filling in of instances to fit someone else's generalization (topic). All this traditional school and college writing only *looks* mature because it is laced with generalizations of a high abstraction level—quotations from the greats, current formulations of issues, and other ideas received from books or teachers. Such haste to score, to make a quick intellectual killing, merely retards learning, because those kids have not worked up those generalizations themselves. This short-circuits the natural circularity between thought and society, bypasses any true mediation by mind, and results in a simply more insidious form of inculcation, less honest than straight formula feeding because book criticism, research papers, and essay exams make students *appear* to be more the authors of the ideas than they really are. Consider too what a deceptive view this conveys to youngsters of both writing and themselves.

I invite the reader to think of writing not only as Lucky's descent into self but also as the ascent from chaos to cosmos. I certainly don't mean to equate the self with chaos, but the inner speech that boils off the self represents some sort of confused concoction of self and society, whereas through writing we may use composition to achieve composure.

A human being is literally *made to order* and will *make* sense of everything that comes into his ken, weird as his cosmology may look to another individual or another culture. The typifying trait of humankind is to "get his head together" even if his only symbolic medium for doing so is iconographic, and no matter how chaotic his environment. Once tool-using includes symbol-making, then people are naturally and necessarily creative in the practical if not esthetic sense. Writing throws out to society samples of the cosmology that any individual has to be making for himself all the time as an ongoing orientation to this world and an unceasingly updated guide for behavior. Writing is a further abstraction, via inner speech, of an involuntary abstracting that the individual engages in constantly for survival anyway. As micro-cosmos he reflects to some degree the cosmos of culture and the macro-cosmos of nature, but he is always in the process of converting chaos to cosmos—or perhaps of discovering the order concealed in apparent disorder—and the particular instance of this composition that we call writing partakes of this general ordering. Writing is an opportunity to find out who I am and what I am to do with my life.

Lest all this sound entirely *too* cosmic to the teacher mired in the pseudo-pragmatic routines of the conventional classroom, the movement from inner speech to the written product gets us into all those familiar alternatives of thought and language that writing teachers call organization, transition, sentence structure, and word choice, or thesis, illustration, and conclusion, but this approach from inner speech shifts the perspective of written composition back downward to where classification and generalization are being spontaneously, even involuntarily, generated and where instances are original; where theses, transitions, and conclusions to thinking chains are all occurring thick and fast (without being assigned) but remain *implicit,* perhaps still in mythic or metaphoric form. Making the implicit appropriately explicit may well be the chief task of writing. Teaching writing is teaching how to *manifest* thought into language, and this requires raising consciousness of all this spontaneous and often unconscious cosmologizing to the point that it passes from verbalizable to verbalized. At the same time, the writer has to become conscious of how the verbalization now manifesting to himself needs to evolve to that degree of explicitness that will make his ideas emerge sharply for others. Also, working deeper in the sources leaves open alternatives about *mode* of discourse that teachers too often foreclose on because of the prejudice about "expository writing." Mythic, imagistic, metaphorical writing does not say *less,* as the highest literary creations show.

Private ways of verbalizing often reflected in rapid note-taking may omit some parts of speech and much punctuation and let a few key words or ideas stand for other unverbalized material that clusters around these saliencies. This inchoate departure point for language use, far from encouraging muddy or solipsistic expression, serves as foil to bring out the real utility of all the parts of speech, the kinds of punctuation, complete sentences, and elaborated sentences, and all the resources of wide-ranging word choice and careful phrasing. Taking-for-granted is the enemy in this regard. Language usually comes across to youngsters as very arbitrary indeed or as picayune "rules." Only when they have to keep adjusting the language of their inner speech to accommodate actual audiences and purposes do the real reasons for language being as it is become clear to novice writers and the full resources of the language become available to them.

People learn to write by practice in conceptualizing and practice in conversing. If these are practiced copiously, realistically, and intelligently, writing itself becomes mere writing down on paper, self-dictation. How much a person actually has to practice with pen and paper depends on how much prior work has gone on with conceptualizing and oral verbalizing. Speaking and writing differ considerably, not least in the opportunity that writing affords to look back over what one has put down, react to it, and revise it. But revision starts much farther back in the inner life as one recapitulates and reformulates experience, reviews and re-states it in his own mind. *The inner speech that presents itself for revision into writing has been much determined in advance by this continual rumination.* Teaching methodology has to be based on this continuity of thought into speech and speech into writing. Progressive revisions at all stages mark this continuity; only *one* kind of revision occurs when someone revises his inner speech as he dictates it to himself. Opportunities for good teaching exist all along this continuity.

True, we learn to write by writing, by realistic practice of the target activity itself, but writing must be construed to begin with self-conversing and the outer conversing that feeds into it not only ideas and attitudes but also vocabulary, sentence structure, and even organization too (consider, for example, the differences in structure between gossip, scolding, interrogation, how-to-do-it directions, etc.). Writing must have continual holistic interplay of many activities over a span of years—of observing and data-gathering, individualized reading, discussion, composition in other media than verbal, and opportunities at any time to practice the whole range of forms of writing practiced in the world beyond school. The subject matter of student writing needs to be material not previously interpreted or abstracted by others—his or her own eyewitnessing, memories, interviews, experiments, feelings, reflections, and reactions to reading. But central is the process of *expatiation* that takes the interplay of inner voices back out into the social world, where the give-and-take of minds and voices can lift each member beyond where he or she started. This requires enormously more small-group interaction than schools now foster—task talk, improvisation, and topic discussion. This global, long-range, and in-depth approach to writing I have already dealt with extensively—as theory in *Teaching the Universe of Discourse,* as teaching methodology in *Student-Centered Language Arts and Reading, K–12,* and *Active Voice: A Writing Program Across the Curriculum,* and as school materials for students in *Interaction.*[7] To the extent that some teachers emphasize "oral-language development" and "pre-writing" and "integrated language arts," they are moving in this direction, but a rationale for teaching writing based on revision of inner speech would support such efforts at a time when schooling trends work against them.

Although I'm not one who believes that improved curriculum waits on further research findings, and in fact see this stand as often really a dodge or a stall, still certain especially germane research with learners may help teachers, I think. Encouraging, I find, are recent trends to look directly at what people do when they try to write—from elementary children (Donald Graves[8] and David Dirlam[9]) to secondary students (Janet Emig[10]) through college (Mina Shaughnessy,[11] Sondra Perl,[12] and Adela Karliner[13]) even to famous professional writers (as, for example, they talk

[7]James Moffett, *Teaching the Universe of Discourse* (Boston: Houghton Mifflin, 1968); James Moffett and Betty Jane Wagner, *Student-Centered Language Arts and Reading, K–12* (Boston: Houghton Mifflin, revised 1976); James Moffett, *Active Voice: A Writing Program Across the Curriculum,* Boynton/Cook Publishers, 1981; and James Moffett, senior author, *Interaction: A Student-Centered Language Arts and Reading Program* (Boston: Houghton Mifflin, 1973).
[8]Donald Graves, "An Examination of the Writing Process of Seven-Year-Old Children," *Research in the Teaching of English,* 9 (1975).
[9]David Dirlam, "The Changing Wisdoms in Children's Writing," unpublished talk delivered May 22, 1980, to the New York State Education Department Conference on Writing Education.
[10]Janet Emig, *The Composing Processes of Twelfth-Graders* (Urbana, Ill.: National Council of Teachers of English, 1971).
[11]Mina Shaughnessy, *Errors and Expectations: A Guide for Teachers of Basic Writing* (New York: Oxford University Press, 1977). She sets a good example of trying to account for the "errors" of student writing by getting into their minds and points of view as much as possible.
[12]Sondra Perl, "The Composing Processes of Unskilled College Writers," *Research in the Teaching of English,* December 1979.
[13]Suzanne E. Jacobs and Adela B. Karliner, "Helping Writers to Think: The Effect of Speech Roles in Individual Conferences on the Quality of Thought in Student Writing," *College English,* January 1977.

about their methods and habits to interviewers in the *Paris Review*). The research of James Britton and colleagues in Britain (now being replicated in Australia) complements this American research.[14] The work of Graves and Karliner may illustrate also a felicitous teaching method which, quite independently of each other, they call "conferencing" and which consists of mid-composition dialogue between a writer and a coach about what the writer is trying to say. Comparisons between transcripts of this supportively groping dialogue with final versions of the compositions demonstrate improvement over first efforts and show again the value of socializing inner speech during writing.

The concept of inner speech will both support and benefit from another relevant research trend called the "psychobiology of writing," because the very nature of inner speech brings together neurophysiological functioning, linguistic structuring of thought, and transitions between personal and social expression. This includes much brain research, most outside the field of education, like the classic work of Wilder Penfield[15] and successors, and some that has moved from outside into education, like that with the hemispherical specialization of the brain[16] as well as the kind of psycholinguistic research that Courtney Cazden[17] summarizes for educators. For too long we have ransacked linguistic, rhetorical, and literary theory for paradigms or even just clues to the teaching of writing, but foremost we should look to the functioning of the human organism. To view writing as revision of inner speech is to see more clearly the way to go in both teaching methods and research procedures and to make this way reciprocal.

Some other advantages of teaching writing from inner speech regard therapy, art, and general self-development. The processes of psychotherapy and of writing both require maximum availability of information from all internal and external sources and maximum synthesizing of this firsthand and secondhand knowledge into a full, harmonious expression of individual experience. This calls for the removal of spells to which the person has not agreed and of which he is unconscious. Freud asked the patient to start talking about anything and just keep uttering as fluently, fully, and spontaneously as possible everything that came into his head— in other words, to attempt to verbalize aloud his stream of consciousness or externalize his inner speech. This technique presupposes that from the apparent chaos of all this disjointed rambling will emerge for analyst and patient an order, eventually "betrayed" by motifs, by sequencing, by

---

[14]J. Britton, T. Burgess, N. Martin, A. McLeod, and H. Rosen, *The Development of Writing Abilities, 11–18* (New York: Macmillan, 1975).

[15]Wilder Penfield, *The Mystery of the Mind: A Critical Study of Consciousness and the Human Brain* (Princeton, N.J.: Princeton University Press, 1975).

[16]A good account for the layman of hemispherical specialization is Howard Gardner, *The Shattered Mind* (New York: Alfred Knopf, 1975).

[17]Courtney Cazden, *Child Language and Education* (New York: Holt, Rinehart and Winston, 1972).

gradual filling in of the personal cosmology. Thus, if successful, the subject's cosmologizing processes, the idiosyncratic ways of structuring and symbolizing experience, stand more clearly revealed and presumably more amenable to deliberate change, if desired. The most important thing a writer needs to know is how he himself does think and verbalize and how he might.

Both writing and psychoanalytic procedure work with discourse to mediate between mind and society, considering society as introjected into the mind of a self that must in turn accommodate itself to that society while keeping its own integrity. More specifically, both tap inner speech to further the individual's dual goals of knowing himself and communicating with others. Regarding method, the critical parallel is that set and setting make enormous practical difference in the effectiveness with which the subject succeeds in getting command over inner speech. Just as the analyst's approach influences strongly what and how the patient will think when he free-associates (they say Jungian patients even start obediently dreaming mandalas), so the way a teacher "sets up the assignment" will influence crucially the focus, level, and selectivity of the student's inner speech. In fact, since writing will be some revision of inner speech, however the teacher conceives composition, it is wiser to create a set and setting that will acknowledge this at the outset and make it work best.

Not for a moment do I suggest that the teacher play psychiatrist. The therapeutic benefits from writing are natural fallout and nothing for a school teacher to strive for. They inhere in the very parallelism described here. Good therapy and composition aim at clear thinking, effective relating, and satisfying self-expression. Precisely because it is not thought of as therapy and works toward another goal, writing can effect fine therapy sometimes. At any rate, self-awareness is the means in both cases, and this requires focusing attention on one's inner speech.

Artful simulation of inner speech occurs much more in literature than merely as a rare technique of modern fiction. In fact, prose interior monologue comes as a late representation of it. As stage soliloquy, it was a mainstay of Greek and Elizabethan drama. Classical Greek theater arrayed beautifully, as a matter of fact, the whole range of vocalization—from inner and outer monologue to staccato dialogue to the chorus, thus uttering individual inner life, exposition, interplay of personality types, and communal attitudes, the whole cycle of personal and social minds. The soliloquy endures today in the one stage convention of modern times that permits anything so "unrealistic" as voicing thoughts aloud to an audience—the musical, where song is the medium for self-verbalization ("If I Were a Rich Man," for example, from *Fiddler on the Roof*).

Song connects drama to the other great literary tradition of artful inner speech, which we find in much lyric poetry of both yesterday and today, such as Keats's "Ode to a Nightingale" and T. S. Eliot's "The Love Song of J. Alfred Prufrock." (Note the titles, incidentally.) Although not so specific as to time, place, and character as Robert Browning's "Soliloquy on a Spanish Cloister," a considerable amount of lyric poetry sustains the outpouring of some soul whose setting and persona simply remain unstated and may or may not be those of the poet. The soul sings itself. This is why the more directly that literature gives it voice, the more lyrical—poetic and musical—becomes the language. Even prose writers like Joyce, Faulkner, and Virginia Woolf moved their language more into poetry the more they simulated inner speech. Joyce's final work, *Finnegan's Wake,* became one long polyglot poem as he attempted to give voice not merely to one person's stream of consciousness but to the race's collective unconscious. Perhaps the use of the aria for soliloquy in opera epitomizes this artful soul vocalization, bringing together as it does drama, poetry, and music.

The literature of inner speech can provide a powerful connection between what students read and what they write. I don't advocate "model writing" if that means fairly close imitation. This connection can, for the most part, operate implicitly. Let's say that, in a general way, as students are learning to capture their inner speech either by jotting down or by speaking spontaneously with partners (perhaps taping), and learning to work this material up for different audiences and purposes, they are also experiencing prose, poetry, drama, and song that simulate inner speech and make an art form of it. Much of this literature, interestingly enough, either was written for performance or readily lends itself to performance. This is so because inner speech moves, like the performing arts, moment by moment in time, so that, if "transcribed," it naturally becomes a script. So students can come to know this literature via a variety of means and media—silent reading, sight reading aloud with partners, giving a rehearsed reading, witnessing a performance live, listening to a recording of the text, or viewing a film or television performance. Thus a literature that might seem less accessible, because inner, turns out, in fact, to be very accessible indeed because inherently dramatic, performable.

This literature of inner speech will accomplish several very valuable services for students. In the first place, it validates this approach to writing at the same time it shows what to do with it. Through the literature closest to the chaos of "random subjectivity," it triumphs as public communication. Partly, it turns to advantage its apparent drawbacks—subjectivity and the moment-to-moment randomness. If the writer grasps the patterns of his own inner life well enough, chances are he will strike responsive chords in others, because patterns abstract experiences to a point where others can share. As shared medium, language makes this easier. And the moment-to-moment movement in time gives drama, vitality, freshness, and novelty of detail. This literature, then, demonstrates for students in a lively way just what teachers would like to help their students learn—to revise inner speech into successful communication. The key is the artfulness, just what the undeveloped or naive learner lacks most, the knacks and skills, the profound tricks of the trade. This literature virtually *enacts* for students, before their very eyes, the process the teacher engages them in. It is unnecessary and unwise to point to strokes of genius and say, "That's what I want you to do too!" Immersion works best. Let them steep in this literature, and they will intuit technique. We are not trying to make little literati—in this respect the chips can fall where they may—but we are, rather, putting to work for us the best teacher in these matters, art. Trust it. Art is, after all, another version of composition, because both are cosmologizing, ordering.

Reciprocally, working at the art of converting one's own inner speech sensitizes students to literary techniques and textures as direct efforts to induce "literary appreciation" (postmortems and vivisections) never can do. For students unused to acknowledging and thinking about inner speech I recommend dealing with it first by improvising a skit in which a made-up character imagined in a definite setting and activity says aloud what he or she is thinking. Since this reverts to familiar play prattle, no one ever finds this activity strange. To get from local speech to paper, students can then either tape and transcribe their own improvised soliloquies or make up new ones on paper in the first place, that is, write down as a kind of script what their character is thinking. A further step at some point is to shift from an imaginary character to oneself and simply write down everything that comes into one's head for a certain length of time.

In revising their self-dictations, students should be reminded that these revisions may take any direction, not only toward drama, poetry, song, or prose but more specific directions within any of these toward lyricism, narrative, or reflection. Seeing these options becomes a real possibility when students start with the matrix itself from which stem all the adult examples they encounter. To see options as a writer facilitates enormously the appreciating of options made by the writers of the works one reads. Role playing the professional is the best way to understand what the professional is doing . . . and to learn his art. The proper relation between literature and composition is not for students to write about the reading but for them to make their own literature and read that of others as a fellow practitioner, however humble the state of their own art at the moment. Such a writing reader more readily attunes to tone, makes out the main point, differentiates voices and styles, follows threads of story or argument, and perceives motifs and patterns.

Most of all, keeping inner speech as the matrix of all writing keeps teaching of writing centered on authentic authorship, so that all these other benefits of writing accrue to the novice as well as to the professional. The novice needs, after all, not fewer but more kinds of motivation.

The student needs to enjoy and value the benefits of self-expression, communication, therapy, and art. The more evident are all these benefits the more easily can learners muster the strength it takes to stick at practice. Writing can be hard work, and until someone does enough of it to find for himself how well it pays off, he needs every enriching connection possible. Too specialized and isolated, writing becomes deadly indeed. Teachers would do well to situate it in those multiple contexts it deserves—of other arts and media, of related investigative disciplines, and of practical self-healing and self-development. The very complexity of writing invites and facilitates the exploitation of these numerous organic connections. Although not easy, this is easier than trying to teach writing within self-defeating conventions not derived from actual learning processes.

Finally, let me crystallize what I may merely have implied so far, that writing does not merely convey what one thinks, it shows what one *is* thinking and even helps to discover what, further, one *might be* thinking. That is, *if* practiced as real authoring, not disguised playback, writing *discovers* as much as it communicates, and this basic benefit must ever be held out and made clear to students. Writing is hauling in a long line from the depths to find out what things are strung on it. Sustained attention to inner speech reveals ideas one did not know one thought, unsuspected connections that illuminate both oneself and the outside objects of one's thought. No better motivation exists, because young people do want to find out what they and the world are like. But only if we construe writing at its maximum meaning will the discovery aspect of it become real for students. Instead of using writing to test other subjects, we can elevate it to where it will *teach* other subjects, for in *making sense* the writer is *making knowledge.* Certainly I'm not alone in arguing that writing should appear to students as a serious learning method itself to discover things about external subjects as well as oneself. Paradoxically, writing does not become an instrument of investigation and discovery of external things until it is acknowledged to be grounded in inner speech, because only when the individual brings some consciousness to the monitoring of the stream of experience does he start to become the master instead of the dupe of that awesome symbolic apparatus that, ill or well, creates his cosmos.

I want now to go beyond *discovery* of one's own mind to *control* of one's own mind, a much less familiar kind of learning that bears special affinity to writing but that will take us into another mental dimension.

Meditation as Control of Inner Speech

It's best to head off at the outset the common notion that meditation comes from another culture, that it is a practice only of strange and dangerous cults, or that it inculcates a particular religious doctrine. Meditation has always been and never ceased to be practiced in Western culture.

All cultures of all times, in fact, have included some forms of it. Though often connected with religions, meditation presupposes such serious intention and self-discipline that it has tended to thrive more outside the church than in, or, if in the church, in special groups well advanced beyond the mass membership. That is, spiritual discipline intended to alter consciousness was too much for most people, even in the ancient world, well before the rise of materialism. Thus each religion spun off an outrider group that became the custodian of the purest spiritual discipline— for Vedanta and Hinduism, yoga; for Mohammedanism, Sufism; for Buddhism, Zen; for Amerindians, shamanism; and for Christianity, the Gnostics, certain early Church Fathers, whose tradition survived in Eastern Orthodox Christianity, and some medieval mystics. When Christ went into the wilderness to fast and meditate, as the Gospel relates, he was following ancient spiritual traditions that from all evidence seem to reach back to the Indus, Tigris/Euphrates, and Nile valleys, "pooling" in the Mediterranean/Balkan basins, and maybe even to stem from an earlier common source.

The modern meaning of meditate—"to turn over in the mind, reflect on"—represents a much more cerebral version of former practices, an idea of which we can gain from the etymology of the word. The Latin *meditari* crosses the words "to heal" in *medicari* and *mederi* via the Indo-European root *med-*, "measure, consider, reflect," and perhaps also in the Avestan (ancient Persian) word *vi-mad,* healer. The shaman and medicine man are one and the same. The association of meditation with healing is truly universal, however, and no doubt expressed what we call today psychosomatic medicine or holistic healing.

It seems clear that the meaning of meditation has changed as our culture has shifted to an emphasis on the new-brain, left-hemisphere, literate, technical, abstract modes of knowing. Consider this reference in Psalm XIX, 14: "Let the words of my mouth and the meditation of my heart be acceptable in Thy sight." This idea that the heart, not the head, is the chief organ of knowledge has been cheapened in modern romanticism but is another serious cross-cultural belief from ancient times, ruling as strongly in yogic emphasis on waking the heart chakra (cardiac plexus or energy center) as in the Christian tradition of the "sacred heart." The Tibetan Rinpoche Thartang Tulkhu once said at a meditation workshop that "Meditation is non-conceptualization," that is, a bypassing of the whole cultural system for filtering reality based on logic and language.[18] My own yoga teacher, Swami Sivalingam, once said it was relaxation, by which he meant a total release of both muscles and thoughts right down practically to the cellular level of functioning.[19]

[18]Founder and head lhama of the Nyingma Tibetan Meditation Center in Berkeley, Ca., and author of many books published there.
[19]Swami Sivalingam, a life-long yogi from South India, is founder of the Prana Yoga Ashram, based in Berkeley with other centers around the world, and author of *Wings of Divine Wisdom,* published by the Ashram, 1977.

Surely, central to any definition of meditation as a spiritual practice would be some notion of transcending intellectual knowledge, which by itself will indeed proceed on the basis, as John Locke stated for the modern age, that "nothing is in the mind that was not in the senses." Sensory experience and hence memory provide grist for the intellectual mill to recombine by ratiocination into inferences. If intellect is the only source of knowledge, then Locke is right, as our epoch of culture tends to assume, although it somehow allows for, without understanding it, the role of intuition, usually chalked off (unscientifically!) to some swifter intellectual shortcutting. But the "higher knowledge" at which meditation aims, although no doubt related to our notion of intuition, cannot be merely relegated to the right hemisphere as just the way the (currently) nondominant half of our head works. It may well depend on unusual collaboration and harmonization of the two hemispheres, as scientific research with the electroencephalograms of meditators today is indicating,[20] but other universal traditions associate higher knowledge with the pineal gland, recently also become an object of serious scientific study,[21] taking us back to Descartes's belief that the pineal gland was the seat of the soul, but far before him to his own source in both the West and the East, according to which advanced meditation awakens dormant power in the pineal gland and opens connections between it, the pituitary gland, and cosmic energy or intelligence. All this suggests that deep meditation causes some "re-wiring" of the neurophysiological circuits and not merely loading up more heavily the existing circuits as conventional education tends to do.

The variety we are confronted with today represents not only alternative techniques preferred by individuals or cultures but also a gradation in depth owing to historical changes. Accordingly, meditation varies all the way from highly focused discursive reflection, close to the current meaning of the word, to rare mystic experiences of ecstasy ("being outside" oneself), but at this upper reach, meditation crosses over into what is called "contemplation." The meaning of *contemplari* was to gaze attentively, to observe (in both senses), but the literal meaning underlying this was, astonishingly, "to mark out an inaugural temple, "to set aside a place for religious observance or initiation, and, of course, the word "temple" for the sides of the head derives from the same source as the temple of contemplation!

But all these allusions to etymology and anatomy, useful as a suggestive framework for definition, cannot make clear the central notions of meditation so well as an account of some of the practices themselves,

[20]The *Brain/Mind Bulletin* of January 16, 1978, summarized such research by a team in Switzerland led by David Orme-Johnson and reported at the Ninth Annual Conference of Electroencephalography and Clinical Neurophysiology at Amsterdam.
[21]The Pineal, a research annual, Eden Medical Research, Inc., St. Albans, Vermont.

which will also move us closer to the reconsideration of writing methodology. My own practical definition of meditation states it as some control of inner speech ranging from merely *watching* it to *focusing* it to *suspending* it altogether. This range of meditative techniques suggests a rough developmental sequence of teaching methods relevant to writing. It starts in the pre-verbal and ends in the post-verbal and runs from uncontrolled to controlled mind.

Researchers at Harvard's Preschool Project reported that the children they observed whom adults described later, in school, as the "brightest, happiest, and most charming" had spent as much as 20 percent of their preschool time "staring" with absorption at some object or another, the largest amount of time the children had allotted to any single activity.[22] "Staring" is the small child's meditation and a chief way he or she learns. This affords direct knowledge, not yet mediated by discourse, and should be encouraged in school. Many bright thinkers and writers don't talk much in the early years but pay such rapt attention that when they do start talking they have a lot to say and know how to say it well. (Recall the etymological connection between gazing and contemplation.) Although it is wise, as we have claimed, to gain awareness of inner speech once it flourishes in oneself, it is unwise to push verbalization the way commercial greenhouses force growth in plants they are readying for the market: you can get a lot of blossoms fast for a short while, but the plant itself weakens and seldom if ever blooms again. The spontaneous gazing of the preschool years can easily continue as a pleasant school activity if children are furnished with engaging materials and encouraged to get deep into them individually, as some Montessori schools do. Besides coming to know things deeply this way, children may also want to gaze at simple positive images such as a star or candle flame.

For this and the following techniques a quiet location and a comfortable sitting position are essential. Although some Christian meditations stipulate kneeling, standing, or even walking, and the Tibetan Buddhist Chogyam Trungpa speaks of "meditation in action,"[23] most techniques require, certainly for the beginner, maximum quiet in the environment and stillness of the meditator. Sitting cross-legged on the floor or sitting on a chair (preferably without touching the back of the chair), one keeps the spine erect but not stiff, releases muscles, and slows and deepens breathing. The key to meditation is a *relaxed body* and an *alert awareness.*

A variation of gazing is visualization. The meditator closes his eyes and transfers the image inward to the middle of the forehead. Alternately gazing outward and visualizing inward teaches one to develop inner attention and imagination without forcing verbalization. Other pure visualization meditations can follow. Staying focused either in or out frees the

[22]Reported in Burton White, *The First Three Years of Life* (Englewood Cliffs, N.J.: Prentice Hall, 1975).
[23]Chogyam Trungpa, *Meditation in Action* (Berkeley, Ca.: Shambala Publications, 1969).

meditator a while from the excitations of the environment and lets him or her feel the strength of the self, the deeper self that abides at least somewhat independently of the outside. Writing presupposes just such inner strength. A writer of whatever age has to feel full of himself and have a degree of confidence, belief that he has something to say, faith in his will, and control of his attention. Gazing and visualizing, finally, develop *vision*—seeing and perceiving in both outer and inner ways prerequisite for writing. These first meditation techniques should help develop selfhood, control, and perception. From here on the techniques run from most discursive to least discursive.

The next simplest and easiest meditation technique consists of letting inner speech flow spontaneously but of *witnessing* it. Instead of floating along on this stream and being borne away from the center of the self, one sits on the bank, so to speak, and watches it flow by, staying separate from it, not trying to influence it, but above all not being "carried away" by it. The meditator centers within his inner sanctum, and focuses attention on the meditation object—in this case, his trains of thoughts. He watches and notes what flows by, as if he were a spectator at someone else's presentation, at a movie, and thus gains new knowledge of his thoughts and detachment from them.

Most of us most of the time do not know what is going on in our minds. The ancient dictum "know thyself" surely meant "know your own mind and the evanescent fluctuations of your temporal existence" as well as "know that thou art divine, despite these evanescent fluctuations." "Know your unconscious," says the psychoanalyst, eliciting the patient's inner speech until this speaker begins truly to hear himself—until both become aware of this incessant inner haranguing and dialoguing and detect the patterns and meaning of it. Swami Sivalingam constantly reminds his students to "watch your mind," in or out of meditation, and says "writing teaches you to watch your thoughts." This is in line with both Eastern traditions of "mindfulness" in keeping constant disciplined attention on the moment and Western traditions of "raising consciousness."

The "summoning" of thoughts about a subject that comes while writing depends on much prior awareness of thoughts that occur in inner speech when one is not writing. To appreciate the value of this mind-witnessing technique, you have to realize how much people normally think without knowing it and consequently how much of their thought they do not have access to at other times for writing or for any other purpose, although these thoughts are unconsciously influencing their behavior. It's important to distinguish the self-consciousness that this technique induces from the awkward self-entanglement associated with young people growing into and through adolescence. The latter sort of self-consciousness comes from unevenness of growth, unsureness of identity and role, and acute concern about how *others* view oneself. Such confusion, in fact, naturally makes clear thinking harder, and posturing is a common resort, on or off paper. Witnessing will actually heal this sort of self-consciousness the homeopathic way, by redirecting it so that another form of the symptom cures the symptom. Periodically settling down and collecting oneself helps to center and balance the inner life while the insights gained from witnessing clarify problems and suggest how best to handle them.

The following techniques require and also develop increasing control of inner speech. Once able to still himself, turn inward, and witness his thoughts, the meditator may deliberately attempt to narrow down and focus his inner speech, to exert some control over it. Will comes more into play. Now, even to observe is to alter, so maintaining the witness distance and not getting "lost in thought" already assert some influence no doubt on the direction and content of inner speech. The present step consists, however, of setting a subject, holding the mind to it without distraction, focusing on it with special intensity, and developing it to an understanding not achievable by ordinary, relatively wayward reflection.

But this focusing differs from just intellectual concentration by a factor that only the most sensitive and original school teachers would ever allow for—the *state of consciousness* in which the meditator beams the topic. Passion, memory, imagination converge with intellect and intuition like rays of different colors coming together to create white light. Drawing on every faculty at once in a kind of all-out effort to penetrate the topic permits reinforcement effects like radiations from variant sources fitting their wave lengths and amplitudes together to make a super ray. Success owes much to set (mental and circumstantial) and setting (physical body and surroundings), to what we might call the assignment conditions. And success evinces itself not just as new ideas but as a more pervasive alteration of the meditator's inner and outer life, this global effect being the real goal rather than an intellectual breakthrough for its own sake.

Orthodox Buddhism and Christianity both have set forth in texts and teachings their methods for this very discursive sort of meditation and the themes they deem appropriate to focus on. Buddhist texts list, for example, such prescribed subjects as the four elements of earth, fire, air, and water; virtues or "stations of Brahma" such as compassion, friendliness, and evenmindedness; "repulsive things" such as skeletons and corpses in various states; and "formless states" of endless space, unlimited consciousness, and nothingness.[24] The death's head or "memento mori" has of course been a widespread Christian meditation object, the reminder of death or mortality, as sometimes depicted in medieval and Renaissance art. In both traditions the purpose may be to break attachment to the body, counter our belief in physical reality, and induce a deeper perspec-

[24]These themes are drawn from Edward Conze, *Buddhist Meditation* (London: George Allen and Unevin, 1956).

tive in which the invisible nature and purpose of human existence can be grasped. Meditating on one's greatest temptation—sex or wealth or power—has the goal of thinking it to death. The meditator may follow specific directions to break down the temptation into parts or aspects, break these down in turn, and thus proceed literally to "analyze the subject to pieces." If successful, the meditator should release himself from this temptation.

In contrast to this use of the destructive potentialities of discourse, some topical meditation is devotional and uses thought trains to lead into a beatific or compassionate state transcending the usual egoistic viewpoint with its limited personal feelings. Christians draw their subjects mostly from the life or sayings of Christ and meditate on one until it reaches its fullest meaning or until this focal intensity elevates feeling to finer levels. Church sermons often try to set a meditation example in how to discourse on a "text." Holding the mind to positive or transcendental topics or objects becomes a way of regulating state of mind and mood, or, as we say today, of altering the state of consciousness, in a beneficial way. Inasmuch as discursive meditation consists of a given subject and a stipulated procedure for focusing inner speech on that subject, it offers a remarkable analogy to school composition assignments, which we call, significantly, "themes," the same term by which church manuals commonly referred to meditation subjects.

Providing a splendid historical parallel between meditation and composition, Louis Martz developed during the 1950s the thesis that the traits our century came to recognize and admire in the so-called "metaphysical poets" of the seventeenth century derived rather directly from very popular meditation practices initiated by Saint Ignatius Loyola, spread by the Jesuits as part of the Counter-Reformation, and taken to heart by these poets. This Jesuitical meditation may best represent what I am calling discursive meditation, the sort most obviously related to writing as a finished product.

At the start of his exposition of this thesis in *The Poetry of Meditation,* Martz quotes Yeats and then summarizes his argument:

> Such thought—such thought have I that hold it tight
> Till meditation master all its parts,
> Nothing can stay my glance
> Until that glance run in the world's despite
>
> To where the damned have howled away their hearts,
> And where the blessed dance;
> Such thought, that in it bound
> I need no other thing,
> Wound in mind's wandering
> As mummies in the mummy-cloth are wound.

> —William Butler Yeats, Oxford, Autumn 1920

"Day after day I have sat in my chair turning a symbol over in my mind, exploring all its details, defining and again defining its elements, testing my convictions and those of others by its unity, attempting to substitute particulars for an abstraction like that of algebra."

Such meditation is the subject of this study: intense, imaginative meditation that brings together the senses, the emotions, and the intellectual faculties of man; brings them together in a moment of dramatic, creative experience. One period when such meditation flourished coincides exactly with the flourishing of English religious poetry in the seventeenth century. There is, I believe, much more than mere coincidence here, for the qualities developed by the "art of meditation" (as Joseph Hall described it) are essentially the qualities that the twentieth century has admired in Donne, or Herbert, or Marvell. Those qualities, some thirty years ago, received their classic definition in the introduction to Grierson's anthology, *Metaphysical Lyrics and Poems,* and in Eliot's essay inspired by that volume. Developed in a series of influential books issued during the 1930s, the definition views Donne as the master and father of a new kind of English poetry, with these distinguishing marks: an acute self-consciousness that shows itself in minute analysis of moods and motives; a conversational tone and accent, expressed in language that is "as a rule simple and pure"; highly unconventional imagery, including the whole range of human experience, from theology to the commonest details of bed and board; an "intellectual, argumentative evolution" within each poem, a "strain of passionate paradoxical reasoning which knits the first line to the last" and which often results in "the elaboration of a figure of speech to the farthest stage to which ingenuity can carry it"; above all, including all, that "unification of sensibility" which could achieve "a direct sensuous apprehension of thought, or a recreation of thought into feeling," and made it possible for Donne to feel his thought "as immediately as the odour of a rose. . . ."

The "metaphysical poets" may be seen, not as Donne and his school, but as a group of writers, widely different in temper and outlook, drawn together by resemblances that result, basically, from the common practice of certain methods of religious meditation. (W. B. Yeats, *A Vision* [New York, Macmillan, 1938], p. 301; T. S. Eliot, "The Metaphysical Poets," *Selected Essays, 1917–1932* [New York, Harcourt Brace, 1932], pp. 242, 245–248. *Metaphysical Lyrics and Poems of the Seventeenth Century,* ed. Herbert J. C. Grierson [Oxford, Clarendon Press, 1921], p. xxxiv.)[25]

The Jesuitical meditation structure that Martz says accounts for these traits of the poetry comprised (1) a prelude called the "composition of

[25]Louis Martz, *The Poetry of Meditation* (New Haven: Yale University Press, 1954), pp. 1–2.

place," (2) a point-by-point analysis of the subject, and (3) a concluding "colloquy." Sometimes more preliminaries were recommended, and sometimes the number of analytic points or colloquies might be five, say, instead of three, but the main format was this trinity.[26] During the famous "composition of place" or "seeing the spot" the meditator tried to create as vividly as possible in his mind some scene or situation such as an incident from the life of Christ, the Judgment Day, the agonies of Hell, the miseries of his own life, the hour of death, or the glory and felicity of the kingdom of heaven. On this spot he brought to bear all the powers of his memory, imagination, and intelligence, to fill out the scene in fullest sensory detail and make it as real as if he were either there or it existed in him. An important specific suggestion of the manuals was to employ "similitudes" of various sorts to enable the meditator to feel the reality of the conjured moment and to relate it to his familiar world. Within this mental stage setting, virtually a controlled hallucination, the intellect made several distinct points by analyzing the scene or situation into components, aspects, causes, effects, and so on. Such points, stimulated by the dramatic and graphic intensity of "seeing the spot," not only deepened the meditator's spiritual understanding but brought on in turn a swelling of "affections" or feeling, a shift from head to heart, that the "colloquies" expressed. These seem to have been not so much dialogue as direct address or petition from the meditator to God, some other spirit or figure, other earthly creatures such as animals, or his own soul or self. In poetic rhetoric the equivalent, I assume, would be called "apostrophe." It was "familiar talke," as St. François de Sales called it, "colloquial," as we would say today.

Preliminaries included "premeditation," often the night before morning meditation, and prayers or petitions between the composition of place and the analysis. Like the Buddhist texts, the manuals enumerated appropriate topics, gave examples of meditations on these topics, and set forth the sequence of steps forming the structure of the whole meditation, frequently encouraging the meditator, however, to depart when spontaneity seemed right. No clear distinction was made between prayer and meditation, and the whole procedure was called "mental prayer" as well as "meditation." Finally, each of the three main steps corresponds to a human faculty and to a person of the Holy Trinity. "The minde is the image of God, in which are these three things, Memory, Understanding, and Will or Love. . . . By Memory, wee are like to the Father, by Understanding to the Sonne, by Will to the Holy Ghost."[27]

Martz relates both the general structure and specific traits of Jesuitical meditation to those of metaphysical poetry. He does not claim, however,

---

[26]Martz included as an appendix to his *The Meditative Poem: An Anthology of 17th Century Verse,* a typical manual of the time, Edward Dawson's "The Practical Methode of Meditation," 1614.
[27] *The Poetry of Meditation,* p. 36.

that the triune structure as an entirety informs more than a few of the poems, but rather that parts of the structure occur in many of the poems and that the typical traits singled out by Grierson and Eliot can be recognized as features of one or another of the three stages. The dramatic scenic openings, for example, for which metaphysical poetry is famous, the sudden, graphic beginnings, were generated, he says, from the poet's experience with the "composition of place, seeing the spot." The imagery drawn from commonplaces of everyday life as well as the daring comparisons, sometimes attenuated into "conceits," arose from this composition when accomplished by "similitude." The wit, the "passionate paradoxical reasoning," the "intellectual, argumentative evolution" derive from the middle, analytic section of the meditation *as set in motion by the graphic opening focus and the similitudes.* And the "colloquy" inspired the characteristic lapses into familiar address, simple and colloquial lines, conversational tone. One has simply to recall well-known poems of Donne or Herbert not only to see the more obvious thematic connections between the meditation and the poetry of the period but also to feel the truth of the thesis that as a mode of discourse the composition of Jesuitical meditations strongly influenced the composition of "metaphysical" poetry. The opening sestet of a holy sonnet by Donne:

> What if this present were the world's last night?
> Mark in my heart, O soul, where thou dost dwell,
> The picture of Christ crucified, and tell
> Whether his countenance can thee affright:
> Tears in his eyes quench the amazing light,
> Blood fills his frowns, which from his pierced head fell.

The "theme" here is both Judgment Day and the Crucifixion. The scene-setting for this meditation is graphically fixed before the mind. Then the argumentative octet, addressed to the soul in a kind of colloquy:

> And can that tongue adjudge thee unto hell,
> Which prayed forgiveness for his foes' fierce spite?
> No, no; but as in my idolatry
> I said to all my profane mistresses,
> Beauty, of pity, foulness only is
> A sign of rigor; so I say to thee:
> To wicked spirits are horrid shapes assigned;
> This beauteous form assumes a piteous mind.

The argument is that as beauty signifies only pity, and foulness only rigor, so the beauteous form of Christ can mean only that the poet-meditator will be forgiven.

Donne's "Good Friday, 1613, Riding Westward" opens with a developed "similitude" that makes concrete the rather abstract subject, in ac-

cordance with meditation procedure when the focus is not on a clear
scene or incident. Then Donne does settle on the image of himself jour-
neying away from the scene of the crucifixion:

> Let man's soul be a sphere, and then in this
> The intelligence that moves, devotion is;
> And as the other spheres, by being grown
> Subject to foreign motion, lose their own,
> And being by others hurried every day
> Scarce in a year their natural form obey,
> Pleasure or business, so, our souls admit
> For their first mover, and are whirled by it.
> Hence is't that I am carried towards the west
> This day, when my soul's form bends towards the east.

Herbert's "Discipline" opens with a colloquy, which often was shifted
around even in the meditations themselves:

> Throw away thy rod,
> Throw away thy wrath.
> Oh my God,
> Take the gentle path.

He opens "The Collar" abruptly and dramatically with a moment of re-
bellion from his own life:

> I struck the board and cried, No more!
> I will abroad.
> What? Shall I ever sigh and pine?
> My lines and life are free, free as the road. . . .

And closes, also in conversational style, but in colloquy with God, not
himself:

> But as I raved and grew more fierce and wild
> At every word,
> Me thoughts I heard one calling, Child!
> And I replied, My Lord.

Martz's argument may be most true for the example he cites who is
both Jesuit and poet, Robert Southey, but who also wrote the least po-
etically. And Martz acknowledges that Renaissance meditation itself derived in turn at least partly from classical logic and rhetoric. Still, even
all these ins and outs of inner and outer speech turning over into each
other—treatises of classical rhetoric and logic, oral public sermons, manuals of meditation procedures influencing the inner speech of individuals
at private devotionals, and these private thought practices returning outward as they influence the ways of writing poetry—all this relates ger-

manely to teaching writing. We have here in Martz's demonstration a relatively clear instance from history of efforts to control inner speech affecting writing. The fact that meditation had another goal than improving writing need not detract from the utility of applying meditation techniques to teaching it. And indeed, is the goal of writing so different from that of meditation?

The metaphysical poets had, like all serious writers, given themselves their own kind of composition course, drawing on those discursive paradigms from society that meant most to them. It was natural. Their utilization of current meditation practices to direct and organize their personal thoughts shows but another way that the individual may internalize outer speech into inner, society into mind. (Part of *Ulysses* is narrated in the question-and-answer form of catechism.) What did writers of other cultures utilize as paradigms for controlling inner speech? Did, for example, the initiation rites and teachings of the Eleusinian, Orphic, Brahmanic, and Odinic "mysteries" exert a comparable influence on the thinking and writing of their time? Manly Hall says that world mythologies are allegories of steps in these rites.[28] What rites and routines today are influencing how writers compose?

I can look upon this historical example as both negative and positive for the teaching of writing. For Donnes, Herberts, Vaughns, and Crashaws, it's all well and good to spell out what to think about and how to think about it. Like the others who made these manuals so popular, they chose freely to follow the meditation procedures. And, as original and creative minds, they knew how to utilize the contents and form for their own growth and self-expression. But *assign* such procedures? And to *school children?* Could it be possible that the American composition tradition of the five-paragraph "theme" preserves some residue of this very historical connection between church teaching and writing? Oh, not of course directly, because this country instituted at the outset the vaunted separation of church and state. But suppose the tradition lingers as a general exploitation of composition for moral inculcation. Look again at the 1978 CEEB topic, "We have met the enemy and he is us." (Confess, you sinner!) The composition is called a "theme" because subjects are essentially given, some allowance, of course, being necessary for individual variation in *which* prelisted topic to write on and in *which* points to make about this familiar topic. A theme is really variations on a theme. Then the tradition prescribes a structure, a sequence, for dealing with this topic, allowance again made for some leeway. Like the meditation structure, the five-paragraph organization calls for an introduction that conveys the theme in some arresting way, makes its three points analytically in the middle (one point per each of three paragraphs, though more of each are

[28]Manly Hall, *The Secret Teachings of All Ages: An Encyclopedic Outline of Masonic, Hermetic, Qabbalistic, and Rosicrucian Symbolical Philosophy* (Los Angeles: The Philosophical Research Society, 1978).

allowed if you want extra credit), then concludes with the uplifting peroration, the emotional dessert after the feast of reason. Some caricature helps us play devil's advocate here so that the dangers may emerge of applying such meditational techniques to the teaching of writing. And surely, at their worst, Renaissance meditation manuals must have locked onto the tendency any of us may have toward sterile exercises and petty piety. And all too easily can we imagine how the church and the society may by this means have reinserted into private minds its authoritative bugging device. The institution always parodies the individual—church, school system, or whatever.

These suggestive glimpses of discursive meditation cannot, of course, do justice to all of its possibilities either as variations of inner speech or as teaching measures. It can run a wide gamut from ordinary concentration or Wordsworthian "experience recollected in tranquillity" through many degrees of the Jesuitical "interior oratory and debate," as Martz once called it, to the edge of silence, into trance. Interestingly, to continue along the meditation scale I am delineating, we have to move backward in history, farther still away from the contemporaneous sense of meditation as merely turning things over in the rational mind. The extraordinary twentieth-century spiritual scholar and philosopher, Rudolph Steiner, has described the Christian mystics of the Middle Ages and early Renaissance—Eckhart, Boehme, Paracelsus, Buso, Silesius, and others—in a way that makes clear that, despite a scientific bent or a scholastic training among some of them, their spiritual thinking began nearer, and carried them farther toward, ecstatic transcendence of thought and language, the merging of the personal mind into cosmic "mind," or God, as they thought of it.[29] But these mystics themselves grew from an earlier tradition that affords an even sharper contrast with the meditation of the Counter-Reformation.

During the first few centuries of Christianity certain of the so-called "Desert Fathers" and "Church Fathers," especially in the Eastern or Byzantine church, practiced nondiscursive meditations, as they described and prescribed in writings collected in the Middle Ages and called *Philokalia*.[30] The central meditation of this Christian strain—called Hesychast and focused on the so-called "Jesus prayer of the heart"—will exemplify nondiscursive meditation. It still survives in certain Greek and Russian traditions, has been revived recently in the United States as part of the Charismatic Movement, and was attempted by Frannie in Salinger's story

---

[29]Rudolph Steiner, *Mystics of the Renaissance* (New York: G. P. Putnam, 1911).

[30]*Writings from the Philokalia on Prayer of the Heart,* trans. E. Kadloubovsky and G. E. H. Palmer (London: Faber & Faber, 1951). For current material see George Maloney, *The Jesus Prayer* and Father David Geraets, *Jesus Beads* (Pecos, N.M.: Dove Publications, 1974 and 1969 respectively). These two books are published by the Benedictine Abbey at Pecos, which also publishes on the Charismatic Movement, in which the Abbey is active.

Frannie and Zooey.[31] The fact is that the meditation of silence has disappeared from view the more our culture has "advanced" into technological and discursive intricacies. Even in the church the mystic has seldom been long welcome. Far from enjoying papal blessing, practitioners of truly mystical meditation either inhibited their ultimate reaches to avoid breaking with the church, as Rudolph Steiner says, became so recluse as to make the whole matter academic, or did, in effect, break away. When his thought moves too far away from society (and the church is always part of society), the individual becomes either mystic or insane, depending on whether he yields his mind or simply loses it. From outside, the distinction blurs to the degree that for practical purposes it's all the same to the society, because the individual has got beyond its control. The individual may say he's now under God's control, but the church is not so sure. Once the agent in the ranks—internalized inner speech—has been silenced, church and society have been bypassed.

The Jesus prayer of the heart typifies the meditation method that consists of repeating over and over to oneself a *single* idea put in a *single* piece of speech until the focus of that idea and the incantation of that verbal sound induce trance. Consciousness is then altered beyond thought and speech. The "prayer" is, "Lord Jesus Christ, have mercy upon me!" This is too simple—and too *religious.* But the holy fathers say, "Sit in your cell and this prayer will teach you everything." This quotation is from St. Simeon The New Theologian, who describes the meditation this way:

> Keep your mind there (in the heart), trying by every possible means to find the place where the heart is, in order that, having found it, your mind should constantly abide there. Wrestling thus, the mind will find the place of the heart. This happens when grace produces sweetness and warmth in prayer. From that moment onwards, from whatever side a thought may appear, the mind immediately chases it away, before it has had time to enter, and become a thought or an image, destroying it by Jesus' name, that is, Lord Jesus Christ, have mercy upon me![32]

But how can just saying something over and over reveal the highest truths about life? And what if you don't happen to believe in Jesus, or even God?

To answer that I will ask a third question: How does meditation differ from prayer? The astonishing healer, Edgar Cayce, answered that

[31]Salinger's Glass family had been reading *The Way of a Pilgrim* and *The Pilgrim Continues His Way,* trans. Helen Bacovcin (Garden City, N.Y.: Doubleday, Image, 1978).
[32]Quoted on p. 79 of *The Spiritual Instructions of Saint Seraphim of Sarov,* ed. Franklin Jones (San Francisco: Dawn Horse, 1973), which puts this tradition in relation to yoga and Oriental thought.

prayer is talking to God; meditation is listening to God.[33] Discourse versus silence. Among other things, people are transmitter/receiver sets, which means they are made both to transmit and to receive but not *at the same time.* If you want to listen, you have to switch the channel over to receiving and keep still. If God or Nature or Cosmic Intelligence is transmitting at the other end, and the individual is holding the line muttering and squawking and debating and petitioning, he is missing a lot! Missing perhaps what he most wants to know, for lack of which he must mutter, squawk, debate, and petition. But as everyone knows who has ever tried to stop thinking, it is very difficult indeed. The mind is a drunken monkey, say the yogis. But one way to cure the habit of ceaselessly speaking to ourselves is—homeopathically—to go ahead and speak to ourselves but to say the same thing over and over.

What Christians often call a prayer the Hindus call a *mantra,* a word or phrase intoned repeatedly in exactly the spirit the Christian Fathers did the Jesus prayer of the heart. When the priest tells the parishioner in need of strength to go say so many Hail Marys or Our Fathers, he is doing the same thing the guru does when he tells the disciple to "go say the mantra." Also like the Jesus prayer, a mantra usually refers to some aspect of divinity. Yogis call the repetition of a mantra *japa;* Westerners unfamiliar with their own spiritual traditions and not realizing the universality of meditation have associated it with the particular form of japa that the Maharishi Mahesh Yogi learned from his guru and introduced into the United States under the name of Transcendental Meditation. Hanging near me as I write is a sandalwood rosary that Swami Sivalingam brought me from India—called a *mala*—which is used to count the number of repetitions of a mantra without having to voice or subvocalize the counting, exactly as the nun "tells the beads" as she "prays." *Om,* sometimes spelled *aum,* the master mantra of Hinduism, has the same origin as the Christian *amen,* which evolved from an earlier word *aumen* and which was a mantra, not merely, as now, an affirmation of what preceded it.[34] Just as monks take vows of silence, the yogis practice *mauna,* the withholding of speech. Controlling outer speech aids the controlling of inner speech. It helps fulfill the aim of mantric meditation, to suspend ordinary thinking. Also parallel in both Eastern and Western spiritual traditions is the widespread practice of chanting or singing mantras aloud, alone or in groups. Much chanting or singing of hymns and prayers is really group recitation of mantras. The *kyrie eleison,* for example, which is Greek for "Lord, have mercy . . . ," fairly represents Christian choral literature as exemplary mantra. In fact, it would be proper to view virtually all West-

---

[33] *A Dictionary: Definitions and Comments from the Edgar Cayce Readings,* compiled by Gerald J. Cataldo (Virginia Beach, Va.: A.R.E. Press, 1973), p. 52.
[34] H. Spencer Lewis, "The Mystical Meaning of Amen," *The Rosicrucian Digest,* February 1976.

ern church services as modeling for the congregation the kinds of meditation—discursive in the sermon, mantric in the liturgy—that they may
practice at home.

The adage "You become what you think" summarizes much spiritual
lore. Christian, Caballistic, Buddhist, or Sufi, a true mantra must always
symbolize the highest spiritual concepts, even though meaning may dissolve during repetition. The repeated word or phrase most often refers to
an aspect of divinity by name or epithet. Thus in arguing that the teaching of Transcendental Meditation in American schools violated the principle separating church from state, the American Civil Liberties Union
technically argued a sound case in those states where some teachers or
schools had introduced TM into the classroom, because the TM mantras
are usually Sanskrit names for different aspects of divinity. This presents
no problem except legally; permitting one church's language and not
those of other churches does violate the law. But in such cases the interpretation of the law should not make *any* practicing of meditation in
schools illegal. The intent of the founding fathers, a very spiritual group,
was not to hinder the growth of the soul! At any rate, the unbelievable
power of the one-pointed meditation resulting from the mantric repetition makes it critical to keep mantras positive and elevated. But mantras
need have no connection whatsoever with a church or religion. What
makes them work fundamentally is *the suspension of inner speech* that they
effect. Any mantra may accomplish this if the meditator succeeds in
holding focus well enough, but in the meantime this tremendous concentration on a negative emblem could have the same bad effects that institutional, commercial, political, or other brainwashing can have.

Through hymns and chants the church attempts to use the internalization of social speech as a way of planting in the individual's mind both
certain uplifting symbols and the internal speech habits that will, through
repetition, remind him of the symbols. Unfortunately, less benevolent
agencies of the society work the same way. Propaganda and advertising
rely on repetition of group chants and rhythmic tunes to set revolving in
the individual the shibboleths, slogans, and brand names they want per-
petuated. Precisely because outer speech converts to inner speech, all
spiritual traditions have come down hard on idle or loose speech, on giving voice to evil things, or, in modern idiom, "talking negatively." The
reason is not superstition but good mental hygiene. The question arises,
however, of what speech shall be repeated to suspend speech so the meditator can pay attention to the transpersonal or divine part of himself for
a change. If a mantra is wrong, the cure could be worse than the disease.
On the other hand, if children are picking up bad mantras from mass media and hate litanies around them, then perhaps school should try to help
them take over more control of their inner speech.

To understand nondiscursive meditation we have to consider both what the mind is aimed at and what it is aimed from. The root meaning of "discourse" is "running to and fro." The meaning of "mystic" derives from *mystos,* "keeping silence," derived in turn from the Greek *myein,* "to keep closed" (of eyes and lips). The mantra substitutes for inner speech, which "runs to and fro," in usual discursive fashion and relatively so even in the focused devotional. During mantra repetition, inner speech continues, in a sense, but changes profoundly from *serial* thoughts, a *train* of thoughts, to a *point* of thought. The voice moves on in time, repeating the same words, but the mind becomes, as yogis say, "one-pointed." Repeating the mantra suspends or at least mitigates inner speech so that nonconceptual intuition can take over in an altered state of consciousness both more receptive and more perceptive. Not only does the idea or object contemplated reveal itself more deeply, but it is as if a whole new and finer attunement occurs, enabling the individual to detect signals from within and from the environment that the ordinary mind drowns out or filters out. Although some people may regard this as a kind of self-hypnosis, which would wrongly put meditation in some category of unconscious vulnerability to others, meditation succeeds actually to the extent that it *de*-hypnotizes the individual from the prior environmental conditioning and acculturation. (Hypnosis has no single brainwave pattern to define it, whereas meditation, like other definite states recognized by science, such as sleeping, dreaming, and waking, yields a distinctive electroencephalographic reading.)[35] This is why spiritual masters refer to the aim of meditation as "awakening" or "liberation."

Many modern people tend to be put off by talk of "higher knowledge" or "awakening" or "direct perception of reality." Let me put the matter this way. Pure light cannot itself really be seen, although it enables grosser things to be seen by illuminating them. Broken down into colors, however, light does manifest itself to normal human vision (although even then, of course, we are not seeing the color in the same sense that we see the object reflecting the color). Just as a prism breaks down light into colors, which we can perceive, so the ordinary verbal/conceptual mind breaks down reality in ways which it can manage, in the terms of its own medium. It translates reality, and because the ordinary mind undergoes such powerful influences from culture and language, it translates reality according to sociohistorical biases. The deepest nondiscursive meditation temporarily turns off that whole information system. Veils fall. Zen masters constantly compare this liberated consciousness to a perfectly still body of water that directly reflects reality, no longer distorting it with ruffles of egoistic feeling or ripplings of the social mind. Or, to use another comparison, the meditator attunes directly to nature

---

[35] Robert Keith Wallace, Herbert Benson, and Archie Wilson, "A Wakeful Hypometabolic Physiologic State," *American Journal of Physiology,* September 1971.

instead of just to human frequencies. But he may at any time switch back on the old information system, which is necessary, and he may tune at will either to the more limited, interpreted world of humankind or to the unrefracted sources themselves. I think that the religious trinity was a practical breakdown of primal unity, to facilitate understanding of what otherwise would be incomprehensible. Trinities like Father, Son, and Holy Ghost or Vishnu, Brahma, and Shiva (or I, you, and it) make a concession to the limitations of conceptualized understanding, which must have parts, categories, and divisions and can do nothing with unity. This is why mystical means silent. But reintegration is essential, and this is why all cultures, as we will see, have developed some way of shifting attunement periodically from the social mediating of nature to nature itself. The breakdown is the process of becoming aware of all the possible divisions within unity. When the mind returns to unity without losing this awareness, this is direct knowledge, higher knowledge, or awakening.

All these meditation techniques may be summarized in the form of a scale progressing from nonverbal to verbal and then, within the verbal, from babble to silence. Put another way, it goes from external focus to internal focus and then, within the internal focus, from uncontrolled to controlled inner speech.

Non- verbal		GAZING—Rapt absorption in outer object, eyes open.
		VISUALIZING—Imagining of inner object, eyes closed.
	Uncon- trolled	WITNESSING INNER SPEECH—Watching as by-stander the inner stream.
Verbal		FOCUSING INNER SPEECH—Narrowing down to and developing a subject intensively with all faculties of mind and heart together.
	Con- trolled	SUSPENDING INNER SPEECH—Holding the mind on one point until it transcends discourse and culture and merges with cosmos, in trance.

If we think of gazing as the small child's "staring," then this progression comes full circle in the sense that it begins and ends in silence and rapture, but the circling rises rather than closes—spirals—because the child's gazing is spontaneous and unaware, whereas the meditator who has succeeded in suspending inner speech goes into conscious voluntary trance. Willed gazing or visualizing can be one means of suspending inner speech, since anything that holds the mind one-pointed will do. Also, we must imagine some gradations on this scale between any two adjacent methods, as some witnessing when one is trying to visualize or trying to focus inner speech, or some focusing when one is trying to suspend inner speech. Likewise, success in intensive focusing of inner speech moves the meditator already into the state of altered consciousness that ultimately becomes ecstatic after inner speech yields completely to silence.[36]

The Grand Paradox

Much scientific experimentation has demonstrated that how people perceive the world even on the sensory level is governed by conceptualization and verbalization. People wearing upside-down glasses will start seeing rightside-up after a while because they *know* that's "the way it s'pozed to be." "Concept dominates percept," as the psychologists say, and the concept is verbal and social. Most thinking is mass thinking carried on in an illusion of privacy. We have so thoroughly learned our lessons, internalized the local cosmology, that because we think alone, the thought seems ours. Most of our "original" thoughts resemble the minute variations, imperceptible to outsiders, that Balinese dancers "improvise" within traditional dances. We live in a verbal-conceptual cage and think we live in the world, which reaches us ordinarily only by some dim translation relayed in changing versions through all the offices of our sensorial, memorial, emotional, and rational bureaucracy. God only knows *what* the truth is. The reason that such rumor-mongering passes for an efficient information system rests on our social dependency: The main thing is to fit in with how everyone else is thinking; we'll get around to the rest of reality when we have a free moment.

According to the extraordinary thesis of psychologist Julian Jaynes, however, until about 3,000 years ago people had no individual consciousness at all, certainly not inner speech as personal as we have described.[37] Rather, members of a culture heard and followed authoritative voices of "gods" of that culture that they hallucinated exactly as today's schizophrenics "hear" the voice of a parent, god or devil, or other introjected authority figure. It was not, he said, until cultures conflicted and the need for individual decision-making arose that consciousness replaced this earlier, "bicameral" or gods-attuned mind, which had "told" one what to do in novel situations not governed by hard and fast custom. Though I believe the date is much too recent, Jaynes's remarkable idea fits a number of reasonable assumptions such as the role of inner speech in guiding behavior, the social origin of inner speech, and the evolution of human be-

[36]For perhaps the best Western book on meditation see Claudio Naranjo and Robert Ornstein, *The Psychology of Meditation* (New York: Viking, 1971). This book benefits from the psychiatric, psychological, and neurophysiological background of the authors and from Naranjo's unusual understanding of Eastern teachings and his personal training in spiritual disciplines. See also Robert Keith Wallace and Herbert Benson, "The Physiology of Meditation," *Scientific American*, February 1972, but this and much other relevant research can be followed currently in *Brain/Mind Bulletin*, P.O. Box 42211, Los Angeles, Ca., 90042.

[37]Julian Jaynes, *The Origin of Consciousness in the Breakdown of the Bicameral Mind* (Boston: Houghton Mifflin, 1976).

ings toward higher consciousness. Jaynes's brilliant and controversial work lends corroboration and perspective to the notion I have advanced of inner speech as social hypnosis and to my contention that the original and fundamental role of the arts was and is to counter the negative effects of inner speech.

Is, then, our rich inner life a lie? Are our "beautiful thoughts" only an illusion? No, these are real, but what mostly gives us the feeling of richness, beauty, and originality, I submit, owes, precisely, to our managing to escape a while from the cage. We would best regard fresh perception and original thinking as *un*thinking prior thoughts that were not so or were too partial, as *removing limitations that we previously "took for granted."* Most scientific breakthroughs push a dent out in the battered sphere of truth by undoing an epoch's "current abstractions," to use Alfred North Whitehead's phrase for the local cosmology.

Modern scientists, artists, and mathematicians have well recognized the limitations of ordinary language and have devised purer symbols to transcend them. But even in common parlance we all acknowledge the inadequacies of verbal-conceptual symbolism to do justice to those extremities of experience lying off the range of the workaday world. We are "struck speechless." "Words cannot express . . ." "I cannot tell you how . . ." The best and worst are "beyond words." Horror is "unspeakable," and bliss is "ineffable." Again, conceptual thought and speech serve the mid-range, socialized experience, and the modern intellectual who might regard as mere superstition the taboo on naming God would overlook the sagacity of this constant reminder that there is more in heaven and earth, as Hamlet says, than dreamt of in our "philosophy," that is, in discourse. The General Semanticist says, "The map is not the territory." Montaigne says, "What do I know?" like a true and, originally, positive skeptic. And nobody appreciates this caution better than today's theoretical physicist contemplating subatomic "particles" that are really processes, not objects, and black holes that tease him out of thought. The reminder is to stay as a small child, who keeps his antennae out and still feels awe and wonder because he hasn't yet put a grid over reality. To the charges against language that it limits, biases, and stereotypes perception according to cultural imperatives, we have to add a second charge, that in reducing reality to the terms of its own symbolism—and all symbols will do this— it devitalizes and negativises experience itself.

Discourse is divisive. Concepts are based on the analogies that the right hemisphere of the brain creates with its metaphorizing capacity. Naming is classifying, and classifying parcels reality into ticketed piles of "like" things (different for different cultures). These named things are then linked via the predicative and conjunctive logics of language to form chains of thought. The left, temporal hemisphere specializes in this chaining or logical sequencing. This entire collaboration of the two halves of the brain—one an analog computer and the other a digital computer—requires and thrives on division. Although the right hemisphere, the analog computer, specializes in synthesizing wholes out of disparate items, these categories or constellations depend of course on selection and exclusion and therefore on dividing. It feeds these categories and constellations to the left hemisphere, which is divisive not only by the very nature of its chief function, to analyze or break down, but also by the fact of sequencing. The discrete items that the right hemisphere brings together as a class of similar things or a figure of interrelated things become available or "discrete" in the first place by virtue of some analytic breakdown instigated by the left hemisphere. And what are wholes as synthesized by the right become parts again when sequenced or serialized by the left into its logical enchainments. This circular processing by the new brain as an entirety generates and depends on division. This is why merely "teaching for the right hemisphere" does not go far enough. These brain functions account for the very nature of discourse—lexicon and syntax and "rules" of operation.

Hindu philosophy distinguishes two kinds of "mind," a lower called *manas,* which probably corresponds to the functions of the cerebrum just described, and a higher mind called *buddhi,* for which Western science or philosophy has no clear equivalent. Outside of mystical literature itself, the closest parallel to *manas* and *buddhi* in the West may be the distinction between *phenomena* and *noumena,* knowledge derived à la Locke from some logical permutation of the evidence of the senses versus knowledge perceived directly, without sensory data, by "intellectual intuition," a dictionary definition[38] of noumena that, significantly, has to collapse a major Western dichotomy to render the concept. This dichotomy between intellect and intuition invokes, in fact, a difference commonly used to distinguish the functions of the left and right brain hemispheres.

Noumenal knowledge may no doubt seem vague or vapid because instead of corresponding to a definite physiological site, like the cerebrum, it cannot be so located. Being unlocatable may indicate, precisely, the nature of being "higher": that is, noumen or buddhi may represent a super-organization of old and new brains, or a whole cerebro-spinal system, with the whole endocrine or glandular system, including activation of dormant functions in the pituitary and pineal glands. Past physiological research loses relevance at this point. The West's three leading brain researchers—Sherrington, Eccles, and Penfield—all concluded at the end of their careers that it is impossible to explain the mind by the brain. Meditation perhaps does not simply switch off the discursive and phenomenal system but switches on a larger system that subsumes and subjugates it.

From a different quarter comes one of the best statements of the negativity of inner speech. Across the tetralogy of his "conversations with

[38] *Webster's New Twentieth Century Dictionary* (New York: Collins World, 1977), p. 1225.

Don Juan," Carlos Castaneda keeps reconceiving the nature and the terms of the spiritual disipline through which the Yaqui shaman is putting him and which he periodically reports. Never does he refer to meditation, and indeed Don Juan seems not to have taught it in any form, at least as we have discussed it here, but he teaches Castaneda a variety of techniques, mostly attentional, that result in *seeing*, supervision, by "stopping the world," as Castaneda earlier called the effect of these techniques. By the fourth book he has recast the terms of his cumulative experience and changed his summary of these techniques to "stopping the inner dialogue."

> "You think and talk too much. You must stop talking to yourself."
>
> "What do you mean?"
>
> "You talk to yourself too much. You're not unique at that. Every one of us does that. We carry on an internal talk. Think about it. Whenever you are alone, what do you do?"
>
> "I talk to myself."
>
> "What do you talk to yourself about?"
>
> "I don't know; anything, I suppose."
>
> "I'll tell you what we talk to ourselves about. We talk about our world. In fact we maintain our world with our internal talk."
>
> "How do we do that?"
>
> "Whenever we finish talking to ourselves the world is always as it should be. We renew it, we kindle it with life, we uphold it with our internal talk. Not only that, but we also choose our paths as we talk to ourselves. Thus we repeat the same choices over and over until the day we die, because we keep on repeating the same internal talk over and over until the day we die.
>
> "A warrior is aware of this and strives to stop his talking. . . ."[39]

Recapitulating all the techniques he has taught him over the years, Don Juan says, "Stopping the internal dialogue is, however, the key. . . . The rest of the activities are only props; all they do is accelerate the effect of stopping the internal dialogue."[40]

In astonishing accord with Don Juan, the classic yoga text, the *Yoga Sutras* (aphorisms) of Patanjali, written probably two or three centuries after Christ but codifying yogic practices and principles transmitted through two or three millennia before, states in a sutra at the very outset:

> Yoga is the restriction of the fluctuations of mind-stuff.
>
> —James Woods, the Harvard Oriental Series

[39]Carlos Castaneda, *A Separate Reality: Further Conversations with Don Juan* (New York: Simon and Schuster), p. 263.
[40]Carlos Castaneda, *Tales of Power* (New York: Simon and Schuster, 1974), p. 233.

Yoga is the suppression of the modifications of mind.
                              —Swami Hariharananda Aranya
Yoga is the control of thought waves in the mind.
                —Swami Prabhavananda and Christopher Isherwood[41]

I have quoted three translations of the same sutra to help the reader distill more surely for himself this key point. Also in common, Don Juan and Patanjali both say the mastery of stopping inner dialogue enables the successful practitioner to assume extraordinary physical and psychical powers (*siddhis*).

The reader can see already the paradox that we have been engaging with. If discourse is "running to and fro," why encourage it—especially if people desire composure? If the deepest and most desirable "meditation" is silence, "nonconceptualization," then why think? If suspending inner speech opens the gate to higher knowledge, who wants to *develop* inner speech? If language just distorts reality through a social lens, what good will it do to learn to write well? Doesn't successful verbal expression conflict with the very goal of expression—to speak the truth? Or is writing just a parlor game, to entertain and blandish, not to symbolize reality?

Certainly we have to face the negative aspects of speech, and even of conceptual thought itself. To do so, however, seems to undermine the main aims of schooling. If we are not trying to teach kids to think and to express themselves, then, hell's bells, what are we up to anyway? How can we old poetry-loving English teachers with our rich inner life and our great investments in language turn around and talk it down? Because, precisely, we have to say the truth, and the truth is that speech is double-edged, a curse and a blessing. (The root of *sacred* means both holy and cursed.)

The teaching of writing must rise to a new sophistication consonant with a new stage in human evolution. A paradox is literally a "double teaching," and that's exactly what we must do—teach two apparently contradictory things at once. Youngsters need to develop inner speech as fully as possible and at the same time learn to suspend it. They must talk through to silence. Of course, I can hear now the teacher who says, "Well, you don't know *my* kids. They come to me so inarticulate they can hardly talk at all—couldn't care less about language—are so brainwashed by TV they hardly have an inner life of their own—and here you talk of making them nonverbal and stopping their inner speech." But this state of affairs is all part of the paradox. Articulation is essential, and silence is golden indeed. Melville's male *ingénu* Billy Budd kills Claggett in a moment of

---

[41]These translations come from the three following sources, respectively: James Haughton Woods, *The Yoga-System of Patanjali,* the Harvard Oriental Series (Delhi, India: Motilal Barnarsidass, 1966); Swami Hariharananda Aranya, *Yoga Philosophy of Patanjali* (Calcutta, India: Calcutta University Press, 1963); and Swami Prabhavananda and Christopher Isherwood, *How to Know God: The Yoga Aphorisms of Patanjali* (Hollywood: Vedanta Press, 1953).

helpless *stuttering* anger. He struck out because he could not speak out. The real goal is control and choice—exercise of will—so that people can avail themselves of discourse and still transcend it.

We can no longer regard schooling as only learning to verbalize. This is naive and irresponsible. It ignores the dangerous side of discourse, which if not balanced can be put into the service, like atomic energy, of the worst motives and phobias. Furthermore, it attunes us to humankind only, not to the whole of nature, leaving us with less than a half truth and therefore not even understanding humankind. ("Human voices wake us, and we drown.") Finally, the best way to teach how to fill out job applications is not to pound away at this as a "minimal criterion" but to help kids connect writing to the whole range of personal and social usage of discourse. Isolating a skill merely deprives it of the context and connections that would teach it. This is true of filling out job applications and of discourse itself. A paradox is not a real but an apparent contradiction. To develop and undo discourse at the same time would not be working against ourselves. Teaching both ways at once, double teaching, has its reason. People are at once both human and what we call divine, that is, they participate in the social subsystem which in turn participates in the total cosmic system. The new stage of evolution at which we are arriving demands education for conscious attunement to both. This means the ability to switch deliberately back and forth and know where one's mind is all the time.

Even if one rejects this dual aim and dual method, it is a practical fact that people who can suspend discourse think and speak better when they turn it back on. Thought straightens and deepens during the hiatus in accordance perhaps with William James's idea that we learn to swim in winter and ice skate in summer, that is, by lying fallow during the off season. Swami Sivalingam can switch with great ease from inner silence to very energetic speech. Given to long meditation all his life, still he thinks and verbalizes with tremendous speed and fluency, although seldom does he have the opportunity today to speak in his native Tamil. It is difficult to keep up with his thoughts and words even though he may be using a lately learned language. When Swami Sivalingam puts pen to paper he writes virtually without pause in a smooth transcription of inner flow. His own guru was the renowned Swami Sivananda, a Western-trained medical doctor turned yogi who wrote over 300 books, most on subtle and difficult subjects. Because their will is lined up behind their mind, and their thought is resolved, advanced meditators talk and write with a combination of depth and fluency that writing teachers should pay attention to and that demonstrates very convincingly how suspending inner speech benefits it.

Harder to believe perhaps is that this truth holds for so-called nonverbal or inarticulate people. Such people do in fact have a busy inner life, but (1) they are less conscious of it, and (2) they are talking to themselves in far more restricted, compulsive ways, telling themselves the same few things over and over, or rerunning in a mental twilight things others have said or shown them. Such people desperately need release from this narrow and uncontrolled repetition, which limits in turn what they can see, say, and do about things outside. So even for the "speechless" person the mind works better if it can be turned down or off from time to time.

Counterspell

It should be clear at this point, in the view developed here, that learning to write well is nothing less than learning to discourse well, and that, educationally, speaking up and shutting up have to be considered together. This means that we would do well not only to take a very broad view of what teaches writing but also to recognize that many of the best ways of teaching writing may be themselves ends as much as means. In any sensible set of humanistic values, meditation deserves a place in schools for its own sake, regardless of its value to writing, and writing might well be regarded as adjunct to meditation rather than the reverse. Aside from clerical maintenance that may be done by computers, what is writing for, anyway, if not to develop understanding? Let's keep this perspective in mind as we approach the question of what methodology may best act as counterspell to teach paradoxically.

First of all, *language* may be used as a counterspell to itself. The incantatory use of language, which is nondiscursive or only half discursive, resolves most directly the paradox of teaching and unteaching discourse at the same time. Rhythm, rhyme, repetition, nonsense, imagery, sheer sound and beat and vocal play—these take a minimum of meaning and charge it with a mental energy that works below the level of symbols and communication (and best appeals to the "nonverbal" or "inarticulate" person). Incantation makes words operate like music or dance or graphic arts. The tense emphasis school usually places on communication alone not only misses the proper entrance point into writing for less verbal people but also misses a key solution to the limitations of discourse, for the incantatory uses of language to undo language cast a counterspell.

Why does poetry always precede prose in the history of literature? Why is it considered the highest form of composition? Because in addition to, or beyond, any symbolization or conveying of meaning, it *summons power.* Vocal potency we no longer think of or think we believe in, although it works its effects on people today as much as ever, on writer as well as reader. Perhaps for the very reason that language is learned in an early state of susceptibility and internalizes the world, it evokes, invokes, conduces, induces, vibrates, and resonates. Yogis associate the energy center of the throat with those just above and below it along the cerebro-spinal chain, at the brain and heart, and regard this place of speech not just as expressing thought and feeling but as a vibrational power source of great influence on what falls within its range. The allegory in Genesis of God *saying* things into existence means likewise that vocalization commands, exerts force like other energy but is directed by intelligence. Magic formulas of the "Open Sesame" sort popularize this ancient and universal conviction about language. "Logos" is translated as "word" in "In the beginning was the word," but an earlier meaning of "logos" than thought (logic) is "energy source of the solar system." In short, teachers will gain enormously from reinstating in school the primal and not merely primitive view of language as not just knowledge but also *power,* a vibratory force that acts on world as well as mind.

Schools need to emphasize, in parity with the symbolic uses of language to express ideas, the forms of language that transcend ideas and alter consciousness, induce trance. This means far more time devoted to song and poetry and to drama and fiction as rhythmic influences, not merely as thematic vehicles. And students should write more in these forms and *perform* such writings of others, not always read them silently. By organizing specialties like "creative drama" and "creative writing," schools have effectively placed them out of bounds for most students most of the time, whereas writing and performing of these art forms of language should occur constantly at all ages as a daily staple. Again, other educators and I have written much about this elsewhere—to no great avail so far because of state doctrines favoring lower goals falsely regarded as utilitarian.

Communicative discourse itself, however, can become a major way of teaching the paradox, in conjunction with silence. We have to think of "developing discourse" as not just throwing open the sluice gates, but of *channeling* discourse and especially *raising the quality* of it. The internalization process itself will accomplish this if well arranged in the classroom. Where can rich variety come from into the inner life? And how can the individual become aware of how he does think and talk and how he might think and talk? From hearing out the world. From listening to and reading or viewing a far broader spectrum of discourse than schools and parents have so far facilitated. Inner speech must be elaborated, refined, and enriched, and this takes a school revolution, for now both student activities and the type and timing of materials are so overcontrolled as to caricature the growth of inner speech. The model of inculcation, dearer perhaps to the public even than to the profession, must go for good. Far from working toward a counterspell, it merely deepens the original social hypnosis, which parents still asleep think they want for their children.

At any rate, in addition to quieting the mind as one method of awakening, we should employ what only appears to be the opposite—namely shaking up the mind, stimulating and activating it so that it *moves.* If the mind *either* holds still enough *or* moves enough it will shake off conditioning, for either liberates, and that is the key. Running to and fro, which is compulsive, must change to running straight on and on along the individual's proper path. If inner speech keeps evolving, people eventually work through the world of words and on out the other side. The more we consciously employ language, the more detached we become from it and know what it can do and what it cannot do. Only after we have spoken up can we shut up. I suspect that when Shakespeare announced his early retirement through Prospero, the magus of his last play, *The Tempest,* he had talked his way into silence and made composition coincide with composure. Teachers don't aim to make little Shakespeares, but we should not miss the lesson that the best way to improve writing is to keep refining inner speech till it evaporates. (A playwright shows most clearly how to set up colloquies in which different aspects of oneself talk toward inner resolution.) A main effect of writing, anyway, is personal growth, which is the best guarantee of effective communication, whether in a job application or a poem. Writing should be taught unabashedly as a spiritual discipline.

But, of course, I'm suggesting that forms of meditation are the main counterspells. To connect meditation more directly with schooling, let's look again at the scale of meditation techniques sketched earlier. This array can serve to find the best meditation for a given writer and topic. The point on the scale closest to the finished composition lies near the middle, where we found the structured discourse of the Jesuits. But if fluency comes hard, maybe one should babble first, just witness the spontaneous production of ideas, words, and images. If depth is needed, perhaps one should aim for silence, try to get beyond what one has already heard and said and read about something and just focus on the subject nondiscursively—that is, just hold, centered in consciousness, some idea, emblem, or phrasing of the subject, sink deep in without trying to have thoughts about it; *then* the meditator could back up on the scale toward discourse and begin to permit trains of thoughts to build up about his subject. More generally, where on this scale, a teacher might ask, can a certain student find himself at the moment, given his verbal and nonverbal development so far?

Gazing, contemplating, may be done at any age as a way to know most fully some object of the material world. The famous biology professor Louis Agassiz, at Harvard, would send a student back repeatedly to look at a fish and describe it until the observer began to see *internal* features of it that he would normally not perceive. Let a learner visually lock into some object he or she has chosen either out of curiosity or deep involvement or as part of a project requiring further knowledge of the object. As a meditation, gazing slips the limits of conceptualization and enables one to see more and hence have more to say when back in the discursive mode.

Students can practice visualizing in connection with many imaginative activities in school, including the already popular "guided fantasy" technique some teachers have adopted. Alone, the meditator imagines, with eyes closed, an inner picture at the "third eye" (Cyclopean) position in the middle of the forehead. Though common to probably all cultures, including Christian, the conjuring and holding of an image before the inner vision has been especially developed in Tibetan meditation, which draws on Buddhism and yoga, especially tantric yoga.[42] Tantra emphasizes transcending rather than shunning the senses as a means to spiritual development. This means that the aspirant subtilizes his sensory vision right onto a higher plane, partly by gazing at "art objects" especially made for this (as indeed was much Christian art) and then by introjecting these, eyes closed, and continuing to see the object. Sometimes one uses a visual construction, called a *yantra,* that is especially designed to be contemplated for its effect on consciousness, being a schema of cosmos as both unity and multiplicity. Carl Jung's mandalas, some Persian rug patterns, and Navajo sand paintings are yantras. Found or student-made yantras can serve to establish visualization as a general practice for imagining anything at will. Through visualization, incidentally, the old link between meditation and healing, buried, as I pointed out, in the etymology of the word, has come alive again in recent years: After Dr. Carl Simonton showed at a military hospital that some "terminal" cancer patients could reverse the disease by meditating and visualizing their cure in some graphic way of their own, Dr. Irving Oyle and many other physicians and therapists have begun incorporating this combination of techniques into general medical practice and into the current holistic health movement.[43]

Since television may well cause some atrophying of the visualizing faculty, as some of us educators have conjectured in regard, usually, to reading problems, visualization practice may improve both comprehension and composition at once. It played an important role in the "composition of place" and no doubt also in the production of "similitudes," which entail *seeing* similarities between points in one's subject and comparable concrete items.

The way in which the Jesuitical sort of discursive meditation might be applied to writing found a spokesman in Gordon Rohman over a decade ago.[44] Rohman lifted out of the ecclesiastical context the essential process that worked for meditators and writers of the seventeenth century and offered it to teachers as one pre-writing technique, leaving subject matter open and capturing the spirit rather than the letter of the

[42]Phillip Rawson, *The Art of Tantra* (Greenwich, Conn.: New York Graphic Society, 1973).

[43]Carl Simonton et al., *Getting Well Again* (New York: J. P. Tarcher, 1978), and Irving Oyle, *The Healing Mind* (New York: Pocket Books, 1976).

[44]Gordon Rohman, "Pre-Writing: The Stage of Discovery in the Writing Process," *College Composition and Communication,* May 1965.

procedure. Doing the same thing in my own way, I would recommend that teachers coach students on how to get themselves into a meditative state of unusual absorption in a subject that interests them and then to visualize, imagine, feel, and think everything they can about that subject without at first concerning themselves about writing something down. After students have brought to bear on a subject all their faculties and thus focused intensively for a time their inner speech, then they would write down some version of these thoughts and proceed from there to work up a composition, presumably with mid-writing response from others and as much repetition of these inner and outer processes as is appropriate for student and subject. So the aim of discursive meditation is to channel and intensify inner speech in a state of heightened consciousness and self-communication that enables the writer to summon all he is capable of saying about the subject. Previous or concurrent practice in visualization will aid this much.

The yogic or Hesychast type of nondiscursive meditation does not have to be done with a mantra. Virtually any focal point that is powerful and positive for the meditator can serve well. When using mantras, students should make or choose their own. Making and discussing mantras should, in fact, become an important classroom activity. What is a good thing to keep saying to yourself? Are we already repeating, consciously or unconsciously to ourselves, certain key words or magic phrases? Are they good or bad for us? What ideas are "elevated" or spiritual? What aspects of language form make for good mantras? Word? Phrase? Sentence? Stanza? Work with mantras can become part of writing and performing song and poetry.

Alternatives to mantras are yantras and other tantra, that is, all arts and sensory avenues. Repetitive external sound may work well to help some individuals to stay one-pointed. Verbal or nonverbal, visual or auditory, physical or imaginary—these are good choices to have for individualizing. A phrase may be sung aloud or intoned within. A verbal person may start to still his inner chatter *only* by vocalizing something. A nonverbal person may achieve good focus best on an image. An unimaginative person may do well to transfer an image by alternately gazing and visualizing. A lonely person may release some anxious "running to and fro" by chanting with others.

Zen Buddhist practitioners of the meditation technique called za-zen focus on their normal breathing, which moves in time but stays the same in the sense that in even respiration one breath is like another. In this respect breath is like a mantra, and in some meditation practices, like the Hesychast, breathing and repetition of the mantra are coordinated. Za-zen emphasizes the here-and-now in contrast with conceptualization, which by its abstract nature necessarily refers out of the present. Holding attention on regular breathing is perfectly safe and may be an easy, fitting focus for many students, offering an alternative to senses.

Breath has a very close connection to thought, almost entirely unsuspected in our era, that I think science will soon begin to rediscover. Though za-zen is simply attending to breathing without altering it, some of the most powerful consciousness-altering exercises entail slowing, holding, or patterning the breath. *Pranayama,* or breath control, has for thousands of years been associated by yogis with mind control, in keeping with the etymological connection in all languages I have heard of between breath and spirit. Pranayama is the specialty of my own teacher, Swami Sivalingam, who has said that it is a "short-cut meditation." So powerful is breath control, in fact, that it can be dangerous without a teacher when carried beyond the more elementary exercises. Some day soon, educators should work out with wise specialists like Swami Sivalingam just which exercises can be safely done at which ages and with how much or how little monitoring by others.

Yogic texts say, "Quiet the breath, quiet the mind."[45] We can notice for ourselves how breath alters as certain emotion-laden thoughts or events occur to us. When the yogi says, "I am in your breath," he means he is following your thoughts and feelings in his concentration. But again, this insight about breath exists in our own heritage as well as in the East. The Christian mystics and fathers refer often enough to control of the breath to show that they too understood very well its connection with the mind and spirit. And it was undoubtedly part of pre-Christian spiritual discipline in the West. Any serious consideration of meditation must in one way or another deal with breathing, since it is likely that thought and breath each can be controlled from either end. I have myself experienced, in common with many others I have talked with, a natural slowing and even stopping of the breath during meditation, but as soon as I become aware of cessation, it starts again, responding directly to the thought. This accompanies a general slowing of metabolic processes, probably related biologically to hibernation processes, that scientific monitoring of meditation corroborates. This is very good for health and might well ease many school problems concerning excitation, emotion, attention, and energy. Aside from its indirect value to writing as an adjunct to meditation, breath control affects clear thinking and expression quite directly by steadying the mind. "Alternate breathing," through one nostril at a time, will, I think, soon be shown to stimulate the respective brain hemispheres through crossed-over neural connections between nostrils and hemispheres. It is nothing less than naive to continue to regard writing as only "mental," and if the trend toward the psychobiology of it succeeds in helping the teaching of writing, it will do so by treating discourse within the total functioning of the organism.

[45]For specific references both to connections between thought and breath and to general doctrines of Tibetan yogic techniques of enlightenment see W. Y. Evans-Wentz, *The Tibetan Book of the Great Liberation or the Method of Realizing Nirvana through Knowing the Mind,* Commentary by C. G. Jung (New York: Oxford University Press, 1954).

Because meditation techniques are the closest to writing, I have featured them, but suspending inner speech as a means to greater knowledge and power underlies a prodigious array of activities of all cultures of all times that may suggest how teachers might go about finding and devising counterspells in lieu of or in league with meditation. The "techniques of ecstasy," as the scholar Mircea Eliade has called them,[46] may be physiological as well as psychological. Physical activity calling for totally external focus of attention or total bodily involvement can make inner speech virtually impossible. In writing about "sports highs" that athletes report, Michael Murphy has recently made this connection.[47] This explains why martial arts like judo and aikido are considered spiritual disciplines. (As my younger daughter said of her high school fencing class, "Your mind doesn't wander!") Think now of the real meaning of Shakers, Quakers, and Holy Rollers, who attempt to bring on this state by dancing of a sort, as do the Sufi Whirling Dervishes, whom I have seen do authentically their gradually accelerating revolving movement with eyes closed and to the accompaniment of chanting. All of the arts originally aimed at trance induction for purposes of enlightenment, as typified by some of the Greek Mysteries, the main source of Western drama, music, art, and dance to the extent that these did not derive more directly from the mysteries of earlier civilizations.

Chemical means were sometimes used in combination with sensorimotor activities. A distinguished scientist/scholar trio has recently asserted, for example, that the mysteries of Eleusis included ingestion of a psychotropic drug from a fungus similar to the peyote mushroom employed since ancient times in Meso-America for shedding the veil of ordinary reality.[48] Aldous Huxley's classic account of the effects of a similar psychotropic drug, "Opening the Doors of Perception," accords remarkably with this ancient chemical approach.[49] But fasting and breath control can also produce liberation from the ordinary mind or "highs" by affecting the chemistry of the brain without the need of ingesting drugs.

There are electrical as well as chemical means for suspending inner speech. Natural sleep produces slow brainwaves of long amplitude that cancel out the higher frequency crackling of thoughts, and electroshock therapy "works" in the brutal fashion it does by shooting through the nervous system a charge so strong that it likewise overwhelms the finer

---

[46]See Mircea Eliade, *Shamanism: Archaic Techniques of Ecstasy*, Bollingen Series LXXVI (Princeton, N.J.: Princeton University Press, 1964). Eliade's remarkable scholarship combines with rare personal understanding to make him one of the most valuable contemporary explainers and presenters of spiritual disciplines. See also his *Yoga: Immortality and Freedom*, Bollingen Series LVI (Princeton, N.J.: Princeton University Press, 1958).

[47]Michael Murphy and Rhea White, *The Psychic Side of Sports* (Reading, Mass.: Addison Wesley, 1978).

[48]R. Gordon Wasson, Carl A. P. Ruok, Albert Hoffmann, *The Road to Eleusis: Unveiling the Secret of the Mysteries* (New York: Harcourt Brace Jovanovich, 1978).

[49]Aldous Huxley, *The Doors of Perception* (New York: Harper & Row, 1970).

neural activities like thinking and literally shocks the patient right out of his mind. Epileptic attacks have been described by brain researcher Wilder Penfield as a kind of electrical storm, which, although they may end in a coma that parodies meditation trance, do seem to occur in people gifted with unusual insight, if not clairvoyance, like Dostoevski. Scientists have found that when psychics are performing their feats while wired to an electroencephalograph they yield unusual brain-wave patterns characterized by the very low frequencies called theta and delta associated with creativity and trance states. (The way most true psychics describe their concentration for a task indicates pretty clearly that they shut off inner speech.) In the case of one famous psychic, Matthew Manning, the electrical activity, which formed a pattern unrecognizable to twenty of the twenty-one scientists present, was traced to the old brain. Also, a common experience reported unexpectedly by some psychics polled for a survey was that they had received a severe electric shock before the age of ten.[50] Although teachers will not want to employ chemical or electrical means, of course, I think knowledge of these means helps teachers to gain insight into such behavior of students as attraction to drugs and into conditions of the body and the environment that in good and bad ways can suspend or reduce students' inner speech.

Other bodily activities are more directly relevant to teaching methods. Pleasantly monotonous craft movements like knitting and weaving or work activities like hauling a rope or wielding a pickaxe or shovel or thrusting seedlings into mud tend to "entrance" the ordinary mind and constitute a natural kind of meditation. Crafts, arts, sports, and many practical self-help activities hold inner speech in abeyance or mute it and thus help attune us beyond discursive thought. Since these possible counterspells should be curriculum candidates anyway, in keeping with the principle that worthy means are also worthy ends, they will offer opportunities to integrate writing with many other kinds of learning to which it is organically related by way of regulating and balancing one's own mind and body.

Let me summarize the value of regarding writing as revised inner speech and of applying meditation techniques to the teaching of writing. We may compare this approach to prevention in medicine as opposed to curing. If health is neglected for years, then at a certain point it appears there is nothing for it but to undergo surgery, consume drugs, or take some other drastic treatment. Good schooling would never let reading or writing get to the point that they are now, where most teaching is remedying, that is, resorting to very artificial "cures" for "weak vocabulary," "ineffective sentence structure," "poor organization," and "short, shallow papers." In effect, schools teach one year of beginning reading and writ-

---

[50]Matthew Manning, *The Link* (Holt, Rinehart and Winston: 1974), pp. 20–26, part of an introduction by Peter Bander.

ing and eleven years of remedial reading and writing, because the approach is based on the mechanistic functioning of inorganic matter instead of on the realistic way that human beings learn to conceptualize and verbalize. Then severe problems of thinking and language arise which it seems only specialized drills will remedy. The causes of this colossal misdirection go well back into the whole culture, beyond the education profession itself, and form another story unto itself. The point here is that we can head off a myriad of learning problems by making the rise, growth, and self-control of inner speech a central focus in curriculum.

Some teachers teach meditation under other names or have initiated related activities. *The Centering Book* and its successor *The Second Centering Book,* pioneering works by education professors, contain many verbatim directions for leading youngsters in exercises of relaxation, concentration, breathing, visualizing, centering, and inner attention.[51] Other books are coming out all the time on the teaching of meditation to young people, usually based on experience in school or community settings. The most educational experimentation with meditation has occurred outside of school, however, in workshops for adults. In his *Intensive Journal* workshops Ira Progoff, a psychotherapist, teaches people how to use writing to discover what they really feel and think and want and are.[52] I have been greatly struck, as have some others, by the similarities between the kinds of writing and the climate for writing of my own approach for school teaching of language arts and Progoff's approach for adult therapy, both developed independently at about the same time. I am struck too that Progoff has also come to use meditation as a method of engaging people in writing.

But to teach meditation one must practice meditation. Though always surprised at how many teachers "come out of the closet" when I talk about meditation, the profession needs far more practitioners. Any interested person can start to meditate without joining an organization, paying money, or necessarily having a teacher, by practicing one of the techniques described in this article. To the extent that schools have the money, projects for changing teachers and the "facilitative behaviors" movement in staff development have tried to improve curriculum by arranging experiences in self-awareness and personal growth for the teachers. Since meditation naturally fulfills this aim, if staff development included it, then schools would simultaneously prepare teachers to improve writing while fostering their general adult growth.

[51]Gay Hendriks and Russel Wills, *The Centering Book* (Englewood Cliffs, N.J.: Prentice-Hall, 1975). Also, Gay Hendriks and T. Roberts, *The Second Centering Book: More Advanced Awareness Activities for Children, Parents, and Teachers* (Englewood Cliffs, N.J.: Prentice-Hall, 1977). For early rationale for introducing meditation into schools see *Phi Delta Kappan,* December 1972, which featured articles on Transcendental Meditation and education.

[52]Ira Progoff, *At a Journal Workshop: The Basic Text and Guide for Using the Intensive Journal* (New York: Dialogue House, 1975). For a useful incorporation of some of Progoff's practices into schools see Mark Hanson, *Sources* (Box 262, Lakeside, Ca. 92040: Interact).

Meditation techniques show how to witness one's own mind, direct one's own mind, and silence one's own mind. Teachers can give no greater gift to their students than to help them expand and master inner speech. Good writing will ensue, whereas fiddling with form alone will teach, if anything, only how to carpenter better the craziness of themselves and their world. Let's direct discourse toward its own self-transformation and self-transcendence. In doing so we will also accomplish better the traditional curriculum goals.

> Meanwhile the mind from pleasure less
> Withdraws into its happiness;
> The mind, that ocean where each kind
> Does straight its own resemblance find,
> Yet it creates, transcending these,
> Far other worlds and other seas,
> Annihilating all that's made
> To a green thought in a green shade.
>> From "The Garden," Andrew Marvell

Appendix

People Reading: A Proposal for the '80s

This is a community project to organize people who can read and write to help others learn to read and write. It involves but is not limited to schools. Those teaching and those learning are of all ages and work together in mixture at whatever times and sites turn out to be feasible for a given community. Professional educators help set up the methods and the collaboration between schools and other community agencies for pooling of resources, but paraprofessionals actually do the teaching—housewives, older students, senior citizens, and other volunteers.

Goals

1. To give literacy free to anyone in the community who wants it.

2. To demonstrate that becoming literate requires only will and a cheap, simple methodology not dependent on professional teachers, esoteric techniques, further research, or special, costly materials.

3. To develop a model of public schooling based on the incorporation of school sites and educators into a community-wide network for sharing all locally available human and material resources.

4. To rekindle through serving and being served a feeling of community and unity.

Methods

The learning methods are essentially two—one aimed especially at reading and the other aimed especially at writing. Both make use of a literate person to provide a temporary bridge for the learner between the vocal medium of speech and the new visual medium of print.

The aide either reads to the learner while the learner follows the text with the eyes, or the aide writes down what the learner has to say while the learner watches. We may call the first the "lap method," to indicate that parents have done it in the tradition of the bedtime story, or the "read-along method" if we wish to indicate a recorded rather than live voice, especially as applied to adolescents or adults.

Taking dictation from a learner while he or she looks on is known in many quarters as the "language-experience approach," meaning that the learner supplies the audio himself by putting his own experience into language. An important part of that method is for learner and aide to read back the dictation together and for the learner to trace over the writing with a transparent-ink pen and try rereading on his own, perhaps to a third person.

Neither of these methods has been employed enough in schools to prove itself or, usually, even to get included in experimental research, whereas a premise of this project is that some combination of the two will suffice to launch literacy.

At an appropriate pace the learner takes over the aide's role by trying to sound out print and spell out his thoughts for himself with the help of the aide when needed. During this transition from aides to independence, novices learn to make use of other human and material resources, chief among them partners and tape recorders. Partners pool their growing knowledge and understanding of how to unlock and spell words by collectively reading aloud to each other (in unison or in turn) and transcribing their own taped speech, collectively also. They can also play certain card, board, and lettered dice games that entail their sounding aloud what they see. For the learner soloing, a tape recorder can gradually replace the aide: the learner listens to a recording of a text that he follows with his eyes, and he talks to a recorder and later transcribes his own speech.

Materials

Since the reading is individualized, virtually any reading matter in any form and of any content can be of use to some learner or another. The organizers of the project solicit from the community the lending or donation of books, magazines, newspapers, brochures, posters, manuals, and so forth. Some of this matter may be left at the sites, and some may be brought temporarily with the volunteer. Effort is made to obtain a great range of subject matter, kind of discourse, format, and difficulty level.

The more tape recorders that can be acquired, the better, although live transcription can always be used if machines are unavailable for all. For "read-along," recordings of texts are important, but these can be made within the community by adults or students with some coaching. Making well-rehearsed recordings by proficient readers for novice readers would, in fact, be a major part of the whole process.

If carefully screened by educators, some game and manipulative materials can serve well if players are asked to sound or listen to what they see and to combine spellings, words, and phrases into whole sentences and stories. Similarly, only those sound films and phonovisual gear would be proper that show and sound simultaneously and that synthesize small-er language units into larger.

Organization

This has to be worked out locally, but the idea is to combine the reg-ular mission of schools to initiate literacy with "adult education" while also bringing more resources of the whole community to bear on this big-ger mission. The organizers will utilize whatever are the best channels for soliciting massive volunteering of service and materials and for arranging times and sites where aides and learners can come together. Educators cast and post the basic directions for the methods so that any volunteer can start anytime, and consult with working parties, helping to decide which learners would benefit from certain human and material resources. It may be that initial and "remedial" learners needn't be segregated by time and site, since any activity or material could be available for mixed groups, which will not be taught as classes but merely share the same area and resources and each other.

Rationale

Generally, schools are having a very hard time teaching literacy, to the point that an unconscionable and unnecessary amount of time and energy go into it. At the same time, the public keeps telling schools to perform better for less money. This project can show an effective way to dispatch literacy so that schools can get on to higher kinds of learning, and it does this by creating a closer collaboration between school and community that will begin to redefine schooling in the direction it must take in the future.

Specifically, to become literate is merely to associate a second medi-um, print, with one already well learned before school, speech, which al-ready bears meaning. What teaches literacy is to *see and hear language at once,* in a motivated and meaningful context, so that the sights and sounds of the language become specifically associated. The two main methods will accomplish this if done continually and copiously, and they have the vir-tue, moreover, that they are ends as well as means, not mere drills alleged to pay off later. Being read to and dictating—while watching—are early forms of reading and writing that allow the learner to assimilate the ex-ternal, social action of the aide into his own inner functioning. This com-bines imitation and internalization. People learn to read and write by successive approximations that more and more nearly become the target solo activities. Thus, the learner at first associates speech with print in gross blocs and imprecisely but progressively refines it to particular as-sociations between sounds and spellings that enable him to unlock or spell words he has not seen before.

Purpose of this Proposal

I make this proposal first to other educators for response and suggestions. Then, in perhaps revised form, it can go to likely school districts, professional journals, and funding sources—if the educators enlisted to support it agree that next steps might be to identify pilot districts (communities), publish it as a public proposal for other places to consider, and seek federal or foundation monies. And this *is* a public proposal, not a personal project. Could such projects be mounted without outside funding? I would be willing to consult free on a project in my own locality. Are others willing to do the same? Perhaps a chain reaction of projects could get going and amount to a significant national movement such as the Bay Area Writing Project has set off. How should we best proceed to generate successful models?

Address replies to me at first, until we know the next organizational step:

James Moffett
4107 Triangle Rd.
Mariposa, CA. 95338
(209) 966-3067